SAT* Reading Comprehension Workbook

Advanced Practice Series

Published by ILEX Publications
www.ILEXPublications.com

On behalf of
Integrated Educational Services, Inc.
355 Main Street
Metuchen, NJ 08840

We would like to thank all the writers and editors at ILEX Publications as well as all of the teachers and students at IES2400 who participated in trials of these passages. Their contributions have been invaluable in the creation of this book. We would also like to thank Sonia Choi for her invaluable input.

Created by
Khalid Khashoggi
Arianna Astuni

Editors
Khalid Khashoggi
Joseph Carlough
John Manna
Rajvi Patel
Arianna Astuni

Design
Joseph Carlough
Ana Grigoriu

Contributing Writers
Chris Holliday
Joseph Carlough
Rajvi Patel
Christopher Carbonell
Vincent Keat
Pooja Patel
Annie Shi
Arianna Astuni

ISBN: 978-0-9913883-0-1

Questions or comments? Email us at info@IlexPublications.com.
We'd love to hear from you!

Table of Contents

Welcome!

IES has spent almost 15 years instructing some of the most advanced high school students in the world—and now we offer our insights to you.

We have found that the greatest score increases come from a combination of good technique and abundant practice. However, the persistent problem for all students is always: "Where can I get more material?"

This Reading Comprehension Workbook is the first volume in the IES Advanced Practice Series of SAT self prep books. It closely mimics every type of SAT Reading Comprehension question, and helps you to spot hidden clues, read for subtext, and discern author's tone and purpose.

Our workbook also includes answer explanations which highlight the visual hints found within a reading comprehension passage. By using this book, you will develop the ability to connect these hints to the correct answer choice—an ability that is crucial to excelling on the SAT.

How to Use This Book

This book is organized into 10 chapters, each with 40 long reading comprehension questions. This reflects the number of long reading comprehension questions on the real SAT. Moreover, these questions mimic the same difficulty levels and question types (tone, inference, implication, etc.) found on the SAT. This means, if you get 90% of the questions right in any given chapter of this book, you can expect the same percentage of correct answers in the reading comprehension sections of the official SAT.

1. Getting Your Feet Wet → Chapter 1 through Chapter 2

First, you will learn to use the technique (found on the following page) for the first time. Break old reading comprehension habits and adopt new ones by utilizing this technique consistently. Train yourself to use this technique on every question. Remember, fill out the Self Evaluation form after checking your answers at the end of each chapter! (You will use these forms in the subsequent steps)

2. Aiming for Accuracy → Chapter 3 through Chapter 4

Here, you will figure out what it is that you are doing wrong and work on those issues. You can hone in on your problem areas through the Self Evaluation forms. You're aiming for accuracy (not speed). If you find your problem is predominantly a lack of vocabulary, please refer to the FREE online vocabulary course. Remember, with accuracy, speed will come!

3. Introducing Time → Chapter 5 through Chapter 6

You are going to be introducing speed for the first time. Give yourself about 1.5 minutes per question. In other words, if the reading comprehension has 6 questions, you will have 9 minutes to complete all 6 questions (which includes the necessary reading of all parts of the passage that are relevant to the line reference). On some questions you will spend more time, on others, less. There is a big difference between rushing and pacing yourself!

4. Speeding Up → Chapter 7 through Chapter 8

Now, you are going to cut down on how long you spend per question. Give yourself only 1.25 minutes per question. So, for the same 6-question reading comprehension, you will only have 7.5 minutes to finish. Remember, continue filling out the Self Evaluation forms!

5. A Minute to Win It → Chapter 9 through Chapter 10

In these chapters, you will further cut down the time spent on each reading comprehension question. Your goal should be to spend roughly a minute per question, or, for the same 6-question long reading comprehension, you will now spend no more than 6 minutes. Remember, do not sacrifice accuracy for speed!

The IES Reading Comprehension Technique

The IES Reading Comprehension Technique is intricate and effective. We have outlined the general steps of our technique for you to apply while you practice these passages. To ensure the best interpretation of these steps do not hesitate to consult a teacher or contact us for an online tutorial.

1. Read the italicized introduction (not the passage itself).

2. Read the first question carefully. If it has a line reference you may proceed to the next step. If it doesn't, skip it and come back to it once all the line reference questions have been answered.

3. For a line reference question, go to the passage and underline the reference. Read all that you need to read before and after the line reference in order to fully understand the line reference.

4. Before you look at the answer choices, ask yourself: "According to the question and the line reference, what will my answer be about?"

    a. **Who** is the answer supposed to be about?
    b. **What** is the answer supposed to be about?
    c. What is the **tone** of the answer supposed to be?

5. Write your answer from step 4 in the margin next to the question. We call this the Margin Answer. Be sure to base your Margin Answer on facts supported by the passage.

6. Now you may look at the answer choices and use a Process of Elimination to rule out any answer that does not address the Who/What/Tone of your Margin Answer.

Note to Teachers:

Be sure to reinforce these steps. Students of different levels may encounter different problems. Watch out for the most common mistakes made by them when using this technique:

- Over-generalized Margin Answers
- Reading too little
- Reading too much
- Not reading the question discerningly
- Not following the question prompt (ie: imply, infer, suggest, primary purpose, etc…)
- Being subjective (not using visual clues)
- Ignoring or misinterpreting tone.
- Using the answer choices to formulate their Margin Answer

Chapter One

Questions 1-6 are based on the following passage.

This passage is adapted from a 2013 essay on the roles played in Shakespeare plays.

Everyone thinks he or she knows the play about the "star-crossed lovers," since it is very difficult for a child in High School to get through the English Lit syllabus without encountering the classic couple either in class or on a rare school trip to the theatre. With the possible exception of *Hamlet*, it is probably the most performed of all the plays that Shakespeare wrote. Every ardent theatergoer carries in his or her head a memory of the actress who, for him or her, was the perfect Juliet. We can all picture her on the balcony, or preparing to swallow the contents of the phial given to her by the Friar, or waking in the tomb to find her lover dead beside her before thrusting the dagger into her breast.

Poor Romeo! His name comes first in the title but it is Juliet that gets all the attention. Why should this be so? After all, apart from Act Four, it is he who is onstage for the most part, it is he who has all the physical stuff to do.

The answer is that Shakespeare was a man who knew the make-up of his company and he wrote to its strengths at any particular time. If we look at the female roles in his plays, we can see when the company was blessed with talented boy actors, and when they were thin on the ground. For example, at the time when he was writing the great comedies, there must have been almost a glut of talented boy players in the company. *Twelfth Night* has three hefty female roles, as does *As You Like It*. In *Romeo and Juliet*, the only roles that can be considered demanding in any way are the Nurse and Juliet. The Nurse would have been played not by a boy actor, but a character actor, one of the comedians perhaps in the company; so we are left with Juliet as the only role for which a boy actor is required. Shakespeare was well aware of a boy actor's limitations.

If you examine the two roles of Juliet and Romeo, it is Romeo who develops as the play progresses. He moves from a boy more interested in playing with words and emotions, striking poses at the beginning of the play, to a man overwhelmed with real love; a boy who hangs back from aggression, defies the rules, and kills, twice, in an attempt to capture the eternity of love. His verse is intricate, passionate, a whirl of different emotions. Throughout the play he is all movement of body and spirit. Frankly, there is no other characterization so accurate of a teenage boy in the whole of literature. In contrast, Juliet is a one note part. She reacts only to what is placed before her. It is her situation the audience sees and with which it has empathy. Her language is uncomplicated and direct. It also simplifies things for the young actor. Juliet's big speech is her soliloquy just before she drinks the potion. It is cleverly written and technically is not difficult: it merely requires a steadily rising inflection throughout the speech. That does not make the speech any less effective. The audience warms to her: they want to protect her vulnerability.

What Shakespeare does so well is to cater to the limitations of his players and utilize what they can do to achieve his effects. Not many dramatists are so accommodating. No wonder today's actresses enjoy playing Shakespeare's heroine. They get all the rave reviews for far less energy expended than Romeo.

1. The primary purpose of this passage is to

(A) present a dilemma
(B) outline a process
(C) resolve a discrepancy
(D) analyze a phenomenon
(E) celebrate a style

2. The word "classic" in line 4 most nearly means

(A) well-known
(B) typical
(C) traditional
(D) vintage
(E) standard

3. The author implies that "every ardent theatergoer" (line 8)

(A) remembers the gruesome scenes
(B) has seen all of Shakespeare's famous plays
(C) carries expectations into all theatre
(D) always loves "Romeo and Juliet"
(E) is smitten with the role of Juliet

4. The word "hefty" in line 28 most nearly means

(A) solid
(B) heavy
(C) portly
(D) substantial
(E) abundant

5. The author explains the roles of Romeo and Juliet in lines 37-51 ("If you…direct") in order to

(A) explain the inherent purpose of a particular play
(B) highlight an anomaly in the audience's reaction to different roles
(C) reunite the reader with characters they already know
(D) describe roles made for actresses in plays
(E) juxtapose teenage male behavior to teenage female behavior

6. In lines 56-58 ("That does…vulnerability"), the author suggests that

(A) the empathy for one character is stronger than the lackluster stage presence of another character
(B) short and direct speeches are better than action
(C) in spite of her simplistic role, Juliet always wins the audience's sympathy
(D) Shakespeare did not mean for Juliet to have any impact on the audience
(E) viewers are wrong about their affinity for a minor character versus the star character

Questions 1-9 are based on the following passage.

This passage, adapted from a study written in 2013, discusses various cultural superstitions.

I have always believed that the human conscience does not just self-extinguish at the point of death. It is a question that has interested scientists, theologians, occultists and philosophers throughout the ages.

Aristotle made clear links between the "existence" and the "essence" in his *Metaphysics*. These ideas had a profound influence not only on the Greeks but on subsequent civilizations: the Romans, Arabs and Medieval Europeans. The concept of the "existence" has remained largely unchanged in the various interpretations over time: that is to say that "existence" is the state of physical being—flesh and blood. The idea of the "essence," however, is not so straightforward.

Philosophers and indeed some psychologists might regard the "essence" as a product of the subconscious or the unconscious mind. Often, the characteristics shown by the "essence" differ greatly from those exhibited by the conscious person. In layman's terms, our "essence" sometimes forces us to act against our better judgment.

A theologian, on the other hand, might regard the "essence" of man as his immortal soul. Some would suggest that at death, our souls are either elevated into the dizzying heights of paradise or to the inferno of Hell. The idea that the way in which one conducts oneself in life determines one's ultimate destiny is one which popular culture is well acquainted with.

In some Eastern cultures, the "ultimate" destiny is not so clearly defined. For instance, one's 'essence' could be reincarnated into one of many forms, and the birth-death-rebirth cycle could be repeated indefinitely. The idea of the "Seven Heavens" also suggests that life after death could indeed be more illustrious than life itself; one would continue to strive to reach the highest level by achieving ever greater degrees of virtue.

In contrast to the spiritual views above, occultists' views are usually considered heretical by mainstream faiths. I suspect this is mainly caused by the fear of the paranormal and mystical. This fear is perhaps due to the tendency of these sects to revere the less celebrated side of the after-life. In reality, many occultists seek to harmonize and manipulate the "essence" in order to benefit the "existence."

How then, do scientists make sense of all these different beliefs? As a scientist, one is obliged to seek an explanation for prevailing conceptions. Early scientific views include the ability of the human body to project its consciousness in the form of electrical impulses that linger on in inanimate objects. These impulses can be then transferred in a finite quantity, subject to the laws of conservation of energy. A less skeptical interpretation of this would point to an explanation for the existence of ghosts or supernatural entities. There is no doubt that our bodies are constantly emitting radiation over a wide range of frequencies. Most of this is in the form of non-visible photons or infrared (heat). On very rare occasions, the radiation can overlap into the visible light region. This could explain the sightings of the human aura, a luminous glow around a person. Arguably, these apparitions have yet to be credibly proven or perhaps can be seen only by individuals with peculiar sight disorders. After all, vampire bats are known to hunt their prey by seeking out infrared wavelength traces and many nocturnal animals are able to track their prey by "seeing" the ultraviolet emissions of excrement.

A recent series of experiments at the University of Hertfordshire in the U.K. suggests the existence of low frequency sound waves or infrasound which can cause phenomena that people typically associate with ghosts. This includes feelings of nervousness and discomfort as well as a sense of a "presence" in the room. The sound waves may also cause vibration in the human eye, causing people to see things that are not there. Usually, these waves are too low-pitched for people to actually perceive so rather than noticing the sound itself, people notice its effects.

Regardless of whether the supernatural exists, many people find it fascinating. This fascination has a number of likely causes, from curiosity about what happens to people after death to the comforting idea that deceased loved ones are still nearby. After all, I refuse to accept the premise that I will eventually just cease to exist!

1. The primary purpose of the passage as a whole is to

(A) investigate the contention between science and mythology
(B) present a scholarly and passionate discussion of popular beliefs
(C) bring an arcane belief system back into the public eye
(D) debunk scientific hypotheses using supernatural evidence
(E) connect ideas about the afterlife to cultural bias

2. In context of the entire passage, the purpose of the second paragraph is to

(A) foreshadow the author's conclusion
(B) introduce an important distinction
(C) deconstruct popular convention
(D) give context to an archaic notion
(E) develop two conflicting ideas

3. In context, lines 27-34 ("The idea…indefinitely") emphasize which respective contrast?

(A) An interesting life versus an infinite circle
(B) A mysterious end versus a known destiny
(C) A final assignment versus a never-ending cycle
(D) A life of celebrity versus a death of anonymity
(E) A constant reincarnation versus a singular rebirth

4. The author uses the phrase "In reality" in line 44 in order to

(A) rectify a misconception
(B) transition to a new topic
(C) propose a theory
(D) mock an idea
(E) define a mysterious concept

5. The scientists' relationship to "these different beliefs" in line 48 is most analogous to which of the following?

(A) An apprentice chef recreates a dish that he temporarily forgot the recipe to.
(B) An architect draws up schematics that don't fit the needs of a client.
(C) A young student tries to answer a math question from his older brother's homework.
(D) A magician amazes a crowded auditorium by making her assistant disappear.
(E) A therapist attempts to account for the source of a patient's deathly fear of snakes.

6. The question in lines 47-48 signals a shift in topic from

(A) popular perception to religious devotion
(B) regular misconception to academic parody
(C) well-known fables to technical understanding
(D) spiritual exploration to scientific inquiry
(E) non-traditional views to conventional wisdom

7. The discussion of the vampire bats in lines 66-69 ("After all…excrement") serves to

(A) provide natural evidence of a seemingly unnatural phenomenon
(B) discredit a scientific approach to a non-scientific issue
(C) supplement the evidence presented with a common superstition
(D) qualify a previously stated fact with a piece of evidence
(E) call attention to a specific contradiction to the argument

8. The theory presented by the University of Hertfordshire (lines 70-81) differs from the other explanations offered in that it

(A) deals with the supernatural, while the others discuss natural phenomenon
(B) is based solely on sound waves, while the other theories are based on sight
(C) is concerned only with sounds, while the others take into account all five senses
(D) deals with natural evidence, while the others are concerned with hypothetical situations
(E) involves physical scenarios, while the others consider intangible experiences

9. Which best describes the author's tone in the final sentence of the passage?

(A) dismissive
(B) empathetic
(C) vehement
(D) capricious
(E) pensive

Questions 1-12 are based on the following passage.

This passage is adapted from a 2013 essay recounting a turning point in English history.

55 B.C.E. and 1066 C.E. are really the only two historical dates that any Englishman remembers. That is quite ironic, really, considering that they are the only times when England was not only invaded but also settled and permanently changed by foreigners. If it did nothing else, the arrival of the Romans under Julius Caesar at least gave the country some straight roads. Later, at the command of the Emperor Hadrian, the Romans built a wall to mark off where England ends and Scotland begins, something that both nations have never failed since to consider as a pretty good idea.

However, it is the date 1066 that really marks the beginning of England as we know it today. It was year of the Norman Conquest, when the French invaded and occupied England, an event that changed the English language, English law, and the English class system irrevocably. It was also responsible for establishing in the natives a determination that "no bloody foreigner" would ever change anything again, and that the stretch of water separating England from the rest of Europe would no longer be regarded as a "sleeve" of France but a channel that was English, a bit like a moat defending a castle (the fact that castles and moats were, in fact, a Norman invention, was allowed to be forgotten).

In one sense, of course, the Norman Conquest was a bit of a relief for the natives after all that time since the Romans had withdrawn and left England under Scandinavian influence. The Vikings and the Danes were far too insecure, irascible, and flighty to settle down and make a go of getting a country properly organized. A bit of pillaging and then they got bored and moved on to something else: it really was not the best way to create a solid, lasting kingdom, let alone an empire. If the Danes had possessed even a little sense of foresight, order, or discipline, then the debacle of 1066 would never have happened. Instead, they allowed Scandinavian gloom and doom to set in: from the moment that Halley's Comet made its first recorded appearance in the night sky above England way back in April of that year, the Danish rulers became convinced that the bright celestial object signaled disaster and bad luck.

The year had begun badly anyway. The king, Edward the Confessor, had died in January, and was succeeded by Harold Godwinson, who claimed that the late King had promised him the throne. However, his claim was disputed by Harald Hardrada of Norway, who said that there had been an agreement among himself and Magnus (a Norwegian king) and Harthacnut (a former King of England) and Tostig (another Norwegian)—you can tell from the names alone that this was going to be a fairly complicated affair—that *he* should be the King. There was also William II, who not only had a sensible name, but was also quite content to let all the Norwegians roar at each other whilst, down in Normandy, he was busy organizing his plan to take over the throne in England.

Tostig and Harald Hardrada sailed post haste from Norway, landed in Northern England, and challenged Harold Godwinson to a battle at Stamford Bridge. Meanwhile, in order to sail from Normandy to the mainland, William set about building a fleet of flat-bottomed boats, onto which he placed his knights and his horses. Horses? Oh, yes. William had horses; Harold did not. William also had knights in chain-mail hauberks (a kind of long shirt), kite-shaped wooden shields, long double-edged swords, a few maces, and plenty of crossbows. William was a professional; Harold was not. He arrived on English soil in late September, knowing that the next king of England would certainly not be called Harold.

He had some time on his hands, for Harold and his men, having dealt with Tostig and company in the North, had to walk all the way down to Hastings in the South, about two hundred miles. William passed the time building a small wooden castle (more fun for the men than sandcastles, one imagines). Harold and his men were pretty exhausted and sulky by the time they arrived in mid-October. The Battle of Hastings started at about nine in the morning. The armies took a couple of hours' break for lunch (a tradition that the French have kept ever since). You can see it all on the Bayeux Tapestry, of course, which was probably the first time anyone recorded a battle visually, but scholars continue to question the record's total accuracy. In the tapestry, Harold is shown being killed by an arrow; some reports claim that he was killed by a lance. Whatever! Either way, it was one in the eye for Harold.

William conquered and swept on to London; the rest is history.

1. The author's attitude toward history as demonstrated in the first paragraph is best be described as

(A) meticulous
(B) nostalgic
(C) cavalier
(D) antagonistic
(E) deferential

2. In the first paragraph, the author mentions the contributions of the Romans in England in lines 6-11 ("If it…idea") in order to

(A) insinuate that the first date mentioned is more important than the other
(B) support a case for national independence and self-determination
(C) refute a popular claim that the Romans damaged England's civilization
(D) invite the reader to question how invading forces affect native people
(E) acknowledge that invaders sometimes leave a positive influence

3. It can be inferred from the characterization of the Norman Conquest in the second paragraph (lines 12-25) that

(A) its consequences survive to this day in English culture and government
(B) it caused the downfall of a bright and promising English culture
(C) it weakened the power of England on the European stage for years to come
(D) it peacefully motivated a struggling nation using diplomacy rather than force
(E) it granted France the opportunity to become the most powerful country in Europe

4. The most significant impact of the "Norman Conquest" in the second paragraph is that

(A) England had found a way to make itself impervious to any outside invasion
(B) the English began to accept all foreign influences on their country
(C) all English castles were supplanted by those built by the French
(D) French culture was irrevocably changed by the English
(E) modern day England was created by this watershed moment

5. The parenthetical statement in lines 23-25 ("The fact that…forgotten") primarily serves to

(A) provide new information that highlights a contentious opinion
(B) add an ironic historical sidenote to the description of English cultural pride
(C) contradict a previous question that the author finds problematic
(D) relate an anecdote about the author's inability to remember historical details
(E) instigate a potential controversy that the author predicts might cross the reader's mind

6. In context of the passage, the author mentions "Halley's Comet" (line 39) in order to

(A) contrast the religious beliefs of the Danes and Normans in the Middle Ages
(B) prove that science was not as sophisticated in the eleventh century as in the twelfth
(C) reevaluate a prior claim about the effectiveness of Scandinavian rulers
(D) suggest that the Danes were crippled by their superstitions
(E) illustrate how the Danes used their knowledge of celestial bodies to craft winning strategies

7. The author lists the names of the men claiming to be king in lines 45-52 ("Edward the...Norwegian") in order to

(A) accurately depict the famous figures in this historical time period
(B) lightheartedly highlight the convoluted nature of royal succession at the time
(C) effectively evaluate the legitimacy of each man's right to the throne
(D) harshly refute scholars who debate which nobles were involved at the time
(E) intently review the political state of Northern Europe in the eleventh century

8. The author's depiction of William II of Normandy in lines 54-58 ("There was...England") can most accurately be described as an example of

(A) metaphor
(B) repetition
(C) dry humor
(D) allusion
(E) hyperbole

9. In line 65, the author uses a question ("Horses?") in order to introduce

(A) a retelling of a historical legend in a factual light
(B) an explanation of Harold's preparations for war
(C) a rebuttal of common theories about the Norman Conquest
(D) a listing of the preparations William made for war
(E) a perspective on the Norman Conquest as determined by modern ideals

10. According to the fifth paragraph (lines 59-72), the author implies that William's success is attributed to

(A) his superior tactical readiness
(B) his popular support in the English countryside
(C) his ruthless nature on the battlefield
(D) his diplomatic success among the French nobility
(E) his soldiers' fierce loyalty to their leader

11. The author's description of William's voyage to England in lines 70-72 ("He arrived…Harold") primarily conveys William's

(A) apprehension and doubt
(B) brutality and diligence
(C) friendliness and jocularity
(D) detachment and severity
(E) self-assurance and conviction

12. The author mentions that William "had some time on his hands" (line 73) in order to explain why the Norman army

(A) "had to walk all the way down to Hastings in the South" (lines 75-76)
(B) "passed the time building a small wooden castle" (line 77)
(C) "were pretty exhausted and sulky by the time they arrived in mid-October" (lines 79-80)
(D) "took a couple of hours' break for lunch" (line 82)
(E) "recorded a battle visually" (lines 85-86)

Questions 1-13 are based on the following passage.

The passages below, adapted from works published in 2012, discuss how technology has affected bullying and the bullying that occurs in school.

Passage 1

The sad truth is that most people can say that they have experienced some form of bullying. I know I have. It can range from mean comments to hallway shoving to threatening text messages, and everything in between. With the emergence of social networking sites, we now not only face bullying in person, but also cyber bullying. These social networking sites are places where a vast majority of the social activities of teen life is both echoed and amplified for better or for worse.

It's no secret that getting bullied is hurtful. But when a student, or any individual, gets bullied in person, there's only so much damage a bully can do before the possibility of someone stepping in and stopping them. In cyberspace, bullying takes on a whole new meaning. Now perpetrators can gain momentum with others chiming in as well. And the others who do decide to join in on the bullying don't need to leave the ease and comfort of their chairs; they simply press a few buttons on the keyboard and they're done. But the impact for those who are bullied is lasting.

Bullying is just as much of a public health problem as it is the victim's or individual's problem, as it causes major concerns for the overall school environment. High schools with a high rate of bullying scored much lower on standardized tests than those with lower rates of bullying. These lower test scores affect the school's capacity to meet federal requirements as well as the educational achievement of many students who do not pass the exams. This is a problem for the schools because of the No Child Left Behind Act, in which students must receive a passing score on the standardized tests to graduate. Under this act, schools are now under pressure to do something about the bullying.

To stop bullying, we need to work together to educate everyone and get everyone involved: administrators, parents, and the students. President Barack Obama recently started a campaign against bullying and Lady Gaga has her own foundation called Born This Way to help spread the message. But these are just some outlets, and unless society as a whole does what is needed to combat this problem, the consequences of bullying will only get worse. We do not permit harassment and the abuse of adults in the workplace, why shouldn't similar protections be afforded to children in school?

Passage 2

After school specials are not as popular now as they were in the 80's, but those who watched them can recall at least one of those specials being on bullying. Today, high profile cases like that of Tyler Clementi have brought bullying to the forefront of America's collective social mind. But what some seem to be forgetting is that bullying has been around long before the media put it in the hot seat. Bullying has not gotten worse over the years, according to studies in the field, but rather the media attention it has received, due to the devastating results of bullying, has highlighted the major problem.

According to a popular website that tracks bullying, "Bullying is unwanted, aggressive behavior…that involves a real or perceived power imbalance. The behavior is repeated, or has the potential to be repeated, over time. Bullying includes actions such as making threats, spreading rumors, attacking someone physically or verbally, and excluding someone from a group on purpose." The argument that these instances are simply children being children is no longer a viable excuse. In an age of interconnectedness, bullying has reached a new plateau. The perpetrators don't just have to pose a physical threat; they now have the internet at their disposal and can do their damage without leaving the comfort of their own homes.

The act of bullying doesn't only have an effect on the victim. For the perpetrators, bullying can be the beginning of a trajectory of trouble. This often includes conduct disorders, skipping school, substance abuse, and eventually, even adult criminal behavior. For the victims, being bullied leads to not simply immediate physical and emotional pain, but many times the impact can extend into later life. The scars don't go away; they stay with the victims into adulthood. The ripple effect doesn't stop at the bully and the bullied, those who are simply witnesses and are not directly involved in bullying are more likely to skip school or abuse alcohol. A climate of fear affects everyone.

Unfortunately, the old way of doing things such as suspension and expulsion doesn't stop bullying. Punishment-based strategies don't give students the tools they need to make lasting behavioral changes. Those who have a tendency to victimize others, usually have weak social skills and no emotional regulation, which can definitely be contributors to bullying behaviors. Therefore, the best strategy to combat bullying is a comprehensive approach. This includes getting the bullies involved. It may sound counterintuitive, but the bullies need help too, maybe the most help. If we can get through to them, we can come close to eliminating the problem altogether.

1. Lines 5-10 suggest that "social networking sites" are places that should be considered

(A) specifically for teens
(B) both beneficial and deleterious
(C) ripe with social activities
(D) loud and raucous
(E) prone to bullying

2. According to the second paragraph of Passage 1, the author implies that cyberspace bullying is

(A) worse than in-person bullying because it is less likely that someone will stop it
(B) less hurtful than in-person bullying because other people in cyberspace chime in to help the victim
(C) indicative of the fact that lazy people bully more than active people do
(D) proof that bullying online has a longer lasting impact than physical bullying
(E) less damaging than being bullied in person because it cannot get physical

3. In Passage 1, the third paragraph (lines 22-35) highlights that

(A) harsher consequences are needed for the perpetrators
(B) social networking sites should be shut down
(C) programs to treat the bullies themselves should be started
(D) bullies respond better to positive reinforcement
(E) bullying is detrimental to academic performance

4. The final paragraph of Passage 1 (lines 36-47) serves primarily to

(A) shift the concern from the ordinary students to celebrities
(B) advocate educational reform and raise awareness with pragmatic comparisons
(C) highlight the historical course of high school bullying and those willing to help abolish it
(D) squash an important issue with the use of a call to arms writing style
(E) place the heart of the problem in a narrow cultural context

5. Which best describes the function of the qualification in lines 42-44 ("But these…worse")?

(A) Deride the use of famous people to highlight a significant social problem.
(B) Subtly hint that certain campaigns or foundations are futile in their efforts.
(C) State that some stars do more to promote bullying than to stop it.
(D) Make a claim that all segments of society must participate in solving this problem.
(E) Extol the president's work in trying to combat this heart-wrenching problem.

6. Lines 51-59 ("Today, high...problem") suggest that greater media attention is due to

(A) the fact that bullying has been going on for years
(B) a lack of television programs to deter bullying
(C) a rising number of high profile cases
(D) the consequences of bullying becoming more severe
(E) an increase in the number of studies devoted to bullying

7. The statement in lines 68-69 ("The argument… excuse") implies that

(A) bullying has gotten worse during the past few decades
(B) children today are more physically aggressive than they once were
(C) bullying is contingent on one victim and one aggressor
(D) children today mature faster than they did before
(E) bullying was previously not considered a real problem

8. The "perpetrators" (line 76) and the "victims" (line 80) are described as

(A) similar in their experience of physical pain
(B) similar in their obvious emotional affliction
(C) similar in that they both suffer in the long term
(D) different in the responsibility they bear toward their predicament
(E) equally embarrassed by social interaction

9. In lines 90-95 ("Punishment-based...behaviors") the author implies that

(A) punishment is not the answer to the problem of bullying
(B) teaching a young child manners will benefit society
(C) most high school students lack social intelligence
(D) bullies are predisposed to having negative emotions
(E) nobody has tried alternative solutions in treating bullying

10. In their opening paragraphs, the two passages differ in that

(A) Passage 1 addresses the cause of bullying, whereas Passage 2 proposes a solution to the problem
(B) Passage 1 offers a personal anecdote, whereas Passage 2 uses statistical data
(C) Passage 1 discusses the changing nature of bullying, whereas Passage 2 underscores the media attention it has received
(D) Passage 1 paints a bleak picture, whereas Passage 2 takes a more optimistic view.
(E) Passage 1 focuses on cyber bullying, whereas Passage 2 only mentions in school bullying

11. The solutions presented in the last paragraph of each passage differ in that

(A) Passage 1 advocates stronger punishment for bullies, whereas Passage 2 advocates more leniency
(B) Passage 1 calls for an increase in funds to solve the problem, whereas Passage 2 suggests a more efficient use of existing funds
(C) Passage 1 advocates more education for the victim, whereas Passage 2 places emphasis on educating the bully
(D) Passage 1 advocates collaboration between authority figures and teens whereas passage 2 advocates focusing on the bully
(E) Passage 1 advocates passing new anti-bullying laws, whereas Passage 2 proposes more enforcement of existing laws

12. The author of Passage 2 would respond to lines 22-25 ("Bullying is…environment") of Passage 1 by

(A) Agreeing and explaining that schools with a high rate of bullying score much lower on standardized tests
(B) Agreeing and citing examples of mental disorders and substance abuse increasing due to bullying
(C) Disagreeing and explaining that the problem is primarily that of the bully, not the victim
(D) Staying neutral and saying that it all depends on if the bullying is done in person or on cyberspace
(E) Equivocating and wavering about the causes and solutions for a so-called social problem

13. The author of Passage 2 would find which of the following important issues missing in the argument presented in Passage 1?

(A) The difference between in person and online bullying.
(B) The discussion of test scores and how they are affected by bullying.
(C) The important work by president Obama and other eminent people.
(D) That bullying is an important issue in our society that must be dealt with.
(E) A comprehensive approach that includes help for the bully.

Self Evaluation

Self Evaluation is important if you want to see an improvement on your next comprehension passage. Each passage has a set of possible reasons for errors. Place a check mark next to the ones that pertain to you, and write your own on the blank line provided. Use this form to better analyze your performance by filling it out regularly and accurately so you can recognize the pattern of your most common mistakes.

If you don't understand why you have made mistakes, there is no way you can correct them!

1st Long Reading Comprehension: # Correct:____ # Wrong:____ # Unanswered:____

- ○ Did not understand the question, line reference, or answers
- ○ Did not underline the line reference
- ○ Read too much or too little around the line reference
- ○ Summarized the line reference instead of answering the question
- ○ Couldn't find the false words
- ○ Couldn't choose between two possible answers
- ○ Did not use tone to help eliminate answers
- ○ When stuck between two answers, guessed instead of looking for additional facts
- ○ Couldn't finish in time
- ○ Other:____

2nd Long Reading Comprehension: # Correct:____ # Wrong:____ # Unanswered:____

- ○ Did not understand the question, line reference, or answers
- ○ Did not underline the line reference
- ○ Read too much or too little around the line reference
- ○ Summarized the line reference instead of answering the question
- ○ Couldn't find the false words
- ○ Couldn't choose between two possible answers
- ○ Did not use tone to help eliminate answers
- ○ When stuck between two answers, guessed instead of looking for additional facts
- ○ Couldn't finish in time
- ○ Other:____

3rd Long Reading Comprehension: # Correct:____ # Wrong:____ # Unanswered:____

- ○ Did not understand the question, line reference, or answers
- ○ Did not underline the line reference
- ○ Read too much or too little around the line reference
- ○ Summarized the line reference instead of answering the question
- ○ Couldn't find the false words
- ○ Couldn't choose between two possible answers
- ○ Did not use tone to help eliminate answers
- ○ When stuck between two answers, guessed instead of looking for additional facts
- ○ Couldn't finish in time
- ○ Other:____

4th Long Reading Comprehension: # Correct:____ # Wrong:____ # Unanswered:____

- ○ Did not understand the question, line reference, or answers
- ○ Did not underline the line reference
- ○ Read too much or too little around the line reference
- ○ Summarized the line reference instead of answering the question
- ○ Couldn't find the false words
- ○ Couldn't choose between two possible answers
- ○ Did not use tone to help eliminate answers
- ○ When stuck between two answers, guessed instead of looking for additional facts
- ○ Couldn't finish in time
- ○ Other:____

Single Long Comprehension
6 Questions Total, Pages 8-9

1. Correct answer: (D)
In the first paragraph, the author introduces the Shakespearean character Juliet, and then continues to describe her role and why it is sought after. Remember: a "phenomenon" is a fact or occurrence.

2. Correct answer: (A)
The clues for this answer come from the LR and the following sentence. The author writes "it is very difficult for a child...to get through the English Lit syllabus without encountering" the story of Romeo and Juliet. He then goes on to say that it is "the most performed of all the plays that Shakespeare wrote."

3. Correct answer: (E)
This LR states that "Every ardent theatergoer carries in his or her head a memory of the actress who, for him or her, was the perfect Juliet." The tone is (+), and suggests that these "theatergoers" feel (+) towards the role of Juliet.

4. Correct answer: (D)
In the sentence immediately after the LR, the author describes only the roles of Juliet and the Nurse to be as "demanding" or "hefty" as those in Twelfth Night and As You Like It. The word closest in meaning to "demanding" is "substantial."

5. Correct answer: (B)
In this paragraph, the author starts out by writing, "If you examine the two roles…it is Romeo who develops as the play progresses." The author then writes, "In contrast, Juliet is a one note part." These quotes introduce how the two roles are different. Then the author writes how the "audience sees" Juliet's "situation" and has "empathy" for her. This shows the audience's reaction.

6. Correct answer: (C)
In this LR, the author states how the audience "warms to" Juliet, and that "they want to protect her vulnerability" towards the end of the play. Look for a positive tone.

Single Long Comprehension
9 Questions Total, Pages 10-11

1. Correct answer: (B)
In (A), both "contention" and "mythology" are false. In (C), "arcane" is false and in (E), "bias" is false. The author provides no support for (D).

2. Correct answer: (B)
In this paragraph, the author discusses a difference between "the existence" and "the essence," which he then goes on to explain further using different belief systems. In (A), "conclusion" is false. In (C), "convention" is false. In (D), "archaic" is false. And in (E), "conflicting" is false.

3. Correct answer: (C)
According to this LR, in many cultures, people determine their "ultimate destiny" by their conduct, while in "some Eastern cultures…the birth-death-rebirth cycle could be repeated indefinitely."

4. Correct answer: (A)
In this LR the author states that "occultists' views are usually considered heretical by mainstream faiths," but that "In reality, many occultists seek to harmonize and manipulate the 'essence' in order to benefit the 'existence.'" In short, the author corrects any misunderstandings the reader may have had.

5. Correct answer: (E)
According to the author, a scientist's job is to find explanations for all "these different beliefs." The only choice that has this same relationship is choice (E), in which the "therapist" is trying to find an explanation for why the "patient" has such a "fear of snakes."

6. Correct answer: (D)
In order to find the answer, the reader must look above and below the LR since the question is asking what shift this LR marks. In the paragraph above the LR, the author begins with "the spiritual views above" and the LR itself is about how "scientists make sense of all these different beliefs." So the shift is between the spiritual and the scientific.

7. Correct answer: (A)
Since the LR begins with "After all," read the previous sentence. The author states that "these apparitions have yet to be credibly proven," and then mentions "vampire bats" which suggests that there may in fact be some credibility to the "phenomenon" mentioned earlier.

P1 - Passage 1 P2 - Passage 2
LR - Line Reference
(+) - Positive
(-) - Negative
All quotes in answer choices can be found in or around the line reference.

8. Correct answer: (B)
When the author delves into scientific explanations, he discusses what we can and cannot see. It isn't until he mentions the information provided by the research at the University of Hertfordshire that he brings up possible explanations of "infrasound."

9. Correct answer: (C)
In the last sentence, the author uses the phrase "I refuse to accept the premise," suggesting he will not change his stance.

Single Long Comprehension
12 Questions Total, Pages 12-14

1. Correct answer: (C)
Starting from the first sentence, the author has an air of arrogance. By saying that these two dates "are really the only two historical dates that any Englishman remembers," the author discounts every other date that is of any importance to anyone else.

2. Correct answer: (E)
In the first paragraph, the author states that the only dates an Englishman remembers are also "when England was not only invaded but also settled and permanently changed by foreigners." Then he mentions the Romans who "at least gave the country some straight roads," suggesting that the "foreigners" sometimes brought beneficial changes to England.

3. Correct answer: (A)
In this paragraph the author uses phrases like "marks the beginning of England as we know it today," and "changed the English language, English law, and the English class system irrevocably," which means that the Norman Conquest not only altered England, but that these alterations can still be seen today.

4. Correct answer: (E)
In the second paragraph the author writes that the date of the Norman Conquest is especially important because it "marks the beginning of England as we know it today," or, it was the "watershed moment" that marked the beginning of "modern day England."

5. Correct answer: (B)
To eliminate the incorrect answers, there is no contentious opinion (A), "problematic" eliminates (C), there is no potential controversy (E), and there is no support for (D).

6. Correct answer: (D)
This is an "in order to question" so the answer will be above or below the LR. In the paragraph in which Halley's Comet is mentioned, author writes that the Scandinavians were too "insecure, irascible, and flighty" to rule a country. But then, to make matters worse, they fueled these traits by allowing Scandinavian "gloom and doom to set in" and "convinced" themselves that Halley's Comet "signaled disaster and bad luck," and thus were "crippled by their superstitions."

7. Correct answer: (B)
In this LR, after the author lists the names of the different kings and their relationships to one another, he writes that "you can tell from the names alone that this was going to be a fairly complicated affair," lightheartedly poking fun at the confusion surrounding the "succession" of possible kings.

8. Correct answer: (C)
When the author first mentions William II, he states that in comparison to the other kings (he had mentioned earlier), William II "had a sensible name," a joke concerning the names of the others.

9. Correct answer: (D)
In the line following the question, the author answers by saying "Oh, yes. William had horses; Harold did not." He then goes on to list William's other military advantages over Harold's weaker army.

10. Correct answer: (A)
The author supports his answer with a description of William's supplies. To eliminate the other choices, there is no popular support (B), we do not know if he was ruthless or not (C), there is no French nobility here (D), and it is not a question of loyalty (E).

11. Correct answer: (E)
The author states that William knew "that the next king of England would certainly not be called Harold." The tone of this LR is (+), eliminating (A), (B), and (D). The statement is not a joke, eliminating (C).

12. Correct answer: (B)
In the sentence following this LR, the author states that with the extra time William built "a small wooden castle."

Double Long Comprehension
13 Questions Total, Pages 15-17

1. Correct answer: (B)
The author states, "Social networking sites are places where…teen life is both echoed and amplified for better or for worse."

2. Correct answer: (A)
The author states, "When a student…gets bullied in person, there's only so much damage a bully can do before the possibility of someone stepping in stopping them." This implies that unlike "in-person" bullying, with cyberspace bullying "it is less likely that someone will stop it," making it "worse than in-person bullying."

3. Correct answer: (E)
According to the author, "High schools with a high rate of bullying scored much lower on standardized tests than those with lower rates of bullying."

4. Correct answer: (B)
The author states, "To stop bullying, we need to work together to educate everyone and get everyone involved: administrators, parents, and the students." The author then mentions President Obama's campaign and Lady Gaga's foundation as examples of "outlets" for bullying. Finally, the author compares bullying to "harassment...in the workplace" and writes that "similar protections be afforded to children in school."

5. Correct answer: (D)
The qualification states that "unless society as a whole does what is needed to combat this problem, the consequences of bullying will only get worse."

6. Correct answer: (C)
The author writes, "Today, high profile cases like that of Tyler Clementi have brought bullying to the forefront of America's collective social mind."

7. Correct answer: (E)
The meaning of this LR is that bullying used to be excused as "children being children" which in turn implies that during that time, it wasn't "considered a real problem," reflected in (E).

8. Correct answer: (C)
The author writes that "For the perpetrators, bullying can be the beginning in a trajectory of trouble." Later in the paragraph, the author writes, "For the victims, being bullied leads to not simply immediate physical and emotional pain, but many times the impact can extend into later life." This "long term" impact is shared by both bully and victim.

9. Correct answer: (A)
Since the LR is the second sentence of the paragraph, the reader should start from the beginning. The author writes that "suspension and expulsion doesn't stop bullying." The author then goes on to write that "Punishment-based strategies don't give students the tools they need to make lasting behavioral changes."

10. Correct answer: (C)
In the opening paragraph of Passage 1, the author writes, "With the emergence of social networking sites, we now not only face bullying in person, but also cyber bullying." In the opening of paragraph of Passage 2, the author writes, "Today, high profile cases…have brought bullying to the forefront of America's collective social mind," and "the media attention it has received, due to the devastating results of bullying, has highlighted the major problem."

11. Correct answer: (D)
The author writes in the last paragraph of Passage 1 that "we need to…get everyone involved: administrators, parents, and the students," whereas the last paragraph of Passage 2 states that "the best strategy to combat bullying is a comprehensive approach [which] includes getting the bullies involved."

12. Correct answer: (B)
In this LR, the author states that "Bullying is just as much of a public health problem as it is the victim's or individual's problem." To this, the author of Passage 2 would say that "The act of bullying doesn't only have an effect on the victim," and that, "The ripple effect doesn't stop at the bully and the bullied…A climate of fear affects everyone."

13. Correct answer: (E)
The author of Passage 1 writes that "To stop bullying, we need to work together to educate everyone and get everyone involved: administrators, parents, and the students," whereas the author of Passage 2 feels that "a comprehensive approach...includes getting the bully involved" because "the bullies need help, too." Therefore the author of Passage 2 would want that specification to be added to the approach advocated in Passage 1.

P1 - Passage 1 P2 - Passage 2
LR - Line Reference
(+) - Positive
(-) - Negative
All quotes in answer choices can be found in or around the line reference.

Chapter Two

Questions 1-6 are based on the following passage.

The following passage discusses the mythology surrounding a small, popular tourist destination in the heart of Lower Normandy, France.

To the West of Lower Normandy, the terrain is gentle and open, with low hills and orchards; but to the East, the land becomes more defensive and suspicious of intruders. Steep crags thrust up between ravines that contain fast moving streams that empty into deep, silent lakes. Brooding forests isolate hamlets which are linked only by narrow and winding roads. Even in winter, it is difficult for the eye to pierce the shadows and barriers created by the closely packed trees. There is a sense of ancient mystery, for this is a land of myth and legend and the powers of magic. It is said that the wizard Merlin paced these woods. Certainly, it is believed that this is the land where Lancelot du Lac grew up before he travelled to Camelot where his encounter with Guinevere helped to destroy the Round Table of King Arthur and his knights. You may scoff at the veracity of this legend, but there is magic working here.

In the forest of the Andaines, part of the landscape that is described above, the road passes through thickets and trees that line the course of the River Vée. Suddenly, it plunges into a ravine between the two high rocky outcrops that tower on either side. This is Monk's Leap (it's another legend of the area, he made the leap to escape a dragon – of course). It is here that the river flows into a lake around which is set the settlement of Bagnolles de l'Orne.

Bagnolles de l'Orne was once two villages. Their combined population stands now at about 2500, the highest it has ever been. You might expect, then, to see a rather pretty little Normandy village with half-timbered buildings nestling in the forested valley bottom. However, there are no homely cottages, but villas dating from the early twentieth century, elegant, fashionable shops and Art Déco hotels redolent of the 1920s. A manicured park, in the center of which lies a lake, marks the center of the town. Here stands the casino with its elegant, terraced restaurant, ballroom, cinema, theatre, slot machines, tables for Roulette and Black Jack and Poker. Bagnolles de l'Órne is a sophisticated Las Vegas situated in the heart of rural Lower Normandy.

How did this happen? The waters of the lake are thermal, essential for hydrotherapy. Naturally, there is a legend attached to the discovery of these therapeutic qualities. However, apart from the Monk who leaped across those rocks, presumably benefitting from the warm waters of the lake, nothing more was done about hydrotherapic bathing until the beginnings of the twentieth century when spas became fashionable all over Europe. Bagnolles was transformed. European nobility and the rich and famous strolled these streets, relaxed in the curing waters, attended the horse trotting meets, teed off leisurely on the golf courses, held elegant soirées, had discreet affairs and gambled the time away. It may have been a little more sophisticated, perhaps, than Las Vegas; but there were gangsters here, too, and there are tales of murders behind the bourgeois facades of the villas.

1. Lines 10-12 ("There is...magic") signify a transition in topic from

(A) a detailed account of the mythology native to a region to a discussion of why that mythology originated there
(B) an explanation concerning the reality of the Middle Ages to a light-hearted discussion of superstition stemming from that reality
(C) a vivisection of a forest as a natural habitat to a brief digression into the political mythos of medieval times
(D) a geographical study of the natural resources in a forest to a dissection of the importance of legends to a society
(E) a description of the physical landscape to a fanciful illustration of the folklore attached to that landscape

2. The phrase in line 17 ("You may...legend") serves to

(A) acknowledge the dubious nature of a claim
(B) refute a mythological explanation
(C) differentiate between myths and legends
(D) instruct the reader on how to use magic
(E) create doubt about superstitious statements

3. The tone of the parenthetical statement in lines 24-25 ("it's another...course") is

(A) optimistic
(B) accusatory
(C) duplicitous
(D) contentious
(E) facetious

4. The description in the third paragraph (lines 28-42) of Bagnolles de l'Orne depicts

(A) France's national munificence
(B) the village's unanticipated prosperity
(C) the licentious nature of Las Vegas
(D) an idyllic forest landscape
(E) a destitute village

5. In line 41, the author mentions "Las Vegas" primarily to

(A) compare France to the United States
(B) underscore a blatant discrepancy
(C) explain a misunderstanding
(D) create a point of reference for the reader
(E) show a historical progression

6. The author's use of the word "Naturally" in line 44 primarily serves to

(A) show a contrast between what is known and what remains unknown
(B) make a connection between the landscape and scientific inquiry
(C) support the author's claim that natural phenomena inspire myths
(D) signal a digression from a discussion on superstition to factual inquiry
(E) emphasize the organic quality of homeopathic remedies

Questions 1-9 are based on the following passage.

This passage is adapted from a semi-autobiographical essay in which the author recalls his attitude towards going to a university and the process of applying.

In one of the few moments when his father felt it necessary to try and communicate with him and find out what he wanted to do with his life, the boy made the mistake of confiding that he wanted to be an actor. From the set of his father's shoulders, the boy understood that perhaps this was not the best profession to have mentioned. The older man grimaced and pointed out that the acting profession was not secure. The majority of actors were out of work for most of the time. Nothing solid in that career. His eyes flicked over the downcast figure before him, overweight, spotty, clumsy and apparently clueless. "Go to university, first," he said. "At least you will have a degree to fall back on." Then, he had shaken the boy's hand, turned on his heel and marched away to catch the last train.

For a moment the boy watched the figure of his father diminish into the distance. Then he shoved his hands deep inside the pockets of his thick grey trousers and slouched away to the nearest toilet. From his pocket he took out a rather crushed cigarette, stuck it in his mouth, lit it, and leaned back against the edge of a racked washbasin. He wondered what he was supposed to do. Exactly what he was told to, he supposed. And then what? He flicked the cigarette butt into the toilet basin opposite.

His teachers were cultured snobs, but they were good at their jobs. During the next few years, they awoke his interest in Shakespeare and E. M. Forster, made History come to romantic life and even taught him to speak a little French with a Yorkshire accent. He took his advanced exams. "Not the top marks, of course," was the verdict of his teachers, "but very acceptable results. He could make a provincial university, perhaps. Definitely not Oxbridge though. He's not a scholar." They were a bit taken aback when, after he had sat the entrance exams for those noble places of learning, he received a summons to attend interviews, not just at Oxford, not just at Cambridge, but at both. They did not tell him what to expect.

Oxford was first. It took him all day to get there on several trains. His interview was in the ugliest building he had ever seen, Keble College. All pretentious buttresses and curlicues, he thought; but his headmaster had told him it was a first rate college, very, very sound academically. The boy had shrugged. He was ushered into a large, dark paneled room full of heavy furniture. A large window allowed the morning light to flood in. Before it was a long table at which several figures sat. He could not make out the faces, for they were "in the dark, with the light behind them."

A voice asked his name. Another asked his date of birth. Another asked him if it had been a difficult journey from "whereabouts in Yorkshire?" Cultured BBC voices they were, patronizing and lordly, trying so hard to communicate with a provincial. The boy felt a wall build in his chest, blocking his voice from speaking clearly. He was aware that he sounded like a sullen Yorkshire tyke, with flat vowels and dropped aitches, as awkward and clumsy as he knew his body to be. Someone asked him about a paragraph he had written in one of the essays for the exam three months previously. What had he meant by that, exactly? Since he could not remember what he had been thinking about during the exam, he had no idea what he had meant – exactly or not exactly. The interviewers, still obscured in the gloom, wished him a safe journey, asking solicitously if he would be able to get all the way home that night.

"Nay," he replied in his thickest accent, "Thar's naw train after ah git to Hull. Ah'm ter stay the neet wi'me Grampah."

"Oh, good," came the imperturbable reply, "So nice to have family, I always think. Safe journey." At Peterhouse College, Cambridge, he was interviewed, in a small but crammed library, by the author, Kingsley Amis.

"Now, Christopher," began the author. The boy was shocked. Always at school he was called by his surname and his parents called him Chris. "Now, Christopher, I want you to imagine you are in this library on a very wet and rainy day." He stared at the author. This sounded like something from "Children's Hour."

"However," continued Kingsley, "it is a very special library."

"It would be," thought Christopher.

"Can you imagine? It only has books from the nineteenth century," chuckled Kingsley.

"Of course it would," thought Christopher, "I hate the nineteenth century."

"Now. Which novel are you going to choose to read on this very wet afternoon? And tell me why you love it," Kingsley oozed bonhomie. The boy's mind went blank. Kingsley offered no help.

A few weeks later, a letter from Keble and a letter from Peterhouse arrived in Yorkshire informing him that regrettably he was not accepted. He showed the letters to the Headmaster.

"Ah, yes. Pity; but I suppose we rather expected this. You are not really Oxbridge material, are you? But I hope you learned something from the experience."

"Yes, sir." Then, after he had closed the door to the headmaster's study behind him, "I learned one thing. The surface is nowt. What's beneath it is all that matters."

1. In lines 1-9 ("In one...secure"), the author's father "felt it necessary" to convey his

(A) advice concerning which degree to pursue
(B) contempt toward all actors
(C) disapproval of the boy's career choice
(D) displeasure at the boy's appearance
(E) desire to become an actor himself

2. In context, the word "set" in line 5 most nearly means

(A) group
(B) pair
(C) size
(D) position
(E) class

3. In the second paragraph, the "boy" (line 17) is best characterized as

(A) a confused adolescent facing a serious dilemma
(B) a rebel who is determined to follow his dreams
(C) an eager young lad looking forward to college
(D) a depressed teenager unwilling to venture out into the world
(E) an idealistic youth who decides to skip college

4. In context, the phrase "but they were good at their jobs" (lines 27-28) primarily serves to

(A) praise a group
(B) qualify a comment
(C) justify a claim
(D) provide evidence
(E) criticize an authority

5. According to lines 32-40 ("He took...expect"), the boy's teachers "were a bit taken aback" (line 36) with the boy because

(A) he knew what his decision was about university even though he was not prepared
(B) his grades were higher than they had expected them to be
(C) the grades on his "advanced" exams were lower than those on his "entrance" exams
(D) he was admitted both to Oxford and Cambridge despite his low grades
(E) his grades did not warrant the quality of response he received from Oxford and Cambridge

6. The description of "Keble College" (line 43) suggests that it was

(A) hideously sprawling and decidedly bright
(B) pretentious in decision yet provincial in spirit
(C) aesthetically drab but academically eminent
(D) architecturally spare and scholastically elite
(E) visually elite and extremely esoteric

7. The accent of the college admission interviewers in lines 52-57 ("A voice...provincial") can best be described as

(A) classy, while the boy's was contrived
(B) educated, while the boy's was cosmopolitan
(C) clumsy, while the boy's was eloquent
(D) spirited, while the boy's was monotonous
(E) stately, while the boy's was parochial

8. The sentences in lines 71-72 ("Thar's naw… grampah") make use of

(A) acerbic wit
(B) foreign language
(C) practiced erudition
(D) regional dialect
(E) intentional circumlocution

9. In context of the passage, the headmaster's tone in lines 100-103 ("Ah, yes…experience") can best be described as

(A) encouraging
(B) condescending
(C) self-effacing
(D) sanctimonious
(E) uncompromising

Questions 1-12 are based on the following passage.

These passages discuss a popular question among birders and avian enthusiasts: what is the fastest bird? The first passage is taken from an essay written in 2009 about the peregrine falcon, the second is excerpted from an article written in 2013.

Passage 1

It is commonly known that the peregrine falcon is able to achieve the highest flight speed of any bird, clocking in at speeds around and over 200 miles per hour during a dive. The falcon is a diverse hunter, preferring the meat of a small or medium sized bird, but is often found feeding upon bats, though only at night, and small mammals, such as squirrels and voles. The more foolhardy of the breed have been known to hunt the larger ibis and stork, and many will feast upon various insect varieties - though this the falcon will do only in the scarcest of situations. A fierce predator, it is not even out of the question for a peregrine to dive into a group of four or five hundred starlings and come out with one in each talon.

Perhaps one of the most recognizable qualities of the peregrine falcon is reverse sexual dimorphism across genders. Females tend to be larger, much larger, and more aggressive than males, a trait common in insects, but not seen as much in the avian world. However, this trait is shared with most bird-eating raptors, and it is not uncommon to see the female of the species chasing a male, particularly when stakes of territory are considered. When determining sex, pay attention to wingspan: the average female's wings will measure 29-47 inches while the male's will measure roughly 19-23 inches.

Another trait to note of the peregrine is the state of its scrape, usually dug into cliff edges or prominently tall human structures, and usually lined with down and fragments of old eggshells or small rocks to keep their own from rolling out. Many of these falcons have even managed to adapt to city life, nesting high above street level in the arches and divots of skyscrapers and churches, hunting starlings and other fliers, sometimes even smaller hawks.

The adaptability of the hawks to human cities, the strategic locations of their scrapes, and the attainment of extreme speeds when diving make the peregrine falcon a nearly perfect hunter. Ian Coestgar, a pioneer in avian field study, has recorded over 150 peregrine attacks, called stoops. "I'd wager," Coestgar wrote in his field diary, "that the peregrine is capable of catching any bird, raptor or not. So fast is its dive and so formidable is its instinct. There are many great hunters in the animal kingdom," Coestgar continues, "I just consider myself lucky that I'm as large as I am, and the falcons are as small as they are."

Passage 2

The peregrine falcon is arguably the fastest creature that flies, depending on how vigorously one will argue semantics: can diving truly be called flying? The dive itself makes no use of the bird's extraordinary wingspan, nor does the attack. Flight must involve the wings; flapping, soaring, somehow using the wings to propel the bird. A falcon doesn't use its wings until after the dive is completed, deploying them as air brakes. The bird doesn't fly. It falls. Is the fastest man alive the one who can run the fastest, or the man who skydives?

Many are now beginning to contest that the White-Throated Needletail, a large variety of swift, is the fastest bird in the animal kingdom, reaching speeds of 105 miles per hour by flapping its wings. This seems a much more realistic statistic when considering which animal is the fastest *flier*.

These birds are so fast that the only real threat to their well-being is their own speed. Many die by crashing head first into windows, reflective surfaces, wires, lighthouses, and other manmade structures that lie outside the scope of avian understanding. The bird is inexorably uncatchable: scientists aiming to study it have to rely heavily on luck, either finding a Needletail nest by chance, or finding a younger bird while it sleeps. This is due to the bird's great speed. Females hunting to find food for their young have been known to travel hundreds of miles just to find a specific breed of locust or beetle. Even the location of the nest can elude researchers and predators alike; most are built in hollow trunks of extremely tall trees, or on small rocky outcrops on the faces of sheer cliffs. The bird makes a cement of twigs, leaves, feathers, and saliva that glues to a rock face, making its nest look like nothing more than a bump protruding just a few inches. The rare snake or mink might find its way to a nest; but most predators pose no threat to a White-Throated Needletail in mid flight due to its great speed and ability to keep a safe roost. Not even man.

1. The primary purpose of both passages is to

(A) propose a theory on which bird is the fastest
(B) broach topics on the difficulty of studying birds in flight
(C) address the human threat to flying wildlife
(D) solidify a theory about nature's fastest creature
(E) describe attributes of various avian species

2. Unlike the author of Passage 2, the author of Passage 1 does which of the following?

(A) Discusses a controversy.
(B) Offers a critique.
(C) Defies a theory.
(D) Quotes an authority.
(E) Admires a species.

3. The author of Passage 2 would most likely respond to the claim made by the author of Passage 1 in lines 1-3 ("the peregrine...bird") by

(A) agreeing, because of the high speeds attained by the peregrine when it dives
(B) disagreeing, because diving should not be considered flying
(C) disagreeing, because the swift dives at a greater speed
(D) agreeing, because the flight speed of the falcon is twice that of the swift
(E) disagreeing, because the male of the species cannot attain the speeds of the female

4. The author's tone in lines 15-26 ("Perhaps one… inches") can best be described as

(A) inspired
(B) effusive
(C) didactic
(D) cautious
(E) confused

5. In context, the word "scrape" (line 28) is closest in meaning to

(A) scratch
(B) feather
(C) call
(D) nest
(E) plight

6. Lines 31-35 ("Many of…hawks") suggest that the human impact on the peregrine falcon's way of life is

(A) threatening
(B) beneficial
(C) unknown
(D) deleterious
(E) negligible

7. Based on lines 41-44 ("'I'd wager…instinct'"), Ian Coestgar's statement "'I just...are'" (lines 46-47) can most likely be interpreted as

(A) a detached observation
(B) a humorous assertion
(C) an honest confession
(D) a snide comment
(E) an objective remark

8. The author of Passage 2 would most likely consider Coestgar's comment in lines 41-43 ("I'd wager... not") to be

(A) correct, because he does admit that the peregrine falcon reaches a higher diving speed than does the White-Throated Needletail
(B) correct, because he does agree with the author of passage 1 that the peregrine falcon is the ultimate bird of prey
(C) incorrect, because the White-Throated Needletail's lateral speeds would make it an impossible target for a dive
(D) incorrect, because the White-Throated Needletail's small size allows it to blend in and hide in most environments
(E) incorrect, because the White-Throated Needletails are always migrating and thus out of reach

9. The opening paragraph of Passage 2 makes use of all of the following EXCEPT:

(A) rhetorical questions
(B) description
(C) argument
(D) analogy
(E) anecdote

10. The author of Passage 2 most likely uses italics in line 63 in order to

(A) mock a term he views as research jargon
(B) emphasize an important distinction
(C) imply skepticism about a technique
(D) reinforce a statistic given in the passage
(E) attribute symbolic meaning to falcons

11. The explanation in lines 65-68 ("Many die… understanding") serves

(A) as a counterargument to a previously made point about threats to the survival of a species
(B) as background information for an in-depth development on a global problem
(C) as supporting evidence for an unpopular position regarding the environment
(D) to underscore a point made about a singular characteristic of a species
(E) to refute a widely held misconception about the destructive role of human development

12. The phrase in lines 81-82 ("The rare...nest") functions primarily as a

(A) concession
(B) comparison
(C) hypothesis
(D) analysis
(E) conception

Questions 1-13 are based on the following passage.

This passage, adapted from a 2013 memoir written by a retired English professor, discusses his formative years at academy.

It is often said that schooldays are the happiest days of one's life. Looking back upon my own years of education, I have reservations about the truth of that axiom. I was unhappy most of the time I was at school, always on the edge of the playground, confused and bewildered, with little idea of how to join in the gangs or coteries that make up much of a schoolchild's environment. In class, I was neither an outstanding pupil and therefore favored by the teachers, nor a complete drop out, relegated to the back row of the classroom where I could have dozed and passed rude notes to confederates who were only interested in crude and inaccurate drawings of the opposite sex. I wanted to leave school when I was fifteen but my exam results were neither so good that it was imperative I should stay on to apply for university scholarships, nor so poor that I could be directed immediately and condescendingly to the local factory. It was agreed (although not by me since I was not consulted) that I should stay on for another three years, mainly because no one knew what other alternative there could be. Nor did I. My parents put me in the boarding section of the school and departed: they had their own lives to get on with—separately, as it turned out.

The boarding house was a very small section of the school, and there were two male teachers in charge of it, Mr. Jones and Mr. Charlton—but we called them "Moe" and "Dez" behind their backs, affectionately, in the same way in which people refer to familiar and famous comedy double acts. Like all good duos, they complemented each other like a well-worn pair of mismatched shoes. Individually, they contrasted each other so sharply in appearance and wit that it was hard to predict how well they worked as a team. Moe was slim, always sharply dressed, holding a pose at the front of the class, apparently imperturbable and in possession of an astringent wit, which never allowed an adversary in conversation a chance to deliver the punch line. Dez, on the other hand, was a sprawling figure, always comfortably rather than smartly dressed. He was most at ease in the worn, coffee-stained leather armchair of his study from which he conversed with rather than lectured to his pupils, always willing to embark on long—and always hilarious—series of reminiscences to illustrate a point. This odd couple also shared the task of teaching my group in English; both had an immense knowledge of their subject, and they balanced out each other's opinions with subtle digs that produced a simultaneous belly laugh from Dez and wry smile of acknowledgement from Moe. They clearly shared the ease, respect, affection, and tolerance that accompany a true friendship.

They saved me. I wanted so much to be like them, and to impress them. So I worked (at least in their lessons), and, as I read the books they discussed, I began to grow up and accept myself in a way I had never done before. They never sat me down and talked to me about my situation, as child psychiatrists and education specialists would do today; rather, they just made me feel, gradually, more secure about myself. Just before I left school, each found a singular moment, quite casually in the middle of a conversation, to slip in a nugget of wisdom that I have always remembered. In the middle of a long story retold to me on the school's main staircase, Dez threw in, *a propos* of nothing, the following remark: "You know, of course, that a lot of people here are quite easily influenced by you, don't you? You should use that." He never expanded on that remark, and I never got the chance to ask him to do so, for I was so dumbfounded by what he had said. Before I had the chance to recover, Dez had moved on to some piece of reminiscence that I have long forgotten. Soon thereafter, as I was leaving the school for the last time, I went to say goodbye to Moe. He shook my hand and looked directly at me, imparting, "We are what we are, for good or ill, so we have to accept and make the most of it."

I never ran into Moe or Dez again, and they're dead now, probably sitting just outside the Pearly Gates, performing one of their routines. I have never forgotten them. I went to university and, eventually, became a teacher, neither as perceptive nor as good as either Moe or Dez, I think. Who would know, anyway? "You. Your pupils, your friends, God. Not a bad public, that," as Sir Thomas More answers when Richard Rich asks that same question in the play "A Man for All Seasons."

I'll agree to that, Mr. Jones and Mr. Charlton... Moe and Dez.

1. The author's primary purpose in writing this passage is to

(A) retell his own experiences as a new teacher in a prestigious boarding school
(B) advocate reforms in schooling based on a difficult experience as a student
(C) advise students in how they can achieve success despite being behind in their studies
(D) lament how lower classes do not prepare students sufficiently for high school
(E) explain that the most important lessons from school do not come from classes

2. The author uses the statement in lines 3-4 ("I have… axiom") to set up his perception of school as

(A) lively and humorous
(B) alienating and perplexing
(C) rigid and rule-driven
(D) pleasant and social
(E) traumatic and pointless

3. The contrast in tone between the first description of school (lines 1-25) and the final description of the author's career (lines 81-90) reflects

(A) the author's own personal growth and new perspective
(B) the change in social attitudes over the period of the author's youth
(C) a decline in the level of education required to become a teacher
(D) an increase in the number of students who move on to college
(E) a shift in curriculum reflecting a need for different types of teachers

4. The nicknames that the author and his classmates give to their English teachers in line 29 convey a sense of

(A) contentious familiarity
(B) inappropriate closeness
(C) covert mockery
(D) jovial reverence
(E) antagonistic competition

5. The author compares Moe and Dez to "a well-worn pair of mismatched shoes" (lines 32-33) in order to highlight

(A) the pair's parallel approach to conveying material in class
(B) an uneasiness prevalent in the lessons given by the pair
(C) the effortless nature of the pair's jibes at each other's lectures
(D) the vicious struggle between the two for the students' affections
(E) the unexpected nature of their comfortable partnership

6. According to the author's description of the teachers' preferences for sharing material, the reader can infer that Moe

(A) glibly and cheerfully incited lively debate, while Dez consistently and thoroughly plodded through dull texts
(B) sternly and severely encouraged proper format, while Dez painstakingly and purposefully discouraged conformity
(C) wryly and carefully dominated discussions, while Dez convivially and unpredictably reacted to his students' inquiries
(D) subtly and judiciously redirected digressions, while Dez spontaneously and ineffectively stumbled through the material
(E) angrily and efficiently disciplined his students, while Dez deliberately and blithely ignored misbehavior

7. According to the author's characterizations, Moe and Dez differ most noticeably in

(A) the relative depth of their lectures and assignments
(B) their particular styles of humor and presentation
(C) their attitudes toward the importance of schooling
(D) their levels of experience in educating teenagers
(E) their expectations of a reasonable amount of schoolwork

8. In context of the passage as a whole, the author implies that Moe and Dez "saved" him (line 55) from which of the following?

(A) An uninteresting, exasperating school with an emphasis on drier subjects
(B) A demanding, arduous battle through a more difficult curriculum track
(C) An aimless, boring future in an uncertain career path
(D) A frustrating, unmannerly home life with his separated parents
(E) A cruel, iniquitous social life plagued by bullies

9. The author mentions that he was "dumbfounded" (line 73) by Dez's advice in order to

(A) consider that Dez was a much more astute figure than he had first thought
(B) contrast Dez's profound idea with anything previously imparted by Moe
(C) encourage the reader's sympathy for his reaction to the teacher's strict dictum
(D) confess a deliberate avoidance of Dez after an awkward encounter
(E) emphasize the unexpected wisdom in the teacher's parting words

10. Based on the information presented in the third paragraph, the quotation in lines 78-80 ("We are...it") serves primarily as

(A) an example of the valuable insights offered up by one of the author's role models
(B) a commonly held attitude that students should strive for an impossible ideal
(C) inspiration for the author to change his intended career path before committing at a university
(D) encouragement for the author to avoid burdening himself with his parents' failing marriage
(E) proof to the author that Moe was the more profound and influential of the two professors

11. In line 79, "ill" most nearly means

(A) harsh
(B) ominous
(C) sickened
(D) unfortunate
(E) hostile

12. The primary function of the quote in lines 87-88 ("You. Your…that") is to

(A) reminisce about a cherished lesson from Moe and Dez's courses
(B) express regret for not contacting Moe or Dez before they passed away
(C) introduce a new argument about the role of religion in the classroom
(D) indicate the satisfaction the author gained from a life as a teacher
(E) advocate a self-critical approach to personal presentation in everyday life

13. Based on the passage as a whole, the author most likely looks back upon his later school days with

(A) regret
(B) frustration
(C) nostalgia
(D) embarrassment
(E) jocularity

Self Evaluation

Self Evaluation is important if you want to see an improvement on your next comprehension passage. Each passage has a set of possible reasons for errors. Place a check mark next to the ones that pertain to you, and write your own on the blank line provided. Use this form to better analyze your performance by filling it out regularly and accurately so you can recognize the pattern of your most common mistakes.

If you don't understand why you have made mistakes, there is no way you can correct them!

1st Long Reading Comprehension: # Correct:____ # Wrong:____ # Unanswered:____

- ○ Did not understand the question, line reference, or answers
- ○ Did not underline the line reference
- ○ Read too much or too little around the line reference
- ○ Summarized the line reference instead of answering the question
- ○ Couldn't find the false words
- ○ Couldn't choose between two possible answers
- ○ Did not use tone to help eliminate answers
- ○ When stuck between two answers, guessed instead of looking for additional facts
- ○ Couldn't finish in time
- ○ Other:____

2nd Long Reading Comprehension: # Correct:____ # Wrong:____ # Unanswered:____

- ○ Did not understand the question, line reference, or answers
- ○ Did not underline the line reference
- ○ Read too much or too little around the line reference
- ○ Summarized the line reference instead of answering the question
- ○ Couldn't find the false words
- ○ Couldn't choose between two possible answers
- ○ Did not use tone to help eliminate answers
- ○ When stuck between two answers, guessed instead of looking for additional facts
- ○ Couldn't finish in time
- ○ Other:____

3rd Long Reading Comprehension: # Correct:____ # Wrong:____ # Unanswered:____

- ○ Did not understand the question, line reference, or answers
- ○ Did not underline the line reference
- ○ Read too much or too little around the line reference
- ○ Summarized the line reference instead of answering the question
- ○ Couldn't find the false words
- ○ Couldn't choose between two possible answers
- ○ Did not use tone to help eliminate answers
- ○ When stuck between two answers, guessed instead of looking for additional facts
- ○ Couldn't finish in time
- ○ Other:____

4th Long Reading Comprehension: # Correct:____ # Wrong:____ # Unanswered:____

- ○ Did not understand the question, line reference, or answers
- ○ Did not underline the line reference
- ○ Read too much or too little around the line reference
- ○ Summarized the line reference instead of answering the question
- ○ Couldn't find the false words
- ○ Couldn't choose between two possible answers
- ○ Did not use tone to help eliminate answers
- ○ When stuck between two answers, guessed instead of looking for additional facts
- ○ Couldn't finish in time
- ○ Other:____

Single Long Comprehension
6 Questions Total, Pages 24-25

1. Correct answer: (E)
This LR signifies a transition. In lines 1-10, the author describes the geography. In lines 10-18, the author discusses legends associated with this area. Look for the false words in (A) ("detailed account of the mythology"), (B) ("reality of the Middle Ages"), (C) ("Political mythos"), and (D) ("Importance of legends to a society").

2. Correct answer: (A)
The author directly addresses the reader and states "You may scoff at the veracity," because he is aware that this claim seems doubtful.

3. Correct answer: (E)
In this statement, the author does not actually believe that the monk "made the leap to escape a dragon." When he says "of course," he is being sarcastic, or in other words "facetious."

4. Correct answer: (B)
Because of Bagnolles de l'Orne's small population, one might expect a "little Normandy Village" upon visiting. But the town is filled with villas, Art Deco hotels, and a grand casino, which suggests that the wealth of Bagnolles de l'Orne is unexpected.

5. Correct answer: (D)
Given that Bagnolles de l'Orne is not as well known worldwide as Las Vegas, the author is providing a point of reference for the reader.

6. Correct answer: (C)
The author is not showing a "contrast," nor is he signaling a "digression," eliminating (A) and (D). There is no "scientific inquiry" (B) and the author does not discuss the "quality" of the care, eliminating (E).

Single Long Comprehension
9 Questions Total, Pages 26-27

1. Correct answer: (C)
This LR states that "The older man grimaced and pointed out that the acting profession was not secure." This suggests that the father was not happy with the decision of his son becoming an actor.

2. Correct answer: (D)
After the boy told his father what he wanted to be, his father's body language changed, which means that set can only mean something reflecting posture, or "position."

3. Correct answer: (A)
In this paragraph, the boy "wondered what he was supposed to do. Exactly what he was told to, he supposed. And then what?" This suggests that the boy was confused about what he was to become.

4. Correct answer: (B)
The author states that "His teachers were cultured snobs," qualifies by saying "but they were good at their jobs." In this case, qualify means "make less severe."

5. Correct answer: (E)
Based on the LR, the boy's teachers expected him to be interviewed for "a provincial university" but not one of the better schools. So when he "received a summons to attend interviews" at both Oxford and Cambridge, the teachers "were a bit taken aback."

6. Correct answer: (C)
The author states in this LR that Keble college was "the ugliest building he had ever seen." Remember, aesthetics always deal with beauty.

7. Correct answer: (E)
In this LR, the boy describes the voices of the college admission interviewers as "cultured," "patronizing," and "lordly." He then describes himself as "a provincial," which is a synonym of parochial.

8. Correct answer: (D)
According to the author, the boy's answer comes out in the "thickest [Yorkshire] accent."

9. Correct answer: (B)
The headmaster's reply to the denial letter was patronizing, putting down the boy's intelligence, and speaking from a place of superiority.

Double Long Comprehension
12 Questions Total, Pages 28-29

1. Correct answer: (A)
The author of Passage 1 begins by writing, "It is commonly known that the peregrine falcon is able to achieve the highest flight speed of any bird," and then ends with, "the attainment of extreme speeds when diving make the peregrine falcon a nearly perfect hunter." The author of Passage 2 begins by writing, "The peregrine falcon is arguably the fastest creature that flies," then contests this by claiming the falcon may dive the fastest, but the white-throated needletail flies the fastest.

2. Correct answer: (D)
The only technique that Passage 1 does that Passage 2 doesn't is quote "Ian Coestgar, a pioneer in avian field study," pointing to (D).

3. Correct answer: (B)
The author of Passage 2 states, "Flight must involve the wings; flapping, soaring, somehow using the wings to propel the bird. A falcon doesn't use its wings until after the dive is completed, deploying them as air brakes. The bird doesn't fly. It falls." This supports that the author would disagree saying that diving is not the same thing as flying.

4. Correct answer: (C)
This paragraph teaches the reader about the peregrine falcon. Didactic means informative, or instructive.

5. Correct answer: (D)
The author describes a "scrape" by saying it is usually "dug into cliff edges or prominently tall human structures, and usually lined with feathers and fragments of old eggshells or small rocks to keep their own from rolling out." The author then goes on to describe nesting habits.

6. Correct answer: (E)
The falcon has "managed to adapt to city life, nesting high above street level in the arches and divots of skyscrapers and churches," suggesting that humans have not interfered much with the falcon's way of life.

7. Correct answer: (B)
The tone here is (+) eliminating (A) and (D). (E) does not have a clear tone, and Coestgar is not making a confession, cancelling (C).

8. Correct answer: (C)
The author of Passage 2 would think this statement is incorrect. The author writes, "Most predators pose no threat…to a White-Throated Needletail in mid-flight."

9. Correct answer: (E)
"Can diving truly be called flying?" and "Is the fastest man alive the one who can run the fastest, or the man who skydives?" are both rhetorical questions and the second one makes use of an analogy, eliminating (A) and (D). The author poses an argument using description here: "Flight must involve the wings; flapping, soaring, somehow using the wings to propel the bird. A falcon doesn't use its wings until after the dive is completed, deploying them as air brakes. The bird doesn't fly. It falls," eliminating (B) and (C).

10. Correct answer: (B)
The word "flier" is italicized because the author questions whether diving should be considered flying.

11. Correct answer: (D)
This LR emphasizes the previous claim about the bird's speed by stating, "These birds are so fast that the only real threat to their well-being is their own speed."

12. Correct answer: (A)
The author makes a fairly sweeping claim stating, "Most predators pose no threat…to a White-Throated Needletail in mid-flight." But the author does state that the "rare snake or mink might find its way to a nest," suggesting that the swift is not without predators. This is a concession because the author admits a point against his own argument.

Single Long Comprehension
13 Questions Total, Pages 30-32

1. Correct answer: (E)
The tone of this passage is ultimately (+), eliminating (D) and (B). This passage is about what the author learned from his boarding school experiences with his two teachers. In the LRs for questions 8 and 10, the author tells us that he learned more from his teachers than from anything else.

2. Correct answer: (B)
Because of the phrase "to set up his perception of school" in the question, the answer will be in the following lines. In the next sentence, the author writes, "I was…always on the edge of the playground," showing his alienation, and "confused and bewildered" means he was perplexed.

3. Correct answer: (A)
The tone for this question goes from (-) to (+) which immediately eliminates (C) and (E). In (B), "social attitudes" is false and in (D), "increase in the number of students" is false.

P1 - Passage 1 P2 - Passage 2
LR - Line Reference
(+) - Positive
(-) - Negative
All quotes in answer choices can be found in or around the line reference.

4. Correct answer: (D)
The author writes that the students "called them 'Moe' and 'Dez'…affectionately" eliminating all (-) toned answers. "Jovial reverence" means good-natured respect.

5. Correct answer: (E)
In the sentence following the LR, the author writes, "Individually, they contrasted each other so sharply in appearance and wit that it was hard to predict how well they worked as a team." At the end of the paragraph the author writes, "They clearly shared the ease, respect, affection, and tolerance that accompany a true friendship."

6. Correct answer: (C)
The tone of the descriptions of Moe and Dez is (+), eliminating (A), (D), and (E). In (B), "encouraged proper format" and "discouraged conformity" are false, as the author provides no support for either.

7. Correct answer: (B)
The author writes that "they contrasted each other so sharply in appearance and wit" which means they were different in their "presentation" and in their "styles of humor."

8. Correct answer: (C)
The author writes that he "wanted so much to be like them" and that "they just made me feel, gradually, more secure about myself." He goes on to write that he "went to university and, eventually, became a teacher," suggesting that Moe and Dez influenced the author a great deal when he was deciding on a career path.

9. Correct answer: (E)
The author writes that he was "dumbfounded by what [Dez] had said," which means he is talking about the "teacher's parting words." The meaning of "dumbfounded" is to make speechless with amazement, which suggests that the "nugget of wisdom" Dez imparted was "unexpected."

10. Correct answer: (A)
This quote is one of the last things that Moe, one of the teachers he "wanted so much to be like," said to the author. This eliminates (B), (C), and (D), as none of them are about something said to the author by one of his teachers. The author provides no support for (E).

11. Correct answer: (D)
Given that "ill" must mean the opposite of "good" or something "we have to accept and make the most of," it cannot be "harsh," "sickened," or "hostile." "Ominous" deals with future events, leaving "unfortunate." Try using it in the sentence.

12. Correct answer: (D)
The tone of the answer to this question is (+) which eliminates (B). The answer is also going to be about the author, eliminating (C) (about religion) and (E) (advice to others). In (A), "courses" is false.

13. Correct answer: (C)
The tone for how the author "looks back upon his later school days" is (+), eliminating (A), (B), and (D). "Jocularity" must involve joking and lightheartedness, and while the author does make use of humor sporadically, it is not how the author "most likely looks back." Remember, nostalgia is a sense of longing for the past.

Chapter Three

Questions 1-7 are based on the following passage.

The following passage investigates possible origins of Valentine's Day, a Western holiday celebrating love and gift-giving.

So many of us around the world celebrate Valentine's Day, but most of us don't think to question where the holiday originated. Why do we give flowers and gifts to our loved ones? And why is the heart so closely associated with Valentine's Day? We all know it's a day of romance and love, but not many of us know why. Overall, the history of St. Valentine, along with the story of its patron saint, is surrounded in mystery. But there are some things we do know.

The Catholic Church recognizes at least two different saints that were both named Valentine, or Valentinus, and who were both martyred. One story goes that Valentine was a priest who served in third century Rome. During this time, the Emperor Claudius II decreed that single men amounted to better soldiers in comparison to married men and those with families. For this reason, he outlawed marriage for young men in hopes of building a stronger army. Valentine saw the injustice of this decision and went against Claudius. He continued to marry young lovers in clandestine ceremonies. Unfortunately, he was discovered, and Claudius ordered Valentine be put to death.

The second origin story of Valentine's Day is about the saint named Valentine who helped Christians escape horrific and inhumane Roman prisons. He was imprisoned, and while there, he allegedly helped heal the blind daughter of his jailer, Julia. Before he was executed, he sent her a note, signed "From your Valentine," signifying what might be the first valentine ever to be sent. Additionally, to "remind them of God's love and to encourage them to remain faithful Christians," legend has it that Valentine cut out parchment hearts and gave them to persecuted Christians and soldiers. This may explain why we still use the heart today.

Valentine's Day is also said to originate from a pagan festival that took place on February 15. The celebration of Lupercalia was a fertility festival dedicated to Faunus, the Roman god of agriculture. During this festival, the Luperci, an order of Roman priests, would collect in a sacred cave where the infants Romulus and Remus, the founders of Rome, were supposed to have been cared for by a she-wolf, or *lupa*. The priests would sacrifice a goat, for fertility, and a dog, for purification. Afterwards, they would strip the goat's hide and dip it into the sacrificial blood. They would then take this hide to the streets, gently slapping both women and crop fields with it. Women welcomed the touch of the hide because it was said to make them more fertile in the upcoming year. According to legend, at the end of the day, all the young women in the city would place their names in a big urn. The unmarried men would then choose a name and become paired with the woman they chose for the year. These matches generally ended in marriage.

Whichever you prefer, the stoic priest who believed in marriage, the healer and savior of the persecuted or the Luperci who granted fertility at festivals, Valentine's Day still holds a special place in our hearts today. Whether we are single or betrothed, it warms our hearts with love and fills our bellies with chocolate - the 21st century answer to a pagan love feast!

1. In the opening paragraph, the author would most likely sum up Valentine's day as

(A) a universal celebration
(B) a mysterious dilemma
(C) a convoluted religion
(D) a romantic salute
(E) an enigmatic holiday

2. What does the author claim that we "know" in the last sentence of the first paragraph?

(A) Records prove that the Christians created the holiday.
(B) Church history records two well known namesakes.
(C) Valentine's day was built upon an ancient tragedy.
(D) The emperor was a catalyst for the celebration.
(E) It was a popular convention to marry on Valentine's Day.

3. According to the second paragraph, Valentine the priest contributed to the theories of Valentine's Day by

(A) disobeying the decree of the authorities and marrying couples secretly
(B) fighting against an unfair and vicious army by targeting specific recruits
(C) bringing religion into an otherwise pagan and war-obsessed society
(D) allowing families to visit during war time and to see their loved ones
(E) helping to build a stronger army that fought against the church

4. The author would say that the "heart" (line 35) synonymous with Valentine's Day most likely came from

(A) the note Saint Valentine sent to Julia just before his execution
(B) Julia's love for the man who miraculously cured her blindness
(C) Asterius' inhumane treatment of the Roman prisoners
(D) adherents of Christianity whose faith never faltered
(E) Saint Valentine's habit of giving paper hearts to condemned prisoners

5. The fourth paragraph (lines 36-55) claims that Valentine's Day originates from a celebration centered on both

(A) mirth and productivity
(B) tradition and spirituality
(C) agriculture and husbandry
(D) harvest and courting
(E) cleansing and protection

6. The author plans his argument by

(A) contrasting three unlikely situations
(B) comparing three men and their good deeds
(C) stating purported facts with supportive anecdotes
(D) explaining politics and religion of the day
(E) creating a mosaic of personal memories

7. In the last paragraph, the author concludes the essay by

(A) arguing that we must commemorate all three of the disparate Valentine namesakes in a modern feast
(B) conceding that we do not know how the holiday started, but should enjoy the festivities nonetheless
(C) stating that all three historical moments may have played a part in the modern day creation of Valentine's Day
(D) implying that Valentine's Day has survived the centuries by shifting its focus to consumerism
(E) detracting from the importance of the holiday by gathering that the origin of a holiday doesn't matter

Questions 1-8 are based on the following passage.

In this passage, the author reflects on the subject of poetry, and the ways in which it should be considered and taught.

Poetry is a thing both revered and hated. It is a distant muse singing the sounds of sirens we are yet to understand but are somewhat willing to appreciate all the more. And the poem is a place where all you thought you knew in daily life ceases to exist–the equivocal, convoluted, foreign, and uncomfortable, all gone! Poetry, undeniably, soothes as much as it challenges.

These statements are not argued. But we must ask, is poetry necessary to the health and wealth of a society? Is there a way to make it more accessible to people far from scholarly pursuits? Must we study the poets of the past to appreciate the present day wordmongers? Do we all have a poet within?

James Dickey, winner of the National Book Award for his poetry collection *Buckdancer's Choice*, offers some timeless and breathtakingly articulated advice: "The first thing to understand about poetry is that it comes to you from outside you, in books or in words, but that for it to live, something from within you must come to it and meet it and complete it." He urges people to explore their connection with other imaginations and the mystical quality of creativity. You cannot approach writing or reading poetry with the same logic, convention, and rules that you do other forms of communication. As Dickey further explains, "Your response with your own mind and body and memory and emotions gives a poem its ability to work its magic; if you give to it, it will give to you and give plenty."

Poetry is a wonderful form of communication that involves not only objective awareness but a deep subjective understanding that comes from every essence of your being and experience. Read a poem today and it means one thing. Read the same poem in ten years and it means another. Read it while falling in love or amidst the horror of a war and again, two entirely different outcomes. Was your analysis wrong or immature the first time around? No! The poem's beauty is such that the words float freely, unattached, only coming to ground through the momentary viewpoint of the reader.

Why then, analyze poetry in a classroom setting? Why participate in a class whose sole purpose is to covet and define that which should be weightless and meaningless until personally beheld and digested? Dickey argues that "the beginning of your true encounter with poetry should be simple. It should bypass all classrooms, textbooks, causes, examinations, and libraries and go straight to things that make your existence exist." The fact is that the university classroom may not be the best place to introduce poetry. Reading other peoples' work may not be the best view point for the novice.

Maybe, poetry should be introduced to young children and teenagers as a form of expression rather than a required course laden with facts and dates and meters and terms. The more your encounter with poetry deepens the more your experience of your own life deepens. You will pick up meaning quickly, and you will create meaning, too, for yourself and others.

What more could we demand from a society - or the world - than the ability to understand the meaning of life from its simplest form to its most complex? What could be better than teaching people to use their words rather than their wars? Is poetry important to society? As Tolstoy most poetically stated, "If you see that some aspect of your society is bad, and you want to improve it, there is only one way to do so: you have to improve people. And in order to improve people, you begin with only one thing: you become better yourself." And to become "better yourself," you need to be in touch with your inner feelings on all that is around you and within you. Poetry, whether read or written, will take you there.

1. The claim made in line 9 ("These statements are not argued") refers to

(A) the author's frustration with poetry
(B) the idea that poetry is hard to understand
(C) the fact that the poet can soothe the reader
(D) the discussion of necessity of poetry
(E) the apparent dichotomy of poetry

2. The function of the second paragraph (lines 9-14) is to

(A) allude to a scholarly style of writing
(B) raise questions for the reader to consider
(C) trace the history of a present day practice
(D) discuss the inaccessability of poetry
(E) reflect on an art form which requires introspection

3. Which is most analogous to the advice reflected in lines 27-30 ("Your response...plenty")?

(A) A heartbroken teenager finds comfort after writing a distressing blog post about love.
(B) A poet writes about astrology and the newest scientific findings in beautiful prose.
(C) A teacher assigns a topic and instructs the students to write a poem using haiku.
(D) A student analyzes a poem using quotes from scholars to back up her ideas.
(E) A writer invents his own meter of poetry, only to discover it's already in use.

4. The author uses the phrases "subjective understanding" (line 33) in the fourth paragraph to refer to

(A) the fact that poetry has no real meaning
(B) the sentiment that nothing ever stays the same
(C) the idea that your reality reflects your perception
(D) the way that poetry is often taught in schools
(E) the difficult part of understanding poetry

5. The tone of the word "No!" in line 39 of the fourth paragraph can best be described as

(A) sarcastic
(B) resigned
(C) emphatic
(D) irritated
(E) derogatory

6. Ultimately, the author views the "classroom setting" (lines 43-44) as

(A) a place where teachers are misinterpreting poetry
(B) the best way to learn about classic poetry
(C) a place devoid of any community existence
(D) a poor introduction to the importance of poetry
(E) a good way to criticize modern poetry

7. Throughout the passage, the author primarily makes use of which technique?

(A) Compare and contrast
(B) Rhetorical questions
(C) Euphemism
(D) Redundancy
(E) Alliteration

8. The author's final remark primarily expresses a sense of

(A) urgency
(B) challenge
(C) insecurity
(D) dedication
(E) confidence

Questions 1-12 are based on the following passage.

The following passage discusses the use of the mercenary Swiss army throughout history, and the various consequences that it had on the nations that employed the soldiers.

In his "Advice to a Young Tradesman," Benjamin Franklin produced the maxim "Time is money." Sound advice indeed, for it is has been followed assiduously in all parts of the world. We pay taxes by the year, schools by the term and teachers by the month. We fork out money for holiday resorts according to season, and hotels for the night (breakfast is extra). We hire cars on a daily basis, and cleaners on an hourly basis. Internet cafés charge by the minute, and phone companies charge by the number of seconds it takes us to inform our family, at the top of our voices, that we "are on the train!" and other such mind-blowing and earth-shattering information.

Of course, this was not a new idea, even in the time of Benjamin Franklin. Way back in the fourteenth century, the Swiss were able to accumulate enough money in order to consolidate their Confederation, by charging for the use of their army: presumably by the season - or however long it took to win a war for the paying customer. They were pretty canny, the Swiss, and very quickly cottoned on to the idea that if one intended to charge for the hiring of an army, the army had better produce not only a high level of success but also a list of "satisfied customers"- the Papal State was a very useful patron in this respect. The Swiss Papal guard, today, is a small but highly colorful battalion that herds and welcomes visitors flocking to St. Peter's square whilst keeping them at a relatively safe distance from the pope himself. Clearly, if you are going to have testimonials, only the best will do.

Mercenary armies were not simply confined to the Swiss, of course. There were enough disputes going on in Europe, for several groups to have a share of the market. "El Cid" probably did not look much like Charlton Heston, but he did lead a mercenary army during his years in exile from the Spanish rulers. Later still, German mercenaries were employed by the British to try and restrain the independent yearnings of upstart, provincial settlers who had felt such deep offence when asked to pay taxes on tea that they created a litter hazard in Boston harbor and needed to be taught a lesson for their impertinence. Sadly, this turned out not to be one of Britain's best ideas.

For governments, the problem with hiring mercenaries was that they were not all as reliable as the Swiss. In addition, they only allowed themselves to be hired by the highest bidder: they could be difficult to control when not paid promptly. Most importantly of all, they felt neither sentimental nor patriotic ties with the country that hired them, and, as a result, could take off from the battle field whenever they felt they had had enough of the whole fracas. Thus, hiring for the season could be very expensive. Better, and certainly cheaper, was to form a national army which could be corralled and controlled by the government of the day. In addition, paying them was simpler: raise the money through taxes that could be imposed "in the national interest." In times of real national crisis, conscription could be introduced so that the populace felt an involvement in the progress of the country. This last idea worked relatively well in the two World Wars of the last century. However, it is a daring leader who entered war without wholehearted backing of the populace, and a leader does so at his or her peril. To take just two examples: Mrs. Thatcher, British prime minister during the Falklands war, got away with it only because of her sweeping victory - it was all done and dusted within a few months - but Tony Blair's popularity began its decline when he urged the UK into the Middle East. The population was divided on the issue. The troops are still there and the cost is enormous.

Time and money. Franklin was right to see that the two are connected not only in our everyday lives, but also in the way we look at our history and our future. We can make jokes about how much each day is measured out in the money we pay out; it is not quite the same when we take a longer consideration of the part they play in our own lifetime or in our development as nations. We cannot be so certain that those two words can be taken quite so light-heartedly. As Benjamin Franklin also wrote in a letter: "But in this world, nothing can be said to be certain, except death and taxes."

The Swiss would not disagree with that.

1. According to the opening paragraph, the phrase "Time is money" (lines 2-3) can best be defined as

(A) money is only relevant to time
(B) each moment of day to day life is costly
(C) money can only be accumulated over time
(D) humanity has fallen victim to the clock
(E) cost is determined by increments of time

2. Which of the following scenarios would NOT fall under the author's definition of "Time is money" (lines 2-3) in the opening paragraph?

(A) A taxi meter increases as its riders sit in traffic.
(B) A person deposits money in a savings account.
(C) A family gets a cell phone plan based on minutes of use.
(D) A college requires a semester's payment.
(E) A gym charges a day-to-day fee instead of monthly.

3. The tone of the statement "other such mind-blowing and earth shattering information" (lines 12-13) can best be described as

(A) exaggerated and sardonic
(B) admonishing and disparaging
(C) conversational and whimsical
(D) informative and disinterested
(E) nostalgic and ambivalent

4. The phrase "cottoned on" (line 21) most nearly means

(A) fought with
(B) grabbed for
(C) caught on
(D) celebrated with
(E) softly approached

5. The author's remark in lines 30-31 ("Clearly, if... do") is made in a tone of

(A) perplexity
(B) compassion
(C) indignation
(D) conviction
(E) astonishment

6. According to the author, all of the following are attributes of the mercenaries described in lines 45-54 ("For governments...expensive") EXCEPT

(A) they are capricious
(B) they are intractable
(C) they are expensive
(D) they are unreliable
(E) they are loyal

7. According to lines 54-62 ("Better, and...country"), which statement best summarizes the author's answer to the problem of mercenaries?

(A) Pay the mercenaries a better salary by increasing taxation.
(B) Create a national army with the support of the citizens.
(C) Encourage patriotism to be instilled in the mercenaries.
(D) Increase the rate of tax return during times of crisis.
(E) Teach citizens to be more accepting of mercenaries.

8. In lines 63-66 ("However, it...peril"), the author conveys a sense of

(A) trepidation
(B) cynicism
(C) imprudence
(D) laziness
(E) community

9. The author uses the phrase "done and dusted" in line 69 to suggest that

(A) England's triumph was decisive and swift
(B) the Falklands war was messy with heavy casualties
(C) Thatcher violated international war protocol
(D) Tony Blair misled his nation in his call for war
(E) British citizens did not support the war unanimously

10. The author references Mrs. Thatcher in line 66 and Tony Blair in line 70 as examples of leaders who

(A) spent enormous sums of money on arms-for-hire
(B) botched a war by not hiring enough mercenaries
(C) trained great armies to fight against tyrants
(D) did not allow their constituents to have a voice
(E) followed the advice of the general populace

11. The author indicates in lines 74-85 ("Time and... taxes") that he is ultimately most concerned with conveying which aspect of time and money?

(A) Their irrelevance concerning personal matters
(B) Their impact on society through the ages
(C) Their connection to matters just of state
(D) Their oft-forgotten jovial nature
(E) Their influence on Benjamin Franklin

12. The author uses the phrase "it is not quite the same" (lines 78-79) primarily in order to

(A) draw a parallel between two unrelated topics
(B) differentiate between fantasy and reality
(C) mark a shift in tone from casual to earnest
(D) add levity to an otherwise serious situation
(E) give necessary background information

Questions 1-13 are based on the following passage.

The following passages are concerned with philosophy and science. In the first passage the author discusses an introduction to relativity by Albert Einstein. The second is a discussion on science and thought.

Passage 1

Albert Einstein, in his work The Meaning of Relativity, explains that what we individually experience is arranged in a series of events. In this series, the single moments that we remember are arranged as happening either "earlier" or "later," which we cannot break down further because these words do not have concrete, universal definitions. Therefore, we, as individuals, experience an "I-time," or subjective time – what is considered earlier to me might be different from what is considered earlier to you. Einstein suggests trying to associate numbers with the events, so that a greater number is associated with a later event than with an earlier one (e.g. the 27th event in my day was dinner, while the 3rd event was breakfast) but ultimately concludes that the "nature of this association may be quite meaningless," because, again, these would be different for different people (dinner might be the 34th thing you do in a day, or, if you are less inclined to be active, the 7th thing).

So we have these experiences. Through talking to each other we can, to a certain extent, compare them. We come to understand that some of our "sense perceptions," as Einstein calls them (which are what we feel and what we experience), can correspond with others' perceptions. But some don't match up quite so well. We tend to believe in shared experiences more easily, as though a common feeling is more real than feelings. This makes them feel more impersonal, more scientific. Einstein suggests that we think of our experiences like a clock: we can all experience and relate to seconds turning to minutes, minutes turning to hours, and hours turning to days (science). But how we actually feel time passing us by is a completely unique experience (not science).

The clock then represents to Einstein the "epitome of our experiences." It can describe our shared experience, but go no further. He states that he is "convinced that the philosophers have had a harmful effect upon the progress of scientific thinking in removing certain fundamental concepts from the domain of empiricism, where they are under our control, where we can observe and determine them." Granted, by philosophizing, we lose what's real and in front of our faces; but without that philosophical thought, what good is science? We want to rationalize what we find, apply it to our lives. Understandably, we want our experiences to be made not only into rigid structures, but also into a seemingly irrational bank of feelings. We are humans, after all.

Passage 2

Scientific thought has taken us further than we've ever been, and we've made remarkable progress in curing disease, in processing technologies, and in explaining evolutionary causalities and theorems. It has, however, made rather unremarkable progress in explaining the human experience: the realm of thought and dream are still relatively untouched, and many scientists scoff at those who explore this research. If it doesn't physically course through your veins, then it cannot be considered "real science." But it is in this way that science has become a processed food: all imaginary thought and personal endeavor has been ousted in lieu of callous facts and unremitting data. The proteins have been broken down, the original fibers have been split. Science has turned the human experience from a living, clucking being to an amorphous chicken nugget. There is a key, though, to finding our humanity.

Philosophic thought, for a long measure of time, was scientific thought. The philosophers of Greece and Rome were highly respected authors who commanded audiences and influenced decisions of the kings. They explained disease and society, often at the same time. They found the answers to natural questions, understanding things like birth, illness, religion and emotion. Who better to experiment than those who had trained themselves to question? But an important and powerful schism occurred, a schism fueled by decidedly unspiritual advancement. Scientific thought began to explain, through proven testing methods, the things that were once only in the domain of the philosophers.

Since that split, it seems that science has effectively made humanity feel more robotic. We view the human experience as something that is quantifiable, something that exists in a world of numbers and reports. But we forget a major component of what it is to be human: thought. Even a daydream is scientifically difficult: where do we go? What are we actually doing while we are there? We aren't quite sleeping—and daydreams aren't physically creating a different reality—but we've gone somewhere. There is much research into the *brain*, sure. But against things like medical theory, pharmaceuticals, engineering and technology, very little emphasis is given to studying the human *mind*. Is scientific thought straying so far from philosophic thought that we are losing our own humanity?

1. Which of the following statements best captures the relationship between the two passages?

(A) The second passage delivers a message that is fundamentally different from that of the first passage.
(B) The author of the second passage calls attention to a significant oversight made by the author of the first passage.
(C) The second passage corroborates points made in the first passage and expands upon them.
(D) The author of the second passage makes use of scientific theory to explain the philosophical musings of the author of the first passage.
(E) The author of the second passage focuses on dissecting one example used by the author of the first passage.

2. How does Albert Einstein's view of the "philosophers" (line 38) in the first passage differ from the assessment of the "philosophers" (line 70) in the second passage?

(A) Einstein sees them as a nuisance, but Passage 2 suggests separating them from scientists.
(B) Einstein acknowledges their importance, but Passage 2 considers scientists to be more deserving.
(C) Einstein accepts their wrongdoings, but Passage 2 thinks they do more harm than good.
(D) Einstein agrees with their philosophical thought, but Passage 2 wishes they were more scientific.
(E) Einstein thinks they are hindering science, but Passage 2 appreciates their positive influence.

3. In the first paragraph of Passage 1, the author states that "I-time" (line 8) is

(A) comparable to common sense perception
(B) understandable through research
(C) dependent on shared experiences
(D) unique to each individual
(E) based on a universal constant

4. The parenthetical statement in lines 18-19 ("dinner might…thing") can best be characterized as

(A) genuine empathy
(B) theoretical illustration
(C) social critique
(D) pointed satire
(E) dry humor

5. Einstein believes the harmful effects of the philosophers in lines 38-42 ("convinced that… them") in the first passage can best be described as

(A) tricking readers into disregarding what they have learned about science
(B) refusing to publish their findings in a way accessible to the public
(C) delving so far into philosophical thought that they are no longer able to analyze concepts in a controlled setting
(D) taking empiric data only at face value so that there can be nothing more
(E) contending that science is nothing more than academic superstition

6. The author's tone in the last two sentences of Passage 1 (lines 46-49) can best be described as

(A) sympathetic
(B) gratified
(C) perplexed
(D) condescending
(E) resigned

7. Einstein, as described in Passage 1, would most likely contribute which of the following to the list in lines 52-54 (" in curing...theorems")?

(A) Understanding language conventions
(B) Quantifying personal experience
(C) Dismissing old religious practices
(D) Advancing the medical sciences
(E) Updating the mechanics behind clocks

8. In line 56, "realm" most nearly means

(A) property
(B) territory
(C) world
(D) field
(E) kingdom

9. The author uses the phrases "the proteins have been broken down" (line 64) and "amorphous chicken nugget" (line 67) primarily in order to

(A) describe a natural process
(B) criticize the popular opinion
(C) incense the reader into action
(D) question the safety of food processing
(E) expand upon a previous metaphor

10. The author of the second passage uses italics in the final paragraph primarily to

(A) imply skepticism about a concept
(B) question the thesis of the passage
(C) highlight an important distinction
(D) redefine two commonly used words
(E) introduce important philosophical ideas

11. “Einstein” (line 29) would most likely respond to the claim made by the author of Passage 2 in lines 85-87 (“We view...reports”) by

(A) disagreeing, because shared personal accounts do not constitute real science
(B) disagreeing, because scientific pursuit is not often based on collected data and reports
(C) agreeing, because the experiences of one person are often universal
(D) agreeing, because objective observation is a common way to record the human experience
(E) agreeing, because written reports are more important than anecdotes

12. The author’s primary purpose in Passage 2 is to argue that

(A) philosophy has become too commonplace
(B) science is becoming too impersonal
(C) philosophy and science should never mix
(D) religion is a necessary part of science
(E) scientific progress should be top priority

13. Which statement about the human experience would both authors most likely agree with?

(A) It relies on both a scientific and a philosophic viewpoint.
(B) The philosophy of human life should be replaced by scientific fact.
(C) It is best left to the philosophers to figure out.
(D) All aspects of the human experience are entirely unique.
(E) It is neither scientific nor philosophical.

Self Evaluation

Self Evaluation is important if you want to see an improvement on your next comprehension passage. Each passage has a set of possible reasons for errors. Place a check mark next to the ones that pertain to you, and write your own on the blank line provided. Use this form to better analyze your performance by filling it out regularly and accurately so you can recognize the pattern of your most common mistakes.

If you don't understand why you have made mistakes, there is no way you can correct them!

1st Long Reading Comprehension: # Correct:____ # Wrong:____ # Unanswered:____

- ○ Did not understand the question, line reference, or answers
- ○ Did not underline the line reference
- ○ Read too much or too little around the line reference
- ○ Summarized the line reference instead of answering the question
- ○ Couldn't find the false words
- ○ Couldn't choose between two possible answers
- ○ Did not use tone to help eliminate answers
- ○ When stuck between two answers, guessed instead of looking for additional facts
- ○ Couldn't finish in time
- ○ Other:____

2nd Long Reading Comprehension: # Correct:____ # Wrong:____ # Unanswered:____

- ○ Did not understand the question, line reference, or answers
- ○ Did not underline the line reference
- ○ Read too much or too little around the line reference
- ○ Summarized the line reference instead of answering the question
- ○ Couldn't find the false words
- ○ Couldn't choose between two possible answers
- ○ Did not use tone to help eliminate answers
- ○ When stuck between two answers, guessed instead of looking for additional facts
- ○ Couldn't finish in time
- ○ Other:____

3rd Long Reading Comprehension: # Correct:____ # Wrong:____ # Unanswered:____

- ○ Did not understand the question, line reference, or answers
- ○ Did not underline the line reference
- ○ Read too much or too little around the line reference
- ○ Summarized the line reference instead of answering the question
- ○ Couldn't find the false words
- ○ Couldn't choose between two possible answers
- ○ Did not use tone to help eliminate answers
- ○ When stuck between two answers, guessed instead of looking for additional facts
- ○ Couldn't finish in time
- ○ Other:____

4th Long Reading Comprehension: # Correct:____ # Wrong:____ # Unanswered:____

- ○ Did not understand the question, line reference, or answers
- ○ Did not underline the line reference
- ○ Read too much or too little around the line reference
- ○ Summarized the line reference instead of answering the question
- ○ Couldn't find the false words
- ○ Couldn't choose between two possible answers
- ○ Did not use tone to help eliminate answers
- ○ When stuck between two answers, guessed instead of looking for additional facts
- ○ Couldn't finish in time
- ○ Other:____

Single Long Comprehension
7 Questions Total, Pages 38-39

1. Correct answer: (E)
The author writes in the first paragraph, "Overall, the history of St. Valentine, along with the story of its patron saint, is surrounded in mystery." This confirms that Valentine's Day is "an enigmatic holiday," because enigmatic means mysterious.

2. Correct answer: (B)
The author explains what we "know" in the second paragraph. She writes, "The Catholic Church recognizes at least two different saints that were both named Valentine, or Valentinus, and who were both martyred."

3. Correct answer: (A)
The author writes, "[Emperor Claudius II] outlawed marriage for young men in hopes of building a stronger army. Valentine saw the injustice of this decision and went against Claudius. He continued to marry young lovers in clandestine ceremonies."

4. Correct answer: (E)
In the sentence before the LR, the author writes, "legend has it that Valentine cut out parchment hearts and gave them to persecuted Christians and soldiers."

5. Correct answer: (D)
The paragraph tells us that the celebration was a "fertility festival dedicated to…the Roman god of agriculture," supporting the word "harvest." It then states that a ceremonial hide was used to bless "both women and crop fields." And finally, "The unmarried men would then…become paired with the woman" This suggests the "courting."

6. Correct answer: (C)
The author gives stories and legends that support three possible explanations. In (A), "unlikely" is false. In (B), "men" is false. In (D), "politics and religion" is false. And in (E), "personal" is false.

7. Correct answer: (B)
The author writes "Whichever you prefer," suggesting that there is no one correct historical moment that marks the meaning behind Valentine's Day, or "conceding that we do not know how the holiday started."

Single Long Comprehension
8 Questions Total, Pages 40-41

1. Correct answer: (E)
Since this LR starts with the word "These," the reader must read up. The author writes, "Poetry is a thing both revered and hated," and later writes, "Poetry… soothes as much as it challenges," suggesting a dichotomy, two contradictory parts.

2. Correct answer: (B)
The author prefaces a list of questions that make up most of this paragraph by saying, "we must ask," bringing up "questions for the reader to consider."

3. Correct answer: (A)
The advice states, "Your response…gives a poem its…magic; if you give to it, it will give to you." In A, the teenager "gives" by writing the blog, and the blog "gives" back by giving the teen "comfort."

4. Correct answer: (C)
The author writes that "Poetry…involves…a deep subjective understanding that comes from…your… experience," and sums up that notion by saying "The poem's beauty is such that the words…only [come] to ground through the momentary viewpoint of the reader," meaning that we derive our meaning of the poem through our "perception" of our "reality" at that time.

5. Correct answer: (C)
The first clue for the tone of this word is the exclamation mark which eliminates (B). The tone of the word is (+) in context. This eliminates all the (-) toned answers, (A), (D), (E).

6. Correct answer: (D)
Because this question starts with "Ultimately," the reader must read on. The author writes, "The fact is that the university classroom may not be the best place to introduce poetry."

7. Correct answer: (B)
The author uses questions throughout the whole passage more than any other technique.

8. Correct answer: (E)
The tone of this last sentence is (+), eliminating (A), (B), and (C). There is no support for (D).

Single Long Comprehension
12 Questions Total, Pages 42-43

1. Correct answer: (E)
Based on the information provided in that paragraph, we pay for services that take time, so our time equals our money. Eliminate (A) and (D), they're outside the scope. (B) and (C) may sound good, but the author does not state that everything in life costs money, nor that money takes time.

2. Correct answer: (B)
According to the author, payment equals the duration of time that passes while a service is being provided. In (B), the "person" depositing the money is the one who ultimately receives it; there is no payment for a service rendered over a predetermined amount of time.

3. Correct answer: (A)
Based on the sentence which contains the LR, the author is being sarcastic by calling fairly commonplace phone exchanges as "mind-blowing and earth-shattering."

4. Correct answer: (C)
Word in context questions should be done as sentence completions. The Swiss were "pretty canny" which means that they were smart, sharp, keen.

5. Correct answer: (D)
The tone of this remark is (+), which eliminates (A) and (C). The author is not being sympathetic, eliminating (B). Nor is the author amazed, eliminating (E). Remember, conviction shows confidence.

6. Correct answer: (E)
In this LR, the author states that mercenaries were "not all as reliable as the Swiss," eliminating (D). Then he states that they were "hired by the highest bidder," eliminating (C). In that same sentence he says "they could be difficult to control" which eliminates (B). And finally, he states that they "could take off from the battle field whenever they felt they had had enough of the whole fracas," eliminating (A).

7. Correct answer: (B)
In the LR, the author claims that "Better, and certainly cheaper, was to form a national army."

8. Correct answer: (C)
The word "peril" signifies that it is dangerous for a leader to enter a war without the backing of his or her country. Imprudence means not thinking of the future, or of repercussions.

9. Correct answer: (A)
In the LR where this phrase appears, the author states that Thatcher (the British prime minister) had a "sweeping victory." This gives us context for the phrase. The only answer choice that has the correct "who" (the British) and the correct "what" (the triumph) is (A).

10. Correct answer: (D)
Before the author gives the examples of Thatcher and Blair, he states that "it is a daring leader who entered war without wholehearted backing of the populace." The correct answer is a flip of this statement. Remember, constituents are supporters.

11. Correct answer: (B)
In this paragraph, the author states that time and money "are connected not only in our everyday life, but also in the way we look at our history and our future."

12. Correct answer: (C)
In this LR, the author states that "we can make jokes" but then says that "it is not quite the same when we take a longer consideration" suggesting a shift in tone from a lighthearted tone to a more concerned tone. Remember, earnest means serious, or honest.

Double Long Comprehension
13 Questions Total, Pages 44-46

1. Correct answer: (C)
The author of the Passage 1 discusses a theory by Einstein and ultimately concludes that philosophy is necessary to science; the author of the Passage 2 builds on that idea, claiming that all science is born from philosophy, and we must keep them intertwined. Because both authors agree, we can eliminate answer choices (A) and (B). The first author is not philosophical, eliminating (D), and the second author does no dissect one example, he builds off of a number of ideas, eliminating (E).

P1 - Passage 1 P2 - Passage 2
LR - Line Reference
(+) - Positive
(-) - Negative
All quotes in answer choices can be found in or around the line reference.

2. Correct answer: (E)
By "removing certain fundamental concepts from the domain of empiricism," Einstein fears that philosophers make understanding physical concepts too difficult. However, the philosophers in Passage 2 were "highly respected authors." With Passage 1 (-) and Passage 2 (+) in mind, we can eliminate (B), (C), and (D). As for (A), the author of Passage 2 actually wants to join philosophy and science, not separate them.

3. Correct answer: (D)
The author of Passage 1 characterizes I-time as "subjective time," meaning it is influenced by personal experiences and opinions.

4. Correct answer: (B)
A quick glance through the passage would establish that the author uses parentheses to explain his points. In this case, he's suggesting situations that haven't happened, making them theoretical.

5. Correct answer: (C)
Einstein fears that the philosophers will get so far into philosophical thought that we will lose the ability to perform tests without bias. To eliminate the others, consider that the philosophers are not attempting to trick anyone (A), they are not publishing their findings (B), they're taking empiric data NOT at face value (D), and they say nothing of superstition (E).

6. Correct answer: (A)
The author begins the LR with the word "Understandably," and then concedes that we are all human. He understands and relates to our attitude towards science.

7. Correct answer: (B)
Einstein, in line 36, Passage 1, is interested in trying to record the "epitome of our experiences." So when considering a list of scientific achievement, he would most likely add "recording human experiences." Remember, quantify means "to determine, measure, or express."

8. Correct answer: (D)
Try removing the word in context from the sentence and trying the others in its place. The "realm" is not a physical place, eliminating (A), (B), and (E). And the author here is talking about the study of thought, not the general concept, eliminating (C).

9. Correct answer: (E)
Because this is an "in order to" question, the answer will lie around the LR. In the previous sentence, the author describes science as becoming "a processed food." These phrases build on that metaphor.

10. Correct answer: (C)
Here the author uses italics to differentiate between the brain, which he considers to be scientific, and the mind, which he considers to be more philosophical.

11. Correct answer: (D)
Einstein's theory, as interpreted by the author of Passage 1, is that the similarities in human experience can be compared in order to create observable data. Only through detached (objective) study can we understand our "shared experience" in line 37.

12. Correct answer: (B)
The author of Passage 2 writes that "science has become a processed food: all imaginary thought and personal endeavor has been ousted in lieu of callous facts" (lines 61-63), and "Is scientific thought straying so far from philosophic thought that we are losing our own humanity?" (lines 97-98) because he is worried science is no longer about being human.

13. Correct answer: (A)
Both authors eventually come to the same conclusion: the author of Passage 1 says "but without that philosophical thought, what good is science?" and the author of Passage 2, "Is scientific thought straying so far from philosophic thought that we are losing our own humanity?" They agree that science and philosophy should not be separate ideas.

Chapter Four

Questions 1-7 are based on the following passage.

The following passage is adapted from a 2013 essay about "The Tempest," a play by William Shakespeare.

Imagine a young man, a student, approaching a play written by Shakespeare for the first time. It can be a little daunting. What approach does he need to take in order to understand what is going on? As an example of his dilemma, how does he approach the first scene of a play like "The Tempest?"

The very first thing the student must do is to empty his mind of all preconceptions. As he begins to read, he should, in his mind's eye, imagine that he is standing in the Globe Theatre watching the play for the first time. What does he see and what does he hear?

"The Tempest" begins with the following stage direction:

A tempestuous noise of thunder and lightning heard.

Clearly in a theatre where there was no curtain Shakespeare needed to attract the attention of the audience to the fact that the play was starting. However, he gives so few actual stage directions in his plays apart from "Enter" and "Exit/Exeunt" that, when he does give directions, we have to assume it was important to him. Here, the word "tempestuous" catches the attention - this is a significant adjective, and a student might recall that, in literature, a storm can have both realistic and metaphorical significance. He may note that the scene is in prose, not verse, which suggests, perhaps, that we are in a place of work. We see two relatively unperturbed sailors, facing the dangers of the storm in a professional, competent and cheerful way. A storm is all part of a day's work at sea.

Their attitude contrasts sharply with that of the passengers who begin to mill about on deck. They are in the way. The Boatswain mentions the word "King:" one could suppose that these passengers are members of a royal household, although we have no idea who the king is, nor of which kingdom he is in charge. They are hustled below decks as the storm appears to worsen. A cry from offstage suggests that the passengers are beginning to panic. During the next thirty lines, the situation becomes more dangerous, and the passengers more volubly frightened. The one we have already met retains a calm, if inappropriate, philosophy, in sharp contrast to the ferocious surliness of the characters with him. It would seem that the ship is about to sink, but not before a last homily from the philosophical passenger.

It is clear that this first scene is thrilling: it makes the audience ask questions about the characters they have seen, to ponder the reason for their situation, and to desire to find out what happens next. If we were only watching the play, that would be a significant start to any play. However, the student needs a moment to consider what the first scene has really suggested to him.

Two groups of people: one is composed of workers who show calm professionalism, respect, unity and competence. The other group is composed of courtiers. However, the supposedly royal party is seen away from its familiar milieu, and appears to lack any sense of appropriate behavior: one might say that the courtiers' are out of their depth. Their remarks are inappropriate and, in two cases, rude, aggressive and offensive. We are aware of the lack of unity. So there is a cultural divide being observed here, in which - just like life - behavior does not necessarily measure degree. This is quite an amount of information to have discovered from an opening scene of only sixty-six lines. We can only hope the student is up to the task.

1. The questions in lines 3-6 are primarily intended to illustrate the

(A) doubt that is cast on a student's ability to understand the true profundity of Shakespeare after study
(B) concerns of a teacher who is attempting to teach Shakespeare in a classroom setting for the first time
(C) worries that a novice student would have when initially approaching Shakespeare's work
(D) common path of inquiry that many Shakespearean scholars take when deconstructing "The Tempest"
(E) level of commitment that is required of any person who decides to read Shakespeare

2. The second paragraph (lines 7-11) functions as

(A) an imagined scenario used by all Shakespearean scholars
(B) an answer to the situation proposed in the first paragraph
(C) a digression from the scenario presented in the first paragraph
(D) a suggestion to all students to visit the Globe Theatre
(E) an anecdote from the author's childhood studies

3. The idea presented in lines 16-18 ("Clearly in… starting") is based on which of the following assumptions?

(A) Generally, the theatre was very punctual.
(B) Most audiences are not really interested in theatre.
(C) Shakespeare was tyrannical about his plays.
(D) Plays did not always start at the beginning.
(E) An audience will not pay attention to a play until a curtain rises.

4. According to the information presented in lines 16-30, the use of the word "tempestuous" (line 22) can best be characterized as

(A) hypothetical
(B) concerning
(C) informative
(D) noteworthy
(E) marginal

5. In lines 31-46, (Their attitude...passenger") it can be inferred that the passengers are

(A) adjusting poorly to a life at sea
(B) not accustomed to a storm at sea
(C) unusual fare for this seasoned crew
(D) insulted by the poor treatment
(E) attending to the panicked crew

6. The function of lines 47-54 ("It is…him") is to

(A) emphasize the levels of meaning in theatre
(B) introduce a new and unrelated topic
(C) question the objectivity of the student
(D) imply that the audience understands the play
(E) highlight the difference between observing and studying a play

7. The contrast between the two groups in lines 55-66 ("Two groups…degree") is one of

(A) composure vs. vulgarity
(B) comfort vs. arrogance
(C) experience vs. elegance
(D) indifference vs. insolence
(E) harmony vs. depravity

Questions 1-8 are based on the following passage.

In this essay, the author develops a theory about the societal usefulness, or lack thereof, of selfishness.

Of course seeing selfishness as evil is nothing new. Avarice, after all, is one of the seven deadly sins. And an entire circle of Hell is dedicated to the horrific punishment of the greedy in Dante's *Inferno*. But I'm going to go a step further and say that there's no such thing as true altruism, the belief in or practice of selfless concern for the well-being of others. We do not exhibit behavior that purely benefits another at our own expense. But is that so bad? And further, can selfishness ever be a good thing?

There is no avoiding the fact: humans are both the most detestable of animals and the noblest. Our ability to exhibit both good and evil has plagued philosophers from Plato to Nietzsche. So far here is what the consensus seems to be: the key to virtue is altruism. But anyone can do what is righteous given the right incentive. What sets apart genuinely good deeds is that they are selfless in nature. Bees and ants exhibit a remarkable level of self-sacrifice, but these insects are so closely related to one another that helping others is synonymous with being selfish, in evolutionary terms anyway. Relatedness can also provide an explanation as to why some other animals, like many birds, will help raise each other's offspring. Then what about humans?

We do at times appear to be selfless. In the 1980s, behavioral economists used a game called the "ultimatum game" to access altruistic tendencies. One player, Player X, is given some money and advised to split it with a second player, Player Y. If Y accepts the division, both keep their share of the money. If not, then neither gets any money. Since it's free money, it would be logical for Y to accept any amount, no matter how small, and for X to split the smallest amount as possible. But what happened instead was that in universities all around the world, the offer that was most often given was 50%. It would appear, at least in a laboratory setting, that humans are very generous, albeit not very smart.

This raises the question, why be nice? One of the most groundbreaking insights of current evolutionary theory is that while our brains are hardwired by self-serving genes, these same inclinations have resulted in behavior that is often altruistic. But those who consider humans to be the worst of creatures will argue that we behave well only if we are being watched, showing that there is no such thing as true altruism. On the contrary, altruistic behaviors do happen, and these behaviors have evolved through natural selection. Furthermore, evolutionary biologists have compiled a list of explanations for human niceness.

The first explanation is that by helping our relatives and families, we are helping to pass down our genes, securing our gene survival. Though we have evolved strong nepotistic instincts and niceness to those who are not our kin, this is simply just an overspill. Another reason may be reciprocity: I do "good" for you so that one day you can do "good" for me. We are not completely independent creatures. Rather, we are highly dependent on others, and we don't forget easily who owes us a favor, so we are in a perfect situation to benefit from reciprocal altruism. Yet a third explanation may be that altruistic behaviors make us look good to others, especially possible mates. This increases our chances of survival and reproduction. We are more likely to do business with and are more attracted to altruistic human beings. And finally, altruistic behavior benefits both the individual and the group; in that unselfish groups were more likely to survive and thrive than selfish groups. If within a group, everyone looks out for one another, that group will do better than say, a group in which each member only looks out for him or herself alone.

Still, natural selection helps those who help themselves, so our egoistic inclinations must still be much stronger than our altruistic ones. So for this, humans have evolved a few strategies to stop free riders, those selfish few who benefit from the altruism of others. From prehistoric times, we have used punishment as the way to keep people in check. Our ancestors used, and some communities still use, capital punishment as the final sanction against free riders. Punishment has made our species a little less evil by removing the most selfish genes from the human gene pool.

Fear of being punished isn't the only thing that keeps us in check. More often than not, we are virtuous because it simply feels good. Most ethical systems advocate altruism. "Turn the other cheek," we are told. And virtue is supposed to be "its own reward."

1. The author's argument is developed primarily by

(A) equivocating over a position and leaving the reader to decide
(B) stating a literary allusion and using science to debunk it
(C) taking an unorthodox position and proceeding to prove it
(D) questioning the theories of evolutionary biology
(E) using social and governmental studies to deride a theory

2. The question "But is that so bad?" (line 9) implies that

(A) our overall definitions of good and bad need to be reexamined
(B) we do exhibit behavior that selflessly helps others
(C) the only way to truly be good is to sometimes be bad
(D) people should not get punished for selfish actions
(E) the audience would think it is bad to state that there is no altruism

3. In context, the author uses the example of "Bees and ants" (lines 18-19) in order to

(A) demonstrate the role of family relation in selfless behavior
(B) distinguish between selfishness and selflessness in the animal kingdon
(C) point out that bees and ants often work together though they are different species
(D) differentiate between apparent altruism and true altruism
(E) argue that humans can learn about selflessness from animal behavior

4. The statement in lines 37-39 ("It would...smart") suggest that

(A) people are inherently nice and generous in their actions
(B) when people are being watched, they will share generously
(C) the contestants were aware that the scenario was fabricated
(D) most people are very cunning when dealing with money
(E) humans tend to act generously after considering the outcome

5. In context, all of the following are reasons for our "niceness" (line 52) EXCEPT

(A) gene survival
(B) personal growth
(C) mutual exchange
(D) public image
(E) community

6. According to the information presented in the passage, evolutionary biologists compiled a list of reasons for human niceness in lines 53-74 most likely in order to

(A) underscore the theory that being watched determines the display of kindness
(B) correct incomplete and biased laboratory experiments
(C) disprove the theory that humans are only capable of altruism if under observation
(D) argue that people can be persuaded to be nice if they see it in others
(E) add a scientific qualification to an ultimately subjective statement

7. In lines 82-84 ("Our ancestors...riders"), the author claims that "capital punishment" is used to

(A) deter those who take advantage of the altruistic
(B) prove how violent and evil humanity truly is
(C) eliminate frugal behavior from society at large
(D) honor the common law set down by mankind
(E) separate the weak from the strong in society

8. The overall tone of the passage is

(A) indignant
(B) righteous
(C) informative
(D) acerbic
(E) optimistic

Questions 1-12 are based on the following passage.

In this passage, the author uses personal anecdotes to discuss the fast pace of changing technology.

When I was a very young boy, in our house, in the hall, at the bottom of the stairs, by the front door, stood a small round table on which sat the telephone. It had a large black base on which was a dial of numbers and letters (ABC 0, DEF 1 and so on), which supported the receiver, one end for listening, the other for talking. It was made of black Bakelite. If one picked up the receiver, one could hear the buzzing sound that meant it was connected and after one had dialed the number, one heard the intermittent ringing tone and then the voice of whomever one had dialed. Should one not know the number of the person to whom one wished to speak, one dialed 0, and spoke directly to the lady in charge of inquiries. She would be able to find the telephone number one needed, even if the person to whom one was telephoning lived at long distance. She could explain how to ring someone abroad or how to reverse the charges. She was always polite and patient and friendly and always seemed concerned to help – just like a neighbor, really.

Naturally, in those days, one did not ring on a whim; one respected the privacy of others. For example, one avoided using the telephone at meal times. Too early in the morning the person to whom one was telephoning might be still in bed or having breakfast: late at night, he may have already gone to bed. Certainly, one never used the telephone after 10 P.M. unless there was an emergency. Indeed, if the phone rang in the middle of the night, one felt quite nervous because one knew that something awful must have happened. There was a definite etiquette about how and when the telephone was used. Certainly, the telephone was not regarded as a substitute for writing a letter. Even, at Christmas, when I was allowed to telephone Grandma and Grandpa to wish them a Merry Christmas and thank them for the ten dollar bill that had been tucked inside the Christmas card they had sent me, I was still expected to write a letter of thanks and post it later in the week. Moreover, I had to write the letter and post it in the mailbox immediately, for the Post Office could be depended upon to deliver it within a day – or two days at the most – unless it was Sunday.

Well, times have changed, that's for sure! Nowadays, it's all "texting" on mobile phones, not to mention, iPod and iPad, and Facebook and Twitter. You walk down any street and weave between an army marching steadfastly and blindly towards you. One hand holds a styrofoam Starbucks carton, the other clutches a device, from which possessor's eyes do not rise. With dextrous thumbs, they flick their way through messages posted and then proceed to text replies. Others stare fixedly ahead, earphones clamped to their heads, apparently chanting madly to themselves - until you realize they are talking to their mobile connection. No matter what time of day it is, it seems, instant thought needs to be transmitted into instant contact. Mealtime used to be a time when the family or friends gathered around a table and chatted intimately to one another. Now, the meal is accompanied by the sound of musical "apps," a muttered "Bear with, bear with," and a long muttered, conversational aside into the mobile in a language incomprehensible to the other diners. Apparently, we live in an instant world, with instant and constant communication. We spend our entire day and night in touch with one another, at work, at home, in the shops, in bed, on the bus, on the train, on the plane, and, one can only assume, on the toilet. Accessibility rules in today's society. We are all, apparently, "friends."

However, friendship is more than accessibility. Even when in a relationship, we need to heed our privacy as much as our need to share. "My true love hath my heart and I have his" wrote the poet. That is true. However, my true love does not need me to be constantly in contact to tell him I am on the train or to pass on to him every wild thought that passes through my head every second of the day. Nor does he need me to send him photos of the ice cream I am eating, nor the details of the consequent effects it may have on my sensibilities. We need moments to be introspective and alone with our thoughts, to respect the boundaries that exist between the individual and the world.

Oh, how often do I long to be back in our house, in the hall, at the bottom of the stairs, by the front door, where stands the small round table on which sits the telephone!

1. The primary purpose of this passage is to

(A) document the evolution of phone technology
(B) suggest ways to improve phone and texting etiquette
(C) comment on the social impact of a trend in communications
(D) describe a family tradition in phone usage
(E) predict the outcome of a technological development

2. The repetitive use of the word "one" in the first paragraph serves to

(A) emphasize the monotonous aspect of life in an era devoid of technology
(B) outline multiple tasks and functionalities performed by and available to any user
(C) mock a cumbersome and old fashioned way of making calls
(D) analyze the psychological effects of an impersonal way of communicating
(E) describe a childhood incident in the most generalized way

3. The function of the sentence "There was…used" in lines 31-32 is to

(A) outline the exact procedure for responding to emergency
(B) introduce a new topic that will contrast the previous topic
(C) lament the passing of a traditional form of communication
(D) advocate letter writing in place of telephoning
(E) summarize the pattern of behaviors previously mentioned

4. According to lines 32-43 ("Certainly, the... Sunday"), which of the following best describes the relationship between the telephone and the letter?

(A) The telephone can supplement but should not replace the letter.
(B) A phone call can sometimes be used in place of a letter.
(C) The telephone is a convenient substitute for letter writing.
(D) Letter writing now bears less significance than the telephone.
(E) One is expected to both write a letter and make a phone call.

5. The use of telephones in the second paragraph differs from that in the third paragraph in that in the third it is suggested that

(A) telephones are used sporadically whereas in the second they are used continuously
(B) the use of telephones in the past has enhanced the practice of texting today
(C) the telephone is depicted as superfluous, yet in the second it is viewed as essential
(D) telephones today are devoid of the conventions adhered to in the past
(E) telephones are used primarily to contact friends, but in the second had a strictly formal purpose

6. It can be inferred from the discussion in the third paragraph that the author believes the "instant and constant communication" in lines 65-66 will ultimately

(A) build gregarious communities based on location
(B) allow a user to connect intimately with acquaintances
(C) inhibit a person's ability for self-reflection and creating boundaries
(D) give people a chance to express their individuality
(E) lead to unemployment due to lack of socialization

7. The author uses quotation marks in line 70 primarily to

(A) highlight esoteric language
(B) emphasize an ironic use of a term
(C) downplay a common confusion
(D) quote a previously made statement
(E) label a modern social movement

8. It can be inferred from the author's characterization of friendship in lines 71-84 ("However, friendship…world") that a friend should

(A) constantly be settling into a state of introspection and solitude
(B) understand the urgency behind the immediate response to a text message
(C) share a description of everyday life in full detail, including pictures
(D) never feel a need to share with or invade the privacy of others
(E) not feel disappointment as a result of a lull in communication

9. The author's use of "accessibility" in lines 69 and 72 suggests that he is

(A) supportive of how widespread it is made by modern technology
(B) critical of the importance it is given in current communication trends
(C) ambivalent about its practical benefits in recent years
(D) optimistic about the future application of digital communication
(E) anxious concerning the potential for a leak of personal data

10. In the fourth paragraph (lines 71-84), the author's primary criticism is that

(A) people have become too fixated on their personal privacy
(B) true love can no longer be attained in this modern age
(C) intimacy should not devolve into obsessive interconnectivity
(D) humanity has become too self-absorbed to nurture relationships
(E) sharing intimate aspects of a relationship can lead to friction

11. According to the passage as a whole, the author implies that the telephone of his youth

(A) symbolizes the lost privacy in the age of technologically driven communication
(B) allows him to reminisce about times spent talking to an old love
(C) represents the aesthetic standards of a typical family household
(D) portrays a feeling of jubilant communication with childhood friends
(E) distinguishes between a loss of privacy and loss of independence

12. The author's tone in the passage shifts from

(A) informal to formal
(B) wistful to disinterested
(C) academic to conversational
(D) nostalgic to critical
(E) flippant to admonitory

Questions 1-13 are based on the following passage.

The following passages are written about the word "Diva." Passage 1 traces the origin of the word while Passage 2 focuses on its modern usage.

Passage 1

Divas are no longer what they used to be. Originally, the soubriquet of "diva" (from a Latin word for "goddess") was used only in the circles of classical opera, applied to the leading female singer in an opera company: later, it was used as a term to separate the really thrilling stars of this genre from the merely good performers of leading roles. However, the word has fallen into more general application to any performer and refers not only to her onstage performing ability, but also for her temperamental, headline-grabbing performances away from the theater, where she often behaves in a manner at best imperious, at worst selfish and spoiled. In the vernacular, a diva can behave very much like a spoiled child when she cannot get what she wants immediately.

In fairness, it should be said that the life of a diva is not easy. The diva is aware that the success of the show rests on the quality of her voice in each performance. Her career is demanding. She has no microphone to help her voice soar above the orchestra and reach the highest circle of the opera house. An operatic aria demands a wide vocal range, but, sometimes more importantly, a wide emotional range of acting. Working in harmony (in all senses of that word) with the leading tenor is key to the success of a performance, as well as with the conductor in the orchestra pit. A diva, in demand all round the world, flies from one venue to another: she must find the ability to gel with new companies and singers. She has to sing in alien languages. She needs not only to cosset her voice but also to find the stamina of a trained athlete. A diva has the highest professional standard to maintain. It is, therefore, unsurprising that she has a low tolerance of incompetence in others and can lash out and make startling demands and scenes, when her own expectations of herself are not equaled. She needs others to have the same dedication as she does towards the next performance. She is only too aware of what her audience demands: only the best, every night. It is an exhausting life.

Although she has now been dead for almost forty years, Maria Callas is still regarded as the greatest diva in the realm of opera. Not only could she succeed in the more traditional romantic soprano roles, but she was also able to encompass the runs in the higher octaves required by Rossini. No soprano was expected to do that. No soprano before her had ever tried. Callas revolutionized the expectations of operatic sopranos from that moment on, and (predictably) became the critical, yet superbly talented, personification of our modern idea of a "diva."

Passage 2

"Diva." Many argue that the utilization of this word in relation to women has been misplaced and used tenuously to grant women empowerment, no matter how justified it may be. What are the dangers if young women were to have a mindset toward power? Should we not encourage that mentality if only to dismantle stratified and rigid gender roles that were never defined by women? Would this be threatening to our "delicate sensibilities" which are ultimately shaped and informed by a patriarchal system touting exclusive male dominance at the expense of the female? Well, yes and no.

Ultimately, the significance of women referring to themselves as Divas is placed in the much needed re-appropriation of power. The criticism of such an espousal as this is often reduced to the neo-liberal and capitalist ideologies (shaped entirely to maintain male supremacy) in a system of "earning." In other words, has the female earned the right to call herself a Diva? Should such a label be based solely on privilege? If the fear is that women are to become autonomous from an often playful utilization of Diva, an act completely contextualized by mirth, there is a serious problem when so little an action can be ever more threatening to a male dominated society.

And while Diva should not spell out insurrection to those who support "proper usage" of the word, it is also indicative of a larger and problematic trend within female self-empowerment. Unfortunately, many women combine the definition of feminism with equal rights. Revolutionary writer and social activist, Frantz Fanon relates this idea to what he calls "the colonial table." Essentially, those affected with the "colonized mind," often stride to ascertain equal rights with those in power, those who set the rules, those who "sit at that table" – never realizing that by striding toward equality, they often solidify and perpetuate an oppressive system which is not intended to remove power from those who mean to keep it. Fanon suggests that the only action for a marginalized people is a critical resistance to such systems, not the participation in them. Would Fanon define the modern usage of Diva as revolutionary? Probably not. Fanon would probably propose that such use would only bind women to a patriarchal system, instead of redefining it.

Yet there should be nothing inherently wrong with women calling themselves Divas, even if such an appropriation of a label is misguided or even baseless. The ultimate truth is that until the patriarchal system which permeates the definition of gender roles can be completely overthrown, it will be nearly impossible for women to redefine their social roles entirely. Instead, all that is left temporarily is an attempt to have the same rights as men, when possibly, that sentiment should be focused more on redefining those rights via the women's perspective.

1. According to lines 7-40 ("However, the...life"), the author of Passage 1 implies that a diva may act spoiled for all the following reasons EXCEPT

(A) she feels pressure to carry the show
(B) she cannot get what she wants
(C) she is looking for personal financial gain
(D) she must always be at her best
(E) she has to achieve utmost quality

2. The phrase, "In fairness" (line 16) serves to

(A) show that the author is defending certain behavior
(B) explain that people in the music industry should be fair
(C) preface a tirade about the negative aspects of being a diva
(D) foreshadow a discussion about theatre
(E) highlight why divas are often disliked

3. The word "gel" in line 29 most nearly means

(A) become firm
(B) bond to
(C) coagulate
(D) work together
(E) materialize

4. In the second paragraph of Passage 1, the parenthetical statement in lines 24-25 ("in all… word") implies that

(A) everyone in the opera must work to match the diva's voice and talents
(B) the word is used in an unconventional way and must be defined by the author
(C) the word conveys the importance of the diva's mental well-being throughout a performance
(D) the symbiotic nature of musical instruments is paramount to the success of the diva
(E) the diva must not only sing in key but also work cooperatively with others in the show

5. In line 48 of Passage 1, "revolutionized," most nearly means

(A) overthrew completely
(B) radically changed
(C) rebelled against
(D) transformed violently
(E) inspired into action

6. In the first paragraph of Passage 2, the author uses a series of questions in order to

(A) introduce a controversial industry
(B) discuss the aptness of a term
(C) belittle a patriarchal society
(D) highlight the pitfalls of being female
(E) dissect the application of gender roles

7. The sentence in lines 71-72 ("Should such… privilege"), reveals the author's attitude of

(A) reverence
(B) modesty
(C) nostalgia
(D) doubt
(E) contempt

8. According to the third paragraph of Passage 2, it can be inferred that the author cites Frantz Fanon's idea of "the colonial table" (line 85) in order to

(A) argue that feminism translates to more than simply equal rights
(B) suggest that patriarchy has pervaded global institutions
(C) agree that feminism is a legitimate form of rebellion
(D) address how feminism usurps socioeconomic power from men
(E) disagree with those critical of the feminist movement

9. The tone of the last sentence of Passage 2 can best described as

(A) critical condemnation
(B) shameless ebullience
(C) qualified resignation
(D) despondent contemplation
(E) jocular inquisition

10. Passage 1 differs from Passage 2 in that

(A) Passage 1 outlines the controversy surrounding divas while Passage 2 downplays that controversy
(B) Passage 1 refers to only modern day divas while Passage 2 alludes to all divas
(C) Passage 1 is a personal take on a word while Passage 2 chronicles the history behind that word
(D) Passage 1 negates the use of a term while Passage 2 unabashedly celebrates it
(E) Passage 1 defines a particular term while Passage 2 discusses the implications of using that term

11. How would the author of Passage 1 answer the question asked in lines 70-71 of Passage 2 ("In other…Diva?")

(A) Yes, only if she has retired after reaching the pinnacle of her career
(B) Yes, only if she is performing as a solo artist in an opera house
(C) Yes, only if she carries the weight of many responsibilities in her given profession
(D) No, because claiming that title is disrespectful to her colleagues
(E) No, because she is playing into typical male stereotypes

12. "Frantz Fanon" (line 84) from Passage 2 would see "The diva" in Passage 1 (line 17) as

(A) a strong feminist changing the modern world
(B) working within the patriarchal system instead of revolutionizing it
(C) challenging the system that otherwise oppresses her
(D) redefining an important term in the history of reaching equal rights
(E) a pointless cog in the propagation of creativity

13. Both the author of Passage 1 and the author of Passage 2 approach the concept of being a Diva with

(A) overt indifference
(B) unequivocal appreciation
(C) blind subjectivity
(D) tempered ambivalence
(E) analytical dryness

Self Evaluation

Self Evaluation is important if you want to see an improvement on your next comprehension passage. Each passage has a set of possible reasons for errors. Place a check mark next to the ones that pertain to you, and write your own on the blank line provided. Use this form to better analyze your performance by filling it out regularly and accurately so you can recognize the pattern of your most common mistakes.

If you don't understand why you have made mistakes, there is no way you can correct them!

1st Long Reading Comprehension: # Correct:____ # Wrong:____ # Unanswered:____

- ○ Did not understand the question, line reference, or answers
- ○ Did not underline the line reference
- ○ Read too much or too little around the line reference
- ○ Summarized the line reference instead of answering the question
- ○ Couldn't find the false words
- ○ Couldn't choose between two possible answers
- ○ Did not use tone to help eliminate answers
- ○ When stuck between two answers, guessed instead of looking for additional facts
- ○ Couldn't finish in time
- ○ Other:____

2nd Long Reading Comprehension: # Correct:____ # Wrong:____ # Unanswered:____

- ○ Did not understand the question, line reference, or answers
- ○ Did not underline the line reference
- ○ Read too much or too little around the line reference
- ○ Summarized the line reference instead of answering the question
- ○ Couldn't find the false words
- ○ Couldn't choose between two possible answers
- ○ Did not use tone to help eliminate answers
- ○ When stuck between two answers, guessed instead of looking for additional facts
- ○ Couldn't finish in time
- ○ Other:____

3rd Long Reading Comprehension: # Correct:____ # Wrong:____ # Unanswered:____

- ○ Did not understand the question, line reference, or answers
- ○ Did not underline the line reference
- ○ Read too much or too little around the line reference
- ○ Summarized the line reference instead of answering the question
- ○ Couldn't find the false words
- ○ Couldn't choose between two possible answers
- ○ Did not use tone to help eliminate answers
- ○ When stuck between two answers, guessed instead of looking for additional facts
- ○ Couldn't finish in time
- ○ Other:____

4th Long Reading Comprehension: # Correct:____ # Wrong:____ # Unanswered:____

- ○ Did not understand the question, line reference, or answers
- ○ Did not underline the line reference
- ○ Read too much or too little around the line reference
- ○ Summarized the line reference instead of answering the question
- ○ Couldn't find the false words
- ○ Couldn't choose between two possible answers
- ○ Did not use tone to help eliminate answers
- ○ When stuck between two answers, guessed instead of looking for additional facts
- ○ Couldn't finish in time
- ○ Other:____

Single Long Comprehension
7 Questions Total, Pages 52-53

1. Correct answer: (C)
Since the LR has a pronoun in it, the reader must read up. The author precedes the series of questions by writing, "Imagine a young man, a student, approaching a play written by Shakespeare for the first time. It can be a little daunting."

2. Correct answer: (B)
The information provided in the second paragraph serves as an explanation to the questions posed in the first paragraph.

3. Correct answer: (E)
In (B), "not really interested" is false. In (C), "tyrannical" is false. In (A), "very punctual" is false. And the author provides no support for (D).

4. Correct answer: (D)
In this LR, the author writes, "Here, the word 'tempestuous' catches the attention - this is a significant adjective," pointing to (D), "noteworthy," which means important or significant.

5. Correct answer: (B)
The author writes that "these passengers are members of a royal household." He then goes on to say that as the storm is brewing "the passengers…begin to mill about on deck" and "are in the way" suggesting that they don't know what to do as this is not a common occurrence for them. He then writes that they "are beginning to panic" and as the storm worsens, are becoming "more volubly frightened."

6. Correct answer: (E)
The author begins the paragraph by saying that the first scene "makes the audience ask questions," but then writes, "However, the student needs…to consider what the first scene has really suggested to him." There is a shift here between the audience simply "observing" and the student "studying" the play.

7. Correct answer: (A)
The author describes the first group as showing "calm professionalism, respect, unity and competence" and the second group by saying that they appear to "lack any sense of appropriate behavior" and whose "remarks are inappropriate and, in two cases, rude, aggressive and offensive." This means that the first group exhibits "composure" or a serene, self-controlled state of mind, and the second group exhibits "vulgarity" or crudeness and a lack of good manners.

Single Long Comprehension
8 Questions Total, Pages 54-55

1. Correct answer: (C)
The author writes, "there's no such thing as true altruism…we do not exhibit behavior that purely benefits another at our own expense." Then the author goes on to ask, "Can selfishness ever be a good thing?" This is an "unorthodox position," because, according to the first sentence, "seeing selfishness as evil is nothing new." The author then goes on to use various studies to prove the "unorthodox position."

2. Correct answer: (E)
Based on the paragraph, we know the author believes that most people see "selfishness as evil." He's asking in this LR, is the notion that we are all essentially selfish such a bad thing? The implication is that yes, "the audience would think it is bad."

3. Correct answer: (D)
The author states that "Bees and ants exhibit a remarkable level of self-sacrifice…[but] helping others is synonymous with being selfish," meaning their "self-sacrifice" is not "real altruism" but rather what only seems like altruism.

4. Correct answer: (B)
The argument is that humans are generous (altruistic) only when "being watched": "at least in a [lab] setting…humans are very generous."

5. Correct answer: (B)
The author writes, "The first explanation is…gene survival," eliminating (A). Next, "Another reason may be reciprocity," eliminating (C). Then, "Yet a third explanation may be altruistic behaviors make us look good," eliminating (D). And finally, "altruistic behavior benefits both the individual and the group," eliminating (E).

6. Correct answer: (C)
In order to find the answer to this question, the reader must read up. The author writes, "[Some] will argue that we behave [altruistically] only if we are being watched…On the contrary…evolutionary biologists have compiled a list of explanations for human [altruism]."

P1 - Passage 1 P2 - Passage 2
LR - Line Reference
(+) - Positive
(-) - Negative
All quotes in answer choices can be found in or around the line reference.

7. Correct answer: (A)
The author writes in this paragraph that "humans have evolved a few strategies to stop free riders, those selfish few who benefit from the altruism of others." The author then goes on to say that "capital punishment [is] the final sanction against free riders."

8. Correct answer: (C)
The tone of this passage is (+), eliminating (A) and (D). There is no support for (E), and while the tone of the last paragraph may be considered "righteous," the author's overall message is not primarily a morally upright one, eliminating (B).

Single Long Comprehension
12 Questions Total, Pages 56-58

1. Correct answer: (C)
In (A), "document" is false. In (B), the author is not giving suggestions "to improve" anything. In (D), "family tradition" is false. In (E), "predict" is false.

2. Correct answer: (B)
In (A), "monotonous aspect of life" is false. In (C), the author is not mocking anything. In (D), "analyze the psychological effects" is false. And in (E), the author is not describing a single "childhood incident."

3. Correct answer: (E)
In the sentence before the LR, the author tells the reader various "rules" one was expected to follow when it came to telephone usage. The LR is a summation of the author's discussion of those rules.

4. Correct answer: (A)
The author states, "the telephone was not regarded as a substitute for writing a letter," but was to be used in addition to writing.

5. Correct answer: (D)
In the second paragraph the author writes, "There was a definite etiquette about how and when the telephone was used," but begins the third paragraph with, "Well, times have changed, that's for sure!" suggesting that the previous "etiquette" is no longer "adhered to."

6. Correct answer: (C)
The word "ultimately" means that the reader must read on. In the fourth paragraph, the author writes, "we need to heed our privacy as much as our need to share." He then writes, "we need moments to be introspective and...to respect the boundaries" between people and "the world."

7. Correct answer: (B)
Quotes in a passage signify one of four things: dialogue, a new term, sarcasm, or skepticism. Here the author is being sarcastic, which is reflected in choice (B) through the use of the word "ironic."

8. Correct answer: (E)
The author quotes a poet and writes, "My true love hath my heart and I have his," and then writes, "However, my true love does not need me to be constantly in contact to tell him...every wild thought that passes through my head every second of the day."

9. Correct answer: (B)
The tone of the author's use of the word "accessibility" is (-), eliminating (A), (C), and (D). There is no support for "anxious," which eliminates (E).

10. Correct answer: (C)
The author starts out the paragraph with, "we need to heed our privacy as much as our need to share," and then sums up his thoughts at the end of the paragraph by saying, "We need...to respect the boundaries that exist between the individual and the world."

11. Correct answer: (A)
The author is reminded of when the phone was a luxury and not an inconvenience. In (B), "old love" is false. In (C), "aesthetic" is false. In (D), "childhood friends" is false. And in (E), "loss of independence" is false.

12. Correct answer: (D)
The tone shifts from (+) to (-), eliminating (A), (C), and (E). In (B), "disinterested" is false.

Double Long Comprehension
13 Questions Total, Pages 59-61

1. Correct answer: (C)
The author writes, "a diva can behave very much like a spoiled child when she cannot get what she wants immediately," eliminating (B). The author then writes, "The diva is aware that the success of the show rests on the quality of her voice in each performance. Her career is demanding," eliminating (A) and (E). Finally, the author writes, "A diva has the highest professional standard to maintain," eliminating (D).

2. Correct answer: (A)
In the paragraph before this LR appears, the author describes the negative aspects behind the term "Diva." But after this LR, the author describes why the diva may behave like "a spoiled child," thereby justifying "certain behavior."

3. Correct answer: (D)
The clue for this "word in context" question comes from the LR itself. In this LR, the author writes, "with new companies and singers." This is the reader's clue that the answer will have to do with cooperation, another way of saying "work together."

4. Correct answer: (E)
The author writes in this LR, "in all senses of that word," suggesting that there is more than one meaning of the word, "harmony." Given that the diva is a singer, the reader can understand that one of the definitions of this word will have to do with performing "in key." The clue for the second definition comes right after the parenthetical in which the author writes, "with the leading tenor." This clue suggests that the tenor and diva must work "cooperatively."

5. Correct answer: (B)
The clue for this answer comes from the sentences preceding the LR. The author writes, about Maria Callas, "Not only could she succeed in the more traditional romantic soprano roles, but she was also able to encompass the runs in the higher octaves … No soprano before her had ever tried." Due to her talents, Maria Callas "radically changed" what was expected of operatic sopranos.

6. Correct answer: (B)
In the first paragraph the author writes, "'Diva.' Many argue that the utilization of this word in relation to women has been misplaced and used tenuously." This statement precedes the "series of questions," suggesting that the author is in fact questioning "the aptness of a term."

7. Correct answer: (D)
In this LR, the author is questioning whether one could be called a Diva based only on "privilege," pointing to "doubt." The tone of this question is (-) eliminating (A), (B), and (C). "Contempt" is too (-).

8. Correct Answer: (A)
The author links "the colonial table" with women "unfortunately" combining "feminism with equal rights," (line 84) suggesting that feminism must be more (+). Eliminate (E) because the author would agree with those who are critical but disagree that (C) feminism is currently legitimate (+). The author never writes about (B) global affairs. (D) is wrong because the author never limits feminism to just socioeconomics.

9. Correct Answer: (C)
In the LR, the "redefining" is out of reach, and possibly unimportant. This suggests the tone is one of resignation. Eliminate (A) and (D) as they are too strongly (-). Eliminate (B) since shameless ebullience, or happiness, is too (+). (E) is wrong because jocular comes from "joking," suggesting that tone is not serious.

10. Correct Answer: (E)
Both passages discuss the "application" (line 9, P1) and the "utilization" (line 53, P2) of "Diva." They differ in the second paragraphs of each passage where P1 explores the origin and P2 considers the meaning. The author of P1 does not write about (A)'s controversy or limits his discussion to (B) only modern day. The author of P2 does not trace (C) the history of "Diva" or suggests that (D) using "Diva" is absolutely (+).

11. Correct Answer: (C)
The author of P1 writes that a diva must "gel" with others, have "stamina," and maintain "the highest professional standard" (lines 30-34), eliminating (B). The author does not refer to (A) retirement, or (E) male stereotypes. The author does not write claiming the title is (D) disrespectful (-), but rather a "more general application" (lines 9-10).

12. Correct Answer: (B)
Frantz Fanon believes that "the only action for a marginalized people is critical resistance" (lines 93-95) to an "oppressive system" (line 91). The diva in P1 does not do that, eliminating (A), (C), and (D). (E) is wrong because the author of P2 does not relate Fanon to creativity.

13. Correct Answer: (D)
Both authors suggest that the utilization of "Diva" is both (+) and (-): P1 states that a diva is "spoiled" (-) (line 18), but has "dedication" (+) (line 38) and P2 states that "there should be nothing inherently wrong with women calling themselves Divas" (+) (lines 100-101), but can also be "problematic" (-) (line 82). Eliminate (B) as the tone is too (+). (A) and (E) are wrong because both are emphatic. (C) is wrong because both offer evidence for their arguments.

P1 - Passage 1 P2 - Passage 2
LR - Line Reference
(+) - Positive
(-) - Negative
All quotes in answer choices can be found in or around the line reference.

Chapter Five

Questions 1-6 are based on the following passage.

This passage is adapted from an essay written by a British man living in Lower Normandy, France. It was written in 2013.

Unlike many of their neighbors in Europe, the French are not noted for their eagerness to work long hours. The British are startled by the French readiness to rest from work not only on Sunday but also on Monday and Wednesday afternoon. The Germans and the Swiss are less naïve but, nevertheless, are scornful of the fact that the whole of France appears to shut down for three weeks in August so that the French citizens may rush, like lemmings, to the Cote D'Azur and squash together on the narrow strips of Mediterranean beach and pay an outrageous amount of money for a small café experience. They desert Paris and other large cities, leaving them empty for tourists to wander around and wonder why everything is closed for "annual vacation." Consequently, most of Northern Europe, perhaps a little sweepingly, dismisses France as an idle nation. The French retort that, at least, they have gotten their priorities in life right. The summer is a time for relaxation and celebration.

The 14th of July marks the start of what the French call "the great escape" - they see no irony in this soubriquet. July 14th is also Bastille Day in celebration of the 1790 uprising by the Parisian citizens who stormed the building to liberate all political prisoners held there. In actual fact, it turned out that there were only seven old men held there, and their escape was plodding and drawn out. Nevertheless, this event marked the end of the old regime and the beginning of modern France, and it was for this reason that, in 1880, it was decided that Bastille Day would become a national holiday, celebrated annually – rather like Independence Day in the United States.

The center of the celebration is The Champs Elysée in Paris. An enormous Tricolor[1] hangs from the Arc du Triomphe. The broad avenue itself is lined with flags of blue, white and red, and smaller versions flutter from every possible vantage point. With great pomp and style, the President of France progresses along the Champs Elysée, which is lined by police officers and applauding Parisians. He takes the salute of the largest military parade in Europe, with cavalry and tanks and weapons not only from France, but also from those territories in the world that still are linked to the "mother country." Jets fly low over the cheering crowds. Later the president meets with the media and talks informally about what has been achieved in the previous year, how France has fared in the previous year, how she stands presently, how she will advance next year. It is rather like the American President's State of the Union speech. The day celebrating the creation and survival of France ends with dancing and concerts and parties and, of course, a huge firework display centered on the Eiffel Tower. The streets are crowded and alive with people calling out to one another, gossiping, examining, buying, laughing, smiling, and reveling in being French: Liberté, Fraternité, Egalité! Vive la France![2]

1 The French Flag

2 Liberty! Brotherhood! Equality! Long live France!

1. According to the first paragraph, the French would most likely respond to the "British" (line 3) and the "Germans and the Swiss" (lines 5-6) by claiming that

(A) vacations and celebrations are both vital to a culture and destructive of it
(B) they have admittedly gotten too listless in their approach to work
(C) maintaining an illustrious career is the most important aspect of life
(D) they have little support for their politics in context of Europe as a whole
(E) national pride and general well-being should be the prime concern

2. The author's use of the words "rush," "lemmings," and "squash" (lines 9-10) suggests a tone of

(A) disapproval
(B) loathing
(C) pity
(D) resentment
(E) excitement

3. The phrase "perhaps a little sweepingly" (line 16) suggests that

(A) the author is tired of having to defend his homeland
(B) the author doesn't believe in this consensus
(C) the author wants to lessen the degree of criticism
(D) the European nations have good cause to dismiss France
(E) the European nations generally approve of France

4. The sentence "The summer…celebration" (lines 18-19) primarily serves to

(A) lend historical credence to a fact
(B) explain a very French attitude
(C) attack a non-French idea
(D) introduce the next topic
(E) digress from the issue at hand

5. According to the second paragraph, the "irony" mentioned in line 21 specifically refers to which idea?

(A) No prisoners were actually freed from their bonds during the event.
(B) "The great escape" describes an event that was not very dramatic.
(C) "The great escape" was the turning point in the French Revolution.
(D) The Parisian citizens entered the city, and no one escaped the city.
(E) The old men being held were being held of their own volition.

6. The third paragraph (lines 33-57) consists primarily of

(A) a categorical study of each element of a festival
(B) a description of a military parade that spans Europe
(C) an illustration of the President of France's power
(D) a detailed account of a French commemoration
(E) the positive and negative outcomes from the celebration

Questions 1-9 are based on the following passages.

The following passages are reprints of short conservation articles. Both authors describe field experiences with big cats.

Passage 1

The radio-collar beacon had been immobile for three days. I was torn. The frequency belonged to my favourite lioness, an old female I'd been studying for two years. She had disappeared here before, a dense wall of spiny num-num thicket where it was impossible to follow in my truck. But, without fail, she had always emerged after a night--a moment I welcomed with relief.

The num-num was close to a large Zulu village and was notorious for wire snares. On the fourth morning, I decided I had to check on her. If she was in a snare, it was already too late, but there was only one way to find out. I abandoned the truck and plunged into the thicket on foot. From the intense sun of the African savanna, I was suddenly submerged in thorn-cloaked gloom. Moving in a clumsy stooping shuffle, I called loudly to my unseen lioness, an absurd monologue to let her know I was coming. If she was alive, I didn't want to surprise her at close quarters.

Every few steps I took, the signal strength grew. So too did the dark barrier of thorns. I had no choice but to get on all fours. The signal was booming: she could not be more than fifty metres away, but I could not see a thing. I dropped to my belly and shuffled deeper on my elbows. Suddenly, a soft grunt. I froze. Flat on my belly, surrounded by thorns.

Through the maze of branches, the silhouette of my lioness abruptly resolved. Ten meters away. She watched me with absolute stillness. She grunted again, and I suddenly saw why. Cubs! Two little lions, a few weeks old, rested between her front legs. It was my cue to leave. She had been astonishingly tolerant but I had asked more of her than I deserved. Her gaze tracked me as I inched back out. As the thorns closed back in around her, she dipped her head to groom her sleeping cubs, my fleeting intrusion forgotten.

Passage 2

As the pinging grew louder in my headphones, I knew that my radio-collared snow leopard was just over the rise. I inched my way toward the ridgeline, ignoring the Gobi desert vista stretching out below. But, as usual, only an empty hillside greeted me when I crested the ridge.

Still, the steady radio ping told me she was close, so I set up my telescope in the shade of a large boulder and watched the valley below. Routinely eluded by these secretive cats, I didn't expect to see her today. Then, like a ghost, she appeared from a brush thicket three hundred yards down slope. For the first two minutes, I didn't breathe, hoping not to attract her attention. Oddly, her interests seemed elsewhere-she kept looking into the thicket.

Then, with no concern for stealth, three balls of fur exploded from the brush, crashing into their mother's legs. Cubs! The 2-month-olds tussled with each other and rolled into a shallow ravine. I tucked myself farther into the shadow of the boulder, but at this distance I was surely well hidden. I thought.

An instant later, the mother leopard turned slowly and looked toward me. She seemed to stare directly into my telescope, clearly not pleased. With that, she abruptly departed, urging the three cubs to follow. Stopping to pick up a straggler in her mouth, she topped the next ridge, and the family disappeared. I tracked her many times over the next 4 months, yet she never allowed another glimpse of those cubs. A dozen years later, I reflect on that day, and am content to have had a moment in the presence of such a rare and precious sight.

1. According to Passage 1, the author uses the word "torn" (line 2) to express

   (A) how angry he was that the radio collar had been ripped off
   (B) his dismay at the unreachable denseness of the thickets
   (C) how he weighed his options between waiting and searching
   (D) whether he should share his news with others or not
   (E) whether he should bury the deceased lioness or not

2. In context, the author felt "relief" (line 8) in the past because

   (A) he was able to continue tracking the lioness
   (B) the lioness was unharmed by the radio collar
   (C) he could use his vehicle again
   (D) the lioness was able to give birth to cubs
   (E) he could continue studying the Zulu

3. The word "plunged" in line 14 most nearly means

(A) plummeted
(B) inserted
(C) jabbed
(D) fell
(E) entered

4. The word "resolved" in line 28 is closest in meaning to

(A) finished
(B) appeared
(C) determined
(D) answered
(E) bound

5. We can assume, in lines 32-34 ("She had... deserved"), that the author feels

(A) he is not worthy of his career as a conservationist
(B) lionesses are extremely tolerant creatures
(C) he was lucky to have come so close to a lioness and her cubs
(D) humbled to receive this animal's affection
(E) he has not tended to the needs of the infant animals

6. Which statement best characterizes the contrast between the lioness in lines 27-30 ("Through the...why") of Passage 1 and the cubs in lines 53-56 ("Then, with...ravine") of Passage 2?

(A) The first displays uncoordinated playfulness while the second portrays graceful stoicism.
(B) The first focuses on animal grooming while the second concerns animal play.
(C) The first alludes to maternal instinct while the second describes a fearful state.
(D) The first describes a wary stealthiness while the second highlights innocent clumsiness.
(E) The first hints at impending doom while the second shows obvious discomfort.

7. In context, the phrase "I thought" (line 58) functions as

(A) validation
(B) foreshadowing
(C) derision
(D) introspection
(E) nostalgia

8. The author of Passage 1 would most likely regard lines 50-51 of Passage 2 ("I didn't...attention") with

(A) appreciation, because tracking leopards will decrease the number of leopard attacks on humans
(B) suspicion, because scientists should put data collection above everything else
(C) admiration, because the author of Passage 2 has the chance to get field experience
(D) contempt, because the author of Passage 2 is too intrusive
(E) respect, because the author of Passage 2 does not disrupt the leopard's way of life

9. Both the author of Passage 1 and the author of Passage 2 would agree with which of the following statements?

(A) Radio collars can be helpful for scientific purposes, but can be a detriment to the animals being studied.
(B) Much information can be gained from tracking an animal, but we must be respectful while doing so.
(C) People should approach big cats and their cubs when given the opportunity.
(D) Patience is required if one attempts to capture a non-domesticated cat.
(E) The information gained by tracking animals is invaluable to hunters who pursue those animals.

Questions 1-12 are based on the following passage.

This passage was adapted from a piece written about the relationship one can develop with dogs. Here, the author discusses four particularly meaningful dogs from his own experience.

It was Christmas and I was five years old. Great Aunt Kate, a formidable spinster and member of the Methodist church, had girded her loins and was coming to stay, rather to my mother's dismay. She telephoned to announce the time of her arrival. "Do you think the boy would like a puppy?" she demanded of my mother before putting the phone down. "Because I have bought him one for Christmas." Two hours later, she was at the front door, a bible in one hand and an ungainly Irish Red Setter puppy tucked under her other arm. "Her name is Molly," said Great Aunt Kate, plonking the dog onto the hall floor. Molly looked around uncertainly, and then ran gawkily to the kitchen, gulped the dish of scraps and bowl of water my mother had hurriedly prepared for her arrival, squatted and left her mark, scooted across to me and excitedly licked my face. It was instant love on both sides. Great Aunt Kate beamed. "Every boy should have a dog," was her verdict.

I am not sure my mother ever forgave Great Aunt Kate. As she was to say later, "The *boy's* dog? I don't notice the boy feeding it, grooming it, cleaning up after it, taking it for walks." In my defense, I can only say that I learned to do all those things in later life. However, I have never been able to refer to a dog as "it." Dogs are not objects, but living, loving, independent personalities who will adapt to the idiosyncrasies of the person with whom they live yet cleverly maneuver the organization of life around them so that their own place in the hierarchy is assured.

I should know. There have been several dogs in my life since Molly. There was Yoschi - or to give him his full nomenclature, for he was pedigree – Yoschi du Planete. A Belgian Boxer, full of curiosity and energy yet in possession of intelligence and manners that were not learned from me. He lived with me in a boarding school, and each morning, I would let him out into the school grounds whilst I woke students and prepared for a day of lessons. Yoschi understood that was my role in the school. His role, he decided, was to patrol the school grounds, greet the school secretaries as they arrived in their office, check with the headmaster that all was well with him and then proceed to the school's kitchen in time to taste whatever the chef may have selected for the day's meals. Later, he would arrive at my classroom, curl up at my feet whilst I taught and lectured the students. He could be critical. When he thought the lesson had been long enough, and perhaps he could feel the agitated energy of the students, he would spring to his feet, stretch, push open the door and leave. The students loved him for that alone.

In contrast, there was Smirnoff, a phlegmatic mongrel who believed that life was a journey that might get rough on occasion, but there would be a happy ending...eventually. Born in Switzerland, he later sailed to England where he spent six months in quarantine, moved to Wales for six years, before enduring another half year in kennels and then flying to Malawi where I was waiting for him. A traveler of some endurance, he made no complaint, just pressed his nose into my hand and gently wagged his tail.

Now, there is Einstein, a Yorkshire Terrier born in Normandy. Fiercely loyal, he patrols the garden, furiously defending it from those pigeons that presume to fly over what he regards as his air-space. On our walks, whilst he acknowledges that I am bigger than he is, he will lead the way, pausing to inspect each tree and lamp post. He decides which of the townswomen are worthy enough to be greeted and flirted with: the Yorkshire part of him appreciates their sensible shoes; the French part of him admires a neat pair of ankles. He believes that a relationship is all about sharing, particularly the sofa by the fire on a winter evening, a bar of chocolate and the cozy recesses of my bed. In addition, like anyone with Yorkshire credentials, he is not afraid to deliver a vocal reprimand. He is unprepared to let anyone else have the last word but will retire to his basket, muttering under his breath. Luckily, he does not bear a grudge and, before long, a little tongue will lick the hand and a small body will snuggle into the forgiving arm.

For me, it would be unthinkable to have been without Einstein, or Smirnoff or Yoschi or Molly or any of the others dogs that have shared my life. Yet, Rudyard Kipling, who so shrewdly understood animals, once warned: "Beware of giving your heart to a dog to tear." He was not wrong. Dogs worm their way into your heart in a way no lover does.

1. The primary purpose of the passage is to

(A) caution others on the seriousness of giving an animal as a gift
(B) discuss the merits and flaws of long-term companionship with dogs
(C) assert that dog ownership should not be taken up lightly and heedlessly
(D) relate experiences demonstrating how ultimately lovable dogs can be
(E) decide that dogs will eventually become a burden to the owner's life

2. The description in the first paragraph suggests that Great Aunt Kate is

(A) domineering, but apologetic
(B) accommodating, but dogmatic
(C) complaisant, but righteous
(D) controlling, but pensive
(E) overbearing, but munificent

3. In context, the mother's question in line 21 implies that

(A) she is considering removing the dog because her son does so little work
(B) she hasn't noticed who the owner of the dog actually is
(C) an animal is a living thing, and no one can really "own" one
(D) she was jealous that the aunt did not get her a dog
(E) ownership should be in direct correlation to care given

4. The statement in lines 26-30 ("Dogs are… assured") indicates that dogs are characterized as

(A) adaptable to whichever situation they are put in but in need of constant support and discipline to survive
(B) accommodating to the equally unique personalities of their owners while maintaining their positions in the household
(C) able to live only with those whose attitudes they find compatible and disagreeable if left in the care of someone else
(D) poorly suited to peculiar situations but capable of adapting as long as they feel that they are in control of the situation
(E) accustomed to meeting the distinctive needs of different owners while accepting of their subservient role in the relationship

5. The author's assessment of Yoschi in lines 34-36 ("A Belgian...me") states that the dog

(A) possessed singular qualities that were not inherited from the owner
(B) took on the personality of whomever was his owner at the time
(C) is of a breed renowned for its intelligence and indomitable spirit
(D) had previously spent time in the care of an excellent dog trainer
(E) was older than the author had originally suspected

6. In context, the students "loved" (line 52) the dog Yoschi because

(A) their teacher usually left him at home
(B) their teacher was annoyed by the dog
(C) he would come sit with them during lunch
(D) he often acted out their own desires
(E) he reminded them of their own dogs at home

7. In the fourth paragraph, the author's dog "Smirnoff" (line 53) is portrayed primarily as

(A) tenacious
(B) complacent
(C) imperturbable
(D) frenetic
(E) needy

8. Lines 63-69 ("Now, there…post") portray Einstein as though he is

(A) a boor
(B) a criminal
(C) an accomplice
(D) a mercenary
(E) a martinet

9. The statement in lines 71-73 ("the Yorkshire… ankles") suggests that the English value

(A) pragmatism, while the French appreciate utility
(B) practicality, while the French appreciate aesthetics
(C) flair, while the French appreciate viability
(D) elegance, while the French appreciate high fashion
(E) functionality, while the French appreciate modesty

10. The quotation from Rudyard Kipling in lines 87-88 is used to

(A) paraphrase a more popular work
(B) reiterate the author's chief complaint
(C) rebut the author's primary thesis
(D) summarize the author's main idea
(E) evaluate the truth in a claim

11. In the passage, the author makes use of all of the following EXCEPT:

(A) anecdote
(B) personification
(C) repetition
(D) quotation
(E) reminiscence

12. The author's overall tone in the passage is best described as

(A) playful
(B) incredulous
(C) emphatic
(D) romantic
(E) confessional

Questions 1-13 are based on the following passage.

This passage discusses Switzerland's relationship to other countries concerning global economics. The author uses two popular Swiss playwrights to develop his main idea.

The Swiss are a very accommodating people. For example, in Switzerland there are four languages: German, Italian, French and Romansch. Or, perhaps, five - thanks to the industries of Tourism and Banking, English is also recognized. As a result, nearly everyone is tri-lingual at least, which, for visitors, is an encouraging ability. In addition, the Swiss treasure their neutrality in times of conflict. They may have started out as citizens of a country noted for its provision of mercenaries to European wars; but, since 1815, the country has studiously avoided direct involvement in any argument.

These two "assets" have not been unprofitable. The Red Cross was founded in this country. Many of the United Nations have their associated organizations based there. International conferences, particularly those concerned with the world's economy, are held in the Alpine resorts. The rich and famous have been encouraged to buy property in the country, to send their offspring to international schools along the shores of Lac Léman, to play on the ski slopes of Gstaad and St. Moritz (unrivaled amongst the natural world, they claim) and to shelter their money in the banks of Geneva, Zurich and Bern. As a result, one of the richest and most secure countries in the world, Switzerland can be regarded as a thriving example to us all of the contentment that can be achieved in life. Paradise is available, if one eschews confrontation and embraces cooperation...a Garden of Eden sheltered by the Alps.

Yet, the original Garden of Eden had its dissenters, and so does Switzerland. Considering the number of languages spoken in Switzerland, perhaps there are fewer critics than one might expect. However, in the mid-twentieth century, both Max Frisch and Friedrich Durrenmatt created plays which examined the fate of the individual in the modern world. The latter is the greater of these two writers and his play, "Der Besuch der Alten Damen" – in English, it is known as "The Visit"- is not only a play of immense irony but also a great example of what is known as Theatre of the Absurd.

Durrenmatt's comic and tragic play is set in a prosperous unnamed European country. The inhabitants of the only town in the country that is still in the midst of economic depression, are awaiting the arrival of the richest woman in the world. She was born and brought up in Guellen and the citizens hope that a reunion with her childhood sweetheart, will encourage her to bestow help and recovery to the town. Claire Zacchanasian arrives, a little prematurely, accompanied by her seventh husband, a butler, two gum-chewing gangsters from New York, two blind eunuchs and a cage containing a black panther. All seems well, if a little bizarre. At the celebration supper in her honor, she announces that she is prepared to give a million to the town and a further million to be shared amongst the inhabitants...on one condition. To gain the money, someone must kill Alfred Ill, who, with the connivance of the town, abandoned and betrayed her when she was an impoverished, pregnant girl. Now she is buying herself justice. The Mayor, for the town, rejects her offer.

"*I'll wait.*" Claire replies.

And wait she does. We watch how the citizens, as the possibility of wealth hangs over them, shift from their initial stance supporting Ill to finding justification in Claire's demands. Even Ill, himself eventually realizes that his life is untenable and accepts the inevitable. In front of the International Press and TV, Claire's "offer" to the town is announced in a traditional Town Hall meeting at which the whole town is asked if they accept Claire's offer – the details of which are not given. They raise their hands in agreement. The Press depart with the women of the village for refreshments, and in a group, the men kill Ill and then announce his death as a heart attack: "*Died of joy*" announces the Mayor. Claire hands the Mayor the cheque and departs with Ill's body. The last line of the play is from the townsfolk: "*Let us go and enjoy our good fortune.*"

Is the play an ironic version of an old Morality play? Or is it a vivid illustration of a world in which man is a mere puppet controlled or menaced by outside forces, unable to find an inherent value in life beyond tangible wealth? Above all, is it perhaps an ironic comment on the values that the Swiss have fashioned in their paradise? A Swiss woman was once asked about how she felt about this comment on her country. She smiled, smoothed the skirt of her Chanel suit, sipped her cocktail and shook her head. "*Ach, nein. Durrenmatt may be a great Swiss dramatist, but his play is not set in Switzerland. No, no. Everyone knows that Guellen is a town in Germany.*"

1. In context of the first paragraph, what does the word "accommodating" (line 1) suggest about the Swiss?

(A) They respond positively to the needs of progressive business.
(B) Their army is always ready to take up war as mercenaries.
(C) They provide a safe haven for international businessmen.
(D) They are allied with neighboring countries.
(E) They are culturally versatile and politically nonaligned.

2. According to lines 8-12 ("They may...argument"), it can be inferred that

(A) prior to 1815, Switzerland participated in every European war
(B) after 1815, there were no more European conflicts that required the use of mercenaries
(C) Switzerland's neutrality was a byproduct of its mercenary agreements
(D) Switzerland ceased all mercenary activities as of 1815
(E) Switzerland became the world expert on the study of neutrality

3. In the second paragraph, the author lists all of the following as examples of the Swiss' neutrality proving profitable EXCEPT:

(A) The wealthy are encouraged to migrate to Switzerland and make use of its resources.
(B) The Red Cross International Foundation was established there.
(C) The country is home to some organizations for international relations.
(D) Conferences pertaining to the general health of the global economy are held there.
(E) The country is a harbor for foreign political dissidents.

4. The word "unrivaled" in the parenthetical statement in line 22 is closest in meaning to

(A) unchallenged
(B) unperturbed
(C) unparalleled
(D) unprovoked
(E) unabridged

5. The author suggests that the "Paradise" in 28 is most likely a result of

(A) economic reliability
(B) international relations
(C) unrivaled affluence
(D) political neutrality
(E) geographic protection

6. "Max Frisch" (line 35) and "Friedrich Durrenmatt" (line 36) serve as examples of

(A) nationalists
(B) detractors
(C) expatriates
(D) entrepreneurs
(E) altruists

7. The author characterizes Claire Zacchanasian's arrival as "a little bizarre" (line 55) because

(A) of the unusual nature of her traveling companions
(B) she proposed to the villagers the murder of Alfred Ill
(C) of her offer to the townspeople of a large sum of money
(D) she arrived to the town at a time earlier than expected
(E) of her want to be reunited with her childhood sweetheart

8. All of the following are given as motivations for Claire imposing the "one condition" in line 58 EXCEPT:

(A) She felt alienated from her childhood town.
(B) She felt the townspeople had conspired against her.
(C) She felt there was a lucrative opportunity.
(D) She felt justified in her reasons for revenge.
(E) She felt the villagers had acted treacherously.

9. The "shift" (line 67) can best be described as a progression from

(A) indifference to self-interest
(B) accommodation to rejection
(C) righteousness to greed
(D) inclusion to exclusion
(E) loyalty to betrayal

10. The mayor's announcement about Mr. Ill in lines 77-78 ("*Died of joy*") implies that the townspeople

(A) feel no remorse for the extreme actions that they have taken
(B) truly believe that Mr. Ill wanted this money for the town
(C) are attempting to mask their sadness at a friend's passing
(D) have a unique attitude among other cultures towards death
(E) determined the death of Mr. Ill stemmed from natural causes

11. Which of the following best personifies the "outside forces" discussed by the author in line 85?

(A) "Max Frisch and Friedrich Durrenmatt" (lines 35-36)
(B) "these two writers" (line 38)
(C) "Claire Zacchanasian" (line 51)
(D) "two blind eunuchs" (lines 53-54)
(E) "the inhabitants" (line 58)

12. Which of the following best defines the "ironic comment" (line 87) about the "thriving example" in lines 26-27?

(A) The pursuit of peace requires sacrifice.
(B) The pursuit of wealth trumps all moral standards.
(C) The lack of money is the source of all crime.
(D) Revenge is only justifiable in matters of money.
(E) The needs of the many outweigh the needs of the few.

13. The tone of the Swiss woman's response in lines 91-94 is

(A) apologetic
(B) confrontational
(C) reflective
(D) smug
(E) self-effacing

Self Evaluation

Self Evaluation is important if you want to see an improvement on your next comprehension passage. Each passage has a set of possible reasons for errors. Place a check mark next to the ones that pertain to you, and write your own on the blank line provided. Use this form to better analyze your performance by filling it out regularly and accurately so you can recognize the pattern of your most common mistakes.

If you don't understand why you have made mistakes, there is no way you can correct them!

1st Long Reading Comprehension: # Correct:____ # Wrong:____ # Unanswered:____

- ○ Did not understand the question, line reference, or answers
- ○ Did not underline the line reference
- ○ Read too much or too little around the line reference
- ○ Summarized the line reference instead of answering the question
- ○ Couldn't find the false words
- ○ Couldn't choose between two possible answers
- ○ Did not use tone to help eliminate answers
- ○ When stuck between two answers, guessed instead of looking for additional facts
- ○ Couldn't finish in time
- ○ Other:____

2nd Long Reading Comprehension: # Correct:____ # Wrong:____ # Unanswered:____

- ○ Did not understand the question, line reference, or answers
- ○ Did not underline the line reference
- ○ Read too much or too little around the line reference
- ○ Summarized the line reference instead of answering the question
- ○ Couldn't find the false words
- ○ Couldn't choose between two possible answers
- ○ Did not use tone to help eliminate answers
- ○ When stuck between two answers, guessed instead of looking for additional facts
- ○ Couldn't finish in time
- ○ Other:____

3rd Long Reading Comprehension: # Correct:____ # Wrong:____ # Unanswered:____

- ○ Did not understand the question, line reference, or answers
- ○ Did not underline the line reference
- ○ Read too much or too little around the line reference
- ○ Summarized the line reference instead of answering the question
- ○ Couldn't find the false words
- ○ Couldn't choose between two possible answers
- ○ Did not use tone to help eliminate answers
- ○ When stuck between two answers, guessed instead of looking for additional facts
- ○ Couldn't finish in time
- ○ Other:____

4th Long Reading Comprehension: # Correct:____ # Wrong:____ # Unanswered:____

- ○ Did not understand the question, line reference, or answers
- ○ Did not underline the line reference
- ○ Read too much or too little around the line reference
- ○ Summarized the line reference instead of answering the question
- ○ Couldn't find the false words
- ○ Couldn't choose between two possible answers
- ○ Did not use tone to help eliminate answers
- ○ When stuck between two answers, guessed instead of looking for additional facts
- ○ Couldn't finish in time
- ○ Other:____

Single Long Comprehension
6 Questions Total, Pages 68-69

1. Correct answer: (E)
According to the first paragraph, the French prioritize relaxation and celebration. To eliminate the others, consider that celebration is not destructive (A), the French are not listless (B), the French do not focus on career (C), and there is no mention of politics (D).

2. Correct answer: (A)
The tone of these words is (-), eliminating E. In the same sentence, the author uses the word "scornful" to describe how the Germans and Swiss feel towards the French taking a three week vacation, bringing us to "disapproval."

3. Correct answer: (C)
The author uses the word sweepingly to show that Europe disregards France without much thought. To eliminate the others, consider that we don't know if the author is tired of defending France (A), that the author agrees, just not fully (B), there is no cause to dismiss France (D), nor does Europe fully accept their lifestyle (E).

4. Correct answer: (B)
In the sentence before the LR, the author writes, "The French retort that…they have got their priorities in life right." So the LR is stating those French priorities.

5. Correct answer: (B)
The event the LR refers to is "the great escape." The author writes, "In actual fact, it turned out that there were only seven old men held there, and their escape was plodding and drawn out," suggesting that the escape was not so exciting.

6. Correct answer: (D)
In this paragraph, the author describes the celebrations. To eliminate the others, look for false words: In (A), "categorical study;" in (B), "spans Europe;" in (C), "President of France's power;" in (E), "positive and negative outcomes."

Double Long Comprehension
9 Questions Total, Pages 70-71

1. Correct Answer: (C)
The question refers to the whole passage. "Torn" sets up the context of choosing between waiting for the lion to show up (paragraph 1) and then going to "check on her" (line 11). The narrator was not (A) angry or (B) upset and (D) never considers sharing this information with anyone. (E) is wrong because the lioness is not deceased.

2. Correct Answer: (A)
The author of P1 writes that he had been "studying" (line 3) the lioness but when it was "impossible to follow" (line 6) her, he felt "relief" when she finally "emerged" (line 7), suggesting he wanted to continue tracking her. The passage does not state that (B) she was hurt by the collar nor that he (E) studied the Zulu. (C) places importance on his vehicle, which was not the source of his relief. (D) refers to the present relief, not one the author felt in the past.

3. Correct Answer: (E)
"Submerged" (line 15) is the context clue for "plunged." This eliminates (B) and (C). (A) and (D) are conditions of falling, which is not referenced in context of the LR.

4. Correct Answer: (B)
The author of P1 writes that her "silhouette" was "ten meters away," indicating that she was now in sight. This eliminates (A), (C), (D), and (E) which do not indicate sight.

5. Correct Answer: (C)
The answer is based on an assumption. The author of P1 writes that the lioness was "astonishingly tolerant" of his presence but it was more than he "deserved," suggesting that the author felt (+) to have gotten so close. The LR does not offer evidence about the author's (A) career or that he had to (E) care for the cubs. (D) is wrong because the author did not receive the lioness's affection. (B) is wrong because the lioness was "astonishingly" or surprisingly tolerant, not "extremely."

6. Correct Answer: (D)
The author of P1 describes the lioness with "absolute stillness" (line 29) while the author of P2 describes the cubs with "no concern for stealth" (line 53). This eliminates (A)'s playfulness, (C)'s fearful state (which refers to the mother leopard, not the cubs) and (E) since the cubs were playing (+), not uncomfortable (-). (B) in P1, the mother grooms the cubs after the authors has begun to leave which is outside of the LR.

7. Correct Answer: (B)
The author of P2 references an expectation that he would be "well hidden" (line 58) from the leopard but "an instant later" (line 60) the author is discovered. Because this is a context question, consider that the LR is used as an omen. An omen concerns the future which eliminates (E). (D) is a literal understanding of the LR, not how the LR is used contextually. (A) is (+) and (C) is (-), but the LR does not offer either tone.

8. Correct Answer: (E)
The author of P1 was respectful when finding the lioness with her cubs. In the LR, the author of P2 is also respectful with the mother leopard, suggesting that the author of P1 would regard this as (+). This eliminates (B) and (C) which are (-). The author of P1 does not state anything about (A) animal attacks or (C) acquiring more field, or career, experience.

9. Correct Answer: (B)
Both authors focus on studying a particular animal. Both regard viewing the cubs as primarily (+), though they both avoid "intrusion" (line 37, P1) and try to remain "hidden" (line 58, P2) respectively. Neither advocate that (C) people should approach, (D) capture, or (E) hunt a wild animal. (A) is wrong because neither indicates that radio collars are (-).

Single Long Comprehension
12 Questions Total, Pages 72-73

1. Correct answer: (D)
The tone of the passage is (+) towards dog companionship, which is enough to get the correct answer. Eliminate all answers with (-) tones. In (A), "caution" and "seriousness;" in (B), "flaws;" in (C), "should not be taken lightly;" and in (E) "become a burden."

2. Correct answer: (E)
Great Aunt Kate is overbearing because she demands responses from the mother, and munificent because she brings a dog for the boy. Eliminate the false words in other answers: in (A), apologetic; in (B), accommodating; in (C), complaisant; in (D), pensive.

3. Correct answer: (E)
The mother does not consider the boy the owner because she is the one who cares for it. There is no stated evidence for (A) or (D), so they can be eliminated. (B) is wrong because she's aware the dog is meant for her son. (C) is an inference based on line 15, not the LR.

4. Correct answer: (B)
According to the LR, dogs "adapt to the idiosyncrasies" of their owners and "maneuver the organization of life around them" to maintain their "place in the hierarchy."

5. Correct answer: (A)
In this LR, the author states that Yoschi was "in possession of intelligence and manners that were not learned from me," and this is all the author tells us. The other answer choices are assumptions, while (A) is based on fact.

6. Correct answer: (D)
The question says "in context" so the answer will not come from the LR alone; it requires reading line before. The children love to see the dog leave a boring lecture. To eliminate the others, consider that the dog is not left at home (A), no one is annoyed by the dog (B), the LR is not about lunch (C), and there is no evidence for (E).

7. Correct answer: (C)
According to the paragraph, Smirnoff is described as "a traveler of some endurance" and said to have "made no complaint." So the dog is imperturbable, which means "not easily agitated or stressed."

8. Correct answer: (E)
In the LR, Einstein is described as the one who tends to "lead the way" while also setting the pace of the walk due to "pausing to inspect each tree and lamp post." He is in control, much like a martinet: disciplined and militaristic.

9: Correct answer: (B)
The LR states that the English part of Einstein "appreciates their sensible shoes" (practicality), while the French part "admires a neat pair of ankles" (aesthetics). Cross out false words in the other answers: in (A), utility; in (C), flair; in (D), elegance; in (E), modesty.

10. Correct answer: (D)
The quote summarizes the author's ultimate idea for writing this essay: the love he has felt for his dogs. To eliminate the other answers, consider the (+) tone. Cross out (B) and (C). In (A), "popular work" is false. The quote is not an evaluation, so cross out (E).

11. Correct answer: (C)
The author uses anecdotes throughout the entire essay (A), Einstein actively decides on his grudges and tantrums (B), the author quotes his mother and aunt (D), and the essay is built around memories (E). But the author makes no attempt at meaningful repetition.

P1 - Passage 1 P2 - Passage 2
LR - Line Reference
(+) - Positive
(-) - Negative
All quotes in answer choices can be found in or around the line reference.

12. Correct answer: (A)
The essay is full of fond and funny memories, heartfelt moments, and lighthearted analysis. The (+) tone can cancel most of the answer choices.

Single Long Comprehension
13 Questions Total, Pages 74-76

1. Correct answer: (E)
After the author says that the Swiss are "accommodating," he writes, "For example, in Switzerland there are four languages…nearly everyone is tri-lingual at least, which, for visitors, is an encouraging ability." This means the Swiss are "culturally versatile." The author then goes on to write, "In addition, the Swiss treasure their neutrality in times of conflict," which means they are "politically nonaligned."

2. Correct answer: (D)
The author writes, "They may have started out as citizens of a country noted for its provision of mercenaries to European wars; but, since 1815, the country has studiously avoided direct involvement in any argument," which means the country no longer involved itself in conflict. It can be inferred that after 1815 they no longer supplied mercenaries.

3. Correct answer: (E)
The author writes, "The rich and famous have been encouraged to buy property in the country," eliminating (A) and, "The Red Cross was founded in this country," eliminating (B). He also writes, "Many of the United Nations have their associated organizations based there," eliminating (C) and finally, "International conferences, particularly those concerned with the world's economy, are held in the Alpine resorts," eliminating (D).

4. Correct answer: (C)
"Unrivaled," in the context of the sentence, means the best, such that nothing else can compare, or "unparalleled."

5. Correct answer: (D)
The author writes, "Paradise is available, if one eschews confrontation," which means "paradise" can be obtained if one avoids conflict or, in other words, maintains "political neutrality."

6. Correct answer: (B)
Before the author gives the example of the two playwrights, he begins the paragraph with, "Yet, the original Garden of Eden had its dissenters, and so does Switzerland." "Dissenters" and "detractors" are synonymous.

7. Correct answer: (A)
The traveling party is described as "a little bizarre" because of its varied members who don't seem to have anything in common. While she did propose a murder and offer money, that was after her arrival, eliminating (B) and (C). Early arrival is not as strange as the members of her group, eliminating (D), and Claire is not intending to meet her former sweetheart, eliminating (E).

8. Correct answer: (C)
The answer can only be (C) because her motivation could not be "lucrative" if she was the one giving the money away.

9. Correct answer: (E)
The author writes that the villagers "shift from their initial stance supporting Ill and find justification in Claire's demands." Meaning that they originally displayed "loyalty" towards Ill but ultimately "betrayed" him for the money.

10. Correct answer: (A)
The author states that "the men kill Ill and then announce his death as a heart attack," and then claim that Ill "Died of joy." This implies that they did not feel regret about killing Ill, justifying their actions.

11. Correct answer: (C)
In this LR, the author describes "outside forces" as those that "control or menace" man as if he were "a mere puppet." Through the context of the story, "The Visit," we see Claire manipulate the townspeople into doing her bidding, eliminating (A), (B), (D), and (E).

12. Correct answer: (B)
The author explains in the first two paragraphs that, by remaining neutral, Switzerland is "regarded as a thriving example to us all of the contentment that can be achieved in life." This is ironic because, in the context of the story, the Swiss were described as abandoning that neutrality, and even committing murder, for monetary gain, meaning that "the pursuit of wealth trumps all moral standards."

13. Correct answer: (D)
Here, the woman speaking is absolute with her answer. The tone of this response is (-), eliminating (C) and (E). The Swiss woman does not feel remorse, eliminating (A). The woman is not argumentative, eliminating (B).

Chapter Six

Questions 1-6 are based on the following passage.

In this passage, adapted from an essay written in 2013, the author discusses the different approaches to political television by the French and the British.

One of the benefits of living in France, but quite close to Britain, is that I have the possibility to watch not only all the TV channels available in France, but also those in the United Kingdom.

Consequently, I am reminded nightly of how the two countries differ completely in their approach to political life. For example, in the UK, the broadcasting organizations constantly examine and criticize the quality of the services that the British government is supposed to provide for the general population. Politicians are scrutinized, interrogated, confronted with their failures, made to defend the reasons for their policies, required to give answers that the general public can take on board. There is a constant interaction between those who govern and those who are governed: this does not always work to the advantage of those who govern. Both Houses of Parliament have seen indiscretions splashed across the headlines of the popular press, discussed in opinion columns of weightier newspapers and debated on television news programs. According to recent polls concerning those bodies in which the British public has least trust, politicians are in the vanguard, slightly behind bankers and the European Union.

In France, on the other hand, politicians on television are listened to politely, their statements rarely questioned. To a large extent, their private lives and activities are neither reported nor examined in the public arena of press and broadcasting. There are rules of respect and etiquette in France which cannot be broached. This does not mean that the population of France believes that the lives of their politicians are impeccable. Everyone knows (although how, it is difficult to fathom) that most presidents have had at least one mistress, that many of them have received considerable amounts of money in exchange for giving aid to various foreign countries. People were much more incensed when a leading French film star who had paid millions of Euros in income tax because of his worldwide success, declared that he was leaving the country as a result of the present government's attempts to raise the amount of tax that the wealthiest in France must now pay.

The British have a deeply rooted belief that those in power have a duty to set a moral example to those who have placed them in power: to work and not to ask for any reward. The French, who are much more pragmatic and phlegmatic as a nation, have no such expectations: they merely shrug their shoulders and murmur, "*C'est comme ca.*" This phrase, loosely translated as "that's how it is," is the basic response to any problem which is, on the surface, insoluble. The British believe that all problems can be resolved if one works hard enough and long enough to do so – hence the British retain a monarch, an upper chamber (the House of Lords) and an elected parliament, all of whom have a role to play in the government of the people. The French believe that if one leaves a problem alone for long enough, it will eventually diminish and disappear, or become irrelevant and, therefore acceptable - which to them is the same thing. Considering that there was once a French Revolution, this might seem, to a foreigner, an astonishing attitude. However, if one looks at the way the French government works today and the way it worked under the Ancien Régime*, one may realize that the only thing to have been changed since 1789 is that a hereditary head of state (the King) has been replaced by a head of state who is elected every five years (the President).

C'est comme ca.

* This refers to the pre-Revolution French monarchy.

1. According to the second paragraph, there is a great public demand in the UK for

(A) a new system of government
(B) better role models for the children
(C) interaction between people and country
(D) accountability from the politicians
(E) more media coverage of political events

2. Which hypothetical situation best characterizes the "rules of respect and etiquette" (line 30)?

(A) A gritty report targeting the stressed family life of a high profile governor
(B) A public forum condemning a political leader for his extramarital affairs
(C) Media that respects a politician's request for discretion after an intimate death
(D) News stories revealing the personal vacation plans of the French president
(E) Photographers who wait outside a politician's home to snap photos of him

3. The statement in lines 31-33 ("This does… impeccable") suggests that the author believes French politicians are

(A) tranquil
(B) dissolute
(C) conscientious
(D) exemplary
(E) temperate

4. In the context of the passage as a whole, lines 44-53 ("The British...insoluble") primarily serve to

(A) express the attitudes that account for contrasting responses between the British and the French
(B) highlight why the French generally find traveling to the UK to be such an arduous task
(C) question the practicality of the French in approaching pivotal political issues
(D) suggest that, as a nation, the British are better at dealing with political indiscretions than are the French
(E) call attention to a popular approach to journalism used by both the French and the British

5. The contrast in attitude of the British and the French, respectively, toward problem solving in lines 53-62 ("The British...thing") can best be described as

(A) unconcerned vs. vigilant
(B) dogmatic vs. objective
(C) unfathomable vs. disinterested
(D) preoccupied vs. attentive
(E) tenacious vs. detached

6. The author's comment in lines 64-70 ("However, if...President") suggests that

(A) the French government quelled the uprising in the 1700s
(B) the politics of France remain relatively unchanged
(C) the political system in France has improved over the last centuries
(D) foreigners were astonished by the French Revolution
(E) French politicians are not an integral part of revolutionary change

Questions 1-9 are based on the following passage.

This passage is adapted from a published piece of correspondence in which the author reflects on his writing process.

The way I work is this: I think of an area I think I want to have a go at. Then I write a long first paragraph, trying to make it striking and invitingly phrased. Then I let the second paragraph develop. Then, I look at what I have and ask the question that I should really have thought about before I started; where do I think this piece is going? Then I start to reread and cut all the unnecessary and show-off stuff I have put in the first paragraph.

For example, when asked about what I actually like about Domfront (where I live) and why it keeps me here (apart from the inability to escape because I cannot drive!), the tone comes from my view of the subject, from writing as honestly as I can. I know that whenever I write anything which is quite good, then it is because I am behaving like a camera and recording what I see in my mind's eye. The energy that comes from doing what you love is inspiring. It is how I used to feel when I was directing plays. The energy spurs on ideas and the honest eye stops me from being too clever for words. And all of it is just fun to do.

The same feeling embraced me when I taught writing. I liked nearly all the classes I used to teach – well, for sure, there were some difficult times, but, on the whole, I looked forward to each day. I treated my classes like they were theatre performances. And, in the theatre you have to work the audience, to engage it, to surprise it, to make the audience want to come back the next time to see what is going to happen. Attack and enthusiasm are the weapons you use. I think (and I don't want to sound arrogant here) that students used to look forward to the next class to find out what was going to happen, and because I had enthusiasm for what I was presenting them, they began to look at it not as a chore but something that was rather fun. It is not just "playing to the gallery" and giving in to the student - too many teachers do that - you have to accompany it with a strictness of quality. You give a student a good grade because what the student has produced is good. You give it a top grade, only when there is nothing further to be said on what the student has produced. You don't use grades as a weapon to make sure the student is sycophantic. I do remember that when anyone in my class got the top mark possible, the news went round the school, and the student felt deservedly proud. A teacher does not tell a student what to think. A teacher helps a student to want to think.

All I know is that my ex-students still write about what they discovered in my lessons, and I feel chuffed about that. I was a useless student at school, ugly, awkward, completely lost and miserable in a boarding house. I wanted to escape and didn't know how to do it. When I did become a teacher, one of the main things I wanted to do was to try to make sure that nobody felt as lost and muddled and awful as I did when I was a teenager (or in my twenties and most of my life, actually!). But I have digressed, once again, carried away by the memories of my life, swept off on a sea of emotion. The tone is clear, no?

1. The author's overall tone in the passage is best described as

(A) indignant
(B) disinterested
(C) conversational
(D) formal
(E) sarcastic

2. According to lines 1-4 ("The way…develop"), the author claims that when he begins writing, he

(A) graphs out a well developed outline
(B) writes in a way that will hook the reader
(C) starts with the conclusion and works backwards
(D) crafts his words to persuade the reader of his argument
(E) tailors his work to be as succinct as it can be

3. In context, the word "show-off" in line 8 most nearly means

(A) creative
(B) arrogant
(C) obnoxious
(D) superfluous
(E) literary

4. The phrase "I am behaving like a camera" (lines 16-17) suggests that the author considers his writing style to be

(A) evasive
(B) convoluted
(C) imaginative
(D) conceited
(E) candid

5. Which of the following would the author consider NOT to be "too clever for words" (line 21)?

(A) A writer walks through the park and writes about what she sees.
(B) A man mimics his favorite author while writing his first novel.
(C) A writer omits damaging information when writing his autobiography.
(D) A medical journal alters the outcome of a study to boost its sales.
(E) An author plagiarizes another author's essays to finish his book.

6. The phrase in line 25 ("well, for…times") functions primarily to

(A) illustrate a preference
(B) qualify a previous remark
(C) contradict a personal view
(D) underscore a popular concept
(E) analyze a writing process

7. In lines 26-31 ("I treated…happen"), the author compares his teaching style to the theatre in that they both

(A) have to captivate the audience
(B) require audience participation
(C) rely on diligent preparation
(D) demand a degree of conviction
(E) involve the sensation of dread

8. Which best describes the way the word "weapons" is used in line 31 and the way the word "weapon" is used in line 44, respectively?

(A) unnecessary vs. intimidating
(B) dangerous vs. provocative
(C) daunting vs. flattering
(D) motivational vs. threatening
(E) inspiring vs. rewarding

9. The author defines "strictness of quality" (lines 39-40) as a situation wherein

(A) a class is renowned throughout the school
(B) a student is appropriately sycophantic
(C) a student emulates a popular work
(D) a teacher feels enthusiastic about teaching
(E) a student's work requires no further editing

Questions 1-12 are based on the following passage.

The following passage was adapted from a series of essays written in 2013 about the 1960s in Britain. Here, the author relates the changes to society.

In the summer of 1956, I went camping with the Boy Scouts. I had never done anything like that before. We went to the South of England and set up our tents about three miles from a town, in a big field, by a stream, with woods nearby. During the day, we did all the things that Boy Scouts did and, I assume, still do. At night, we snuggled into our sleeping bags under canvas tents and fell asleep to the music floating from the rides and swings of a nearby travelling fair. Most of it was pretty familiar until, one night, I found myself the only one in the tent still awake, and I heard a new sound that animated me. It was raw, edgy and, above all, incredibly sensual. It was the sound of Elvis.

Musically, of course, this was really where the sixties started. The sounds of Elvis, Jerry Lee Lewis, Buddy Holly, and, above all, the Gibson Les Paul electric guitar carried music from Rock 'n' Roll to the development of Hard Rock, by way of Motown and elsewhere. I guess, in the UK, kids were ready for it: no young teenager could afford to miss a chord. Of course, when the calendar changed to 1960, I was no longer a teenager, so I guess most of this excitement passed me by. However, the Beatles and the Rolling Stones stole the scene for everyone: they inflamed the young and infuriated the old with their attitudes so free, adventurous, daring and demanding—on and offstage. We could neither ignore nor dismiss them: people were either "disgusted from Tunbridge Wells" or "dedicated followers of fashion."

Ah, yes... fashion. Most men noticed that skirts became shorter and tops skimpier as the decade developed, but they themselves were also becoming more adventurous in dress. I distinctly remember wearing Cuban heeled boots and long limp-collared and full-sleeved shirts in paisley, not to mention bell-bottom trousers... and very silly I looked, too. Clothing in the sixties for the young heavily demanded the slimmer figure to be effective. I let my hair grow, of course: not quite to my shoulders, for I was always a conservative at heart. Still, I thought I looked the "bees' knees"—in words my grandmother would have used—as I tottered down the street, an overweight bear, bulging at every pore. I can't say that I noticed an improvement in my level of attractiveness despite the clothing... or perhaps because of it.

It was all a bit of fun really. Heaven knows there really had not been much of that since the war ended in 1945. Perhaps it is difficult to realize now, but in the sixties, there were still cities in the UK where the evidence of the bombings during the war was still evident. It was only in the sixties that the High Streets in England began to take on a Technicolor aspect, rather than the drab dullness of scanty window dressing they had held until then. Even British films were improving: the first James Bond film came out in 1962 starring Sean Connery, who was seedy and flippant—and spoke with a Scottish accent, for Heaven's sake! That was a breakthrough from the monotone, repressed, repetitive movies of how British stiff upper lips had won the war. Traditional, conservative attitudes were replaced by optimism and even an apparent confidence. People began to say what they thought. Satire was popular, even on television with shows where politicians' pomposity was mocked—along with almost everything else. Things were going to be different from then on.

I celebrated my twenty-third birthday in 1963 by going to the theatre to see a revue that had been written by a friend of mine. Lots of silly sketches, some satirical acts, some old jokes revisited, a couple of funny songs and cleverly worked dance routines. Great fun. There was one sketch I shall never forget. The curtain rose to reveal a typical middle-class room where a man was preparing his meal. There was a radio on the table, playing the usual radio music from an actual broadcast. As the man sat down to eat his breakfast, the music on the radio faded and an announcer began to speak: "We interrupt this program to take you to the news studio for a breaking news announcement." The actor reached over and switched off the radio. We chuckled: that was the usual reaction to such interruptions. After the show ended to tumultuous applause and I left the theatre, the streets outside were crowded with vendors selling special editions of the newspaper.

"American President Kennedy assassinated" was the headline.

1. The author describes a camping trip in the first paragraph in order to

(A) relate how impressive the music of the late 1950s was compared to what had come before
(B) describe a typical night of camping with the boy Scouts in the 1960s
(C) point out how little the Boy Scouts have evolved with the times
(D) set up the scene where he first heard the music that would launch the 1960s
(E) describe his first impression of rock as reminiscent of music he's loved before

2. The author mentions Elvis, Jerry Lee Lewis, and Buddy Holly in lines 15-16 as

(A) popular instrumentalists with unsavory personal lives
(B) traditional singers whose careers failed in the 1960s
(C) representative figures performing in new musical styles
(D) artists whose work influenced The Beatles and The Rolling Stones
(E) young musicians who led a social revolution among their fans

3. The author explains his age "when the calendar changed" (line 21) in order to

(A) highlight that young people were the strongest force of cultural change
(B) denounce the strict attitudes of his fellow young adult traditionalists
(C) clarify his membership in the youth movements of the 1950s
(D) convince the reader that he was a core player in political events
(E) muse about how different his involvement would have been had he been younger

4. In the third paragraph (lines 30-45), the author suggests that he

(A) fit in with neither the revolutionary youth nor the conventional adults
(B) exploited the new fashion to the best of his physical ability
(C) criticized the ridiculous fashions certain designers promoted to the young
(D) ignored the dizzying number of variations on classic looks for men
(E) pioneered a number of fashion trends that were popular through the 60s

5. Based on the third paragraph (lines 30-45), the author would most likely describe men's fashion in the 1960s as

(A) conspicuous and comfortable
(B) provocative and sensual
(C) beautiful and expensive
(D) eccentric and awkward
(E) economical and tawdry

6. Based on his statement in lines 40-45 ("Still, I… it"), the author most likely believes that he was

(A) indistinguishable from other young men in his age group
(B) unable to keep up with fashion because of his physique
(C) blissfully ignorant of how ridiculous he looked
(D) unattractive in spite of his attempts at fashion
(E) encouraged in his fashion choices by his grandmother

7. The author mentions the war in lines 46-51 ("Heaven knows… evident") in order to imply that British youth in the 1960s were

(A) finally ready to let go of a difficult past and enjoy themselves
(B) unconscious of their parents' tribulations during the war years
(C) deliberately avoiding traumatic memories of the war
(D) looking to have fun rather than enlisting in the army
(E) insensitive because of their lack of patriotism

8. The author articulates that "British films were improving" (lines 54-55) because the writers and directors

(A) treated the subject of politics more seriously
(B) emulated the style of the Scottish film industry
(C) avoided inaccessible fantasy in favor of more realistic dramas
(D) availed themselves of more modern visual and auditory technology
(E) no longer focused only on representing the successes of the war efforts

9. Based on his statements in the fourth paragraph (lines 46-66), the author most likely believes that changing attitudes in the 1960s

(A) inspired the youth to become more accepting of foreigners
(B) degraded a strong sense of nationalism by questioning officials
(C) exchanged the tension of the war years with hope for the future
(D) resulted in waves of structural and political reforms
(E) were the result of Scottish cultural influence on British society

10. In context of the passage, the author most likely asserts that the "sketch" mentioned in line 72 is so unforgettable because it

(A) satirized middle class social values through the use of song and dance routines
(B) depicted disdain for the media coincidentally at the time of a major news event
(C) was the funniest and wittiest performance he had witnessed in his life
(D) showed the reaction of the man to the radio as most unusual given the nature of the news announcement
(E) demonstrated the carefree attitude of society towards significant political change

11. In the context of the passage, the audience members most likely responded to the "usual reaction" (lines 81-82) with amusement because they

(A) recognized the actor's subtle satire of a famous event
(B) were bored with the sketch itself and welcomed a change
(C) identified and agreed with the actor's response to the news
(D) had become inured to the severe tone of news announcers
(E) did not care what might have been going on in society

12. Throughout the passage, the author characterizes his role in the changes of the 1960s as

(A) a detached observer
(B) an atypical participant
(C) a charismatic leader
(D) a disgruntled opponent
(E) a confused outsider

Questions 1-13 are based on the following passage.

The following passages discuss the impact of standardized testing on society. The author of Passage 1 speaks from a personal point of view, while the author of Passage 2 takes a more journalistic approach.

Passage 1

Life today is littered with exams. From the day we are born, our progress is measured at nearly regular intervals, moments when we find ourselves trapped in a chilly hall, our bodies tense with nerves, mouths rigidly tight, hearts beating fast. We sit at a desk, a closed booklet before us, a pen gripped in one hand. The other hand fiddles with the lucky charm we brought with us. Scribble, scribble, scribble: our future depends on this exam! For many of us, an exam is a torture far worse than anything invented by the Spanish Inquisition.

The author Michael Morpurgo once said, "One of the great failings of our education system is that we tend to focus on those who are succeeding in exams, and there are plenty of them. But who we should be looking at–and a lot more urgently–are those who fail." He puts his finger accurately on the limitation of any examination system. If you pass an exam, you are eligible for the next step in life: if you fail, then hard luck! You're finished. Thank you so much for your effort, but your future is terminated.

Of course, that is a sweeping statement. We all know and admire people who have been successful in life, despite their failures in the exam hall. For example, many of our best actors left school without any success in the exam stakes. A famous actress once said, "You don't take exams for acting: you take courage." She was right. One of the ironies in life today is that many of the great actors, and businessmen, and authors, and pop-singers, who never made it to university because they failed exams, are offered honorary degrees by universities in recognition of their success. Am I alone in thinking that this is a rather patronizing gesture?

For, intended or not, there is often an elitism implied in the system of exams that we enforce at every step of people's lives. To some people, letters before or after one's name suggest that one has arrived at a level which somehow implies that one is better intellectually, economically, socially and perhaps even morally, than those who have not made the grade. Common sense should tell us that it isn't necessarily so. We are individuals and each one of us approaches life in a different way. We should not feel bullied and dragooned by a system that insists we conform to a set pattern or be dismissed.

Passage 2

With the "No Child Left Behind Act," recent concerns have arisen amongst educators about the role that exams play in determining a school's federal funding. With this act, teachers must adjust their lessons plans to prepare their students for standardized exams. Consequently, some question whether this act is merely a superficial quick fix since its aim is to ensure a school's pecuniary stability and not necessarily improve its educational approach. This act forces educators to focus on their school's Adequate Yearly Progress, or AYP. Since AYP has become a "hot button" issue, factious quarrels have pervaded even the most common of educators' conversations.

However, meeting or exceeding AYP objectives is a significant step toward educational reform. AYP sets reasonable goals for each school and is a steadfast method for keeping educators accountable. And these goals are actually quite reasonable because each AYP plan is specified to an individual school's target areas. Experienced educators, commissioned via the "No Child Left Behind Act," compile data based on the median student of his or her state. The AYP's criteria is then utilized to set the troubled school's progress plan for the next year. Ultimately, those critical of the standardized examination tend to forget that the word "adequate," within the acronym AYP, is not tantamount to nuclear fission or organic chemistry. "Adequate" simply means satisfactory. No one is proposing that the school become an International Baccalaureate overnight. Such hyperbole is often used, however, to refute the necessity of examination.

Because public schools rely on federal funding to operate, it is imperative that they provide the necessary proof (in particular, sufficient AYP results) to secure that money. However, some disagree. "This type of 'education' only works to gloss over the crux of a systematic problem detailed by the almighty dollar," said Anna Thompson, a high school teacher for more than twenty years. She believes that there are possible correlations between a school's socioeconomic background and AYP results. Ergo she asks, "how can a school acquire the much needed funding to succeed their AYP objectives, if it relies on that same funding to reform its teaching staff? It's a Catch-22 in which teachers who are needed in failing districts are instead hired in more affluent towns because these districts can offer higher salaries. 'Bubbling up' the answer key, taking the cash, and cashing the check – this is not education."

Yet, Anna and her supporters tend to forget a very important detail. Schools in need of AYP are below standards that are set in place by their respective states. Thus, while some teachers may feel the pressure to conform their lessons plans toward a standardized test, the concepts that they are preparing their students for are not abstract, collegiate, erudite theories. Rather, they are basic practices and applications that any school should be able to sustain. Otherwise, what can we reasonably expect from our students if our educational system doesn't look out for them?

1. The rhetorical device primarily used in lines 9-11 ("For many…Inquisition") is

(A) anecdote
(B) hyperbole
(C) flashback
(D) irony
(E) personification

2. The author's statement in line 22 ("Of course… statement") serves to

(A) assert that a claim is entirely correct
(B) admit to a personal bias against an idea
(C) acknowledge that a view might seem unreasonable
(D) recognize that an opposing argument is convincing
(E) digress into an unrelated topic not previously mentioned

3. According to the third paragraph of Passage 1, the author believes that offering "honorary degrees" (line 32) to the "great actors, and businessmen, and authors, and pop-singers" (lines 29-30) is

(A) condescending
(B) commendable
(C) understandable
(D) inappropriate
(E) uninteresting

4. According to the information presented in the last paragraph of Passage 1, the author most likely considers the system of test-taking to be

(A) a necessary evil
(B) a logical requirement
(C) a celebrated tradition
(D) a monotonous procedure
(E) an oppressive practice

5. The phrase "factious quarrels have pervaded" (line 59) suggests that

(A) students are embracing AYP standards
(B) contention over the AYP debate is widespread
(C) educators are in general agreement over AYP
(D) public schools take issue with AYP while private schools do not
(E) disagreement is inevitable between students and teachers

6. In the second paragraph of Passage 2, the author believes that "AYP" (line 61) is

(A) an exaggerated and impossible goal to reach
(B) the cause of problems in troubled schools
(C) a dangerously strict standard for high schools
(D) a means to improve long term educational goals
(E) a clever money-making tool for failing schools

7. The "type of 'education'" discussed in line 84 refers to education that

(A) incorporates a rigorous physics and chemistry curriculum
(B) inspires creative solutions to problems in the education system
(C) is ultimately dictated by the federal funding a school gets
(D) directs educators to schools that are in need of quality teachers
(E) challenges the notion that educators must teach to a test

8. The tone of lines 96-97 ("'Bubbling up'… education") can best be described as

(A) regretful
(B) inspirational
(C) skeptical
(D) derisive
(E) amused

9. Unlike the author of Passage 1, the author of Passage 2 explicitly expresses a view about the

(A) bureaucracy behind standardized testing
(B) controversy surrounding elitism in education
(C) impact on the individual student
(D) importance of a college degree
(E) author's experiences as a test taker

10. Which of the following best characterizes the tone of Passage 1 and that of Passage 2, respectively?

(A) Righteous indignation vs. lighthearted banter
(B) Outright disdain vs. qualified skepticism
(C) Subtle derision vs. caustic railing
(D) Detached analysis vs. academic objectivity
(E) Formal objectivity vs. dry humor

11. How would "Anna Thompson" (line 86) of Passage 2 respond to the statement in lines 37-42 ("To some…grade") of Passage 1?

(A) Life achievement is not based on the grades that a student will obtain throughout years of standardized testing.
(B) The letters before or after one's name are indicative of how hard an individual is willing to work to achieve goals.
(C) The system of test taking is engineered to appeal to students who learn based on their own set of individual standards.
(D) Student grades rarely have an impact on the Adequate Yearly Progress of the average high school.
(E) There may be a connection between an institution's socioeconomic background and the students' academic performance.

12. The concluding sentence of each passage makes its point by

(A) citing scholarly analysis
(B) detailing personal experiences
(C) inciting collective interest
(D) questioning accepted opinions
(E) quoting a authority

13. Both authors mention all of the following EXCEPT

(A) socioeconomic class
(B) federal funding
(C) the education system
(D) unsatisfactory grades
(E) supplementary commentary

6

Self Evaluation

Self Evaluation is important if you want to see an improvement on your next comprehension passage. Each passage has a set of possible reasons for errors. Place a check mark next to the ones that pertain to you, and write your own on the blank line provided. Use this form to better analyze your performance by filling it out regularly and accurately so you can recognize the pattern of your most common mistakes.

If you don't understand why you have made mistakes, there is no way you can correct them!

1st Long Reading Comprehension: # Correct:____ # Wrong:____ # Unanswered:____

○ Did not understand the question, line reference, or answers
○ Did not underline the line reference
○ Read too much or too little around the line reference
○ Summarized the line reference instead of answering the question
○ Couldn't find the false words
○ Couldn't choose between two possible answers
○ Did not use tone to help eliminate answers
○ When stuck between two answers, guessed instead of looking for additional facts
○ Couldn't finish in time
○ Other:____

2nd Long Reading Comprehension: # Correct:____ # Wrong:____ # Unanswered:____

○ Did not understand the question, line reference, or answers
○ Did not underline the line reference
○ Read too much or too little around the line reference
○ Summarized the line reference instead of answering the question
○ Couldn't find the false words
○ Couldn't choose between two possible answers
○ Did not use tone to help eliminate answers
○ When stuck between two answers, guessed instead of looking for additional facts
○ Couldn't finish in time
○ Other:____

3rd Long Reading Comprehension: # Correct:____ # Wrong:____ # Unanswered:____

○ Did not understand the question, line reference, or answers
○ Did not underline the line reference
○ Read too much or too little around the line reference
○ Summarized the line reference instead of answering the question
○ Couldn't find the false words
○ Couldn't choose between two possible answers
○ Did not use tone to help eliminate answers
○ When stuck between two answers, guessed instead of looking for additional facts
○ Couldn't finish in time
○ Other:____

4th Long Reading Comprehension: # Correct:____ # Wrong:____ # Unanswered:____

○ Did not understand the question, line reference, or answers
○ Did not underline the line reference
○ Read too much or too little around the line reference
○ Summarized the line reference instead of answering the question
○ Couldn't find the false words
○ Couldn't choose between two possible answers
○ Did not use tone to help eliminate answers
○ When stuck between two answers, guessed instead of looking for additional facts
○ Couldn't finish in time
○ Other:____

Single Long Comprehension
6 Questions Total, Pages 82-83

1. Correct answer: (D)
The author writes that "Politicians are scrutinized, interrogated, confronted with their failures, made to defend the reasons for their policies, required to give answers that the general public can take on board," because the British have little trust in their politicians.

2. Correct answer: (C)
The author writes about politicians that "their private lives and activities are neither reported nor examined in the public arena of press and broadcasting," which he describes as the French's attempt to adhere to "rules of respect and etiquette." Take note of the (+) tone.

3. Correct answer: (B)
The tone is (-), eliminating (A), (D), and (E). In the lines that follow the LR, the author describes how the French politicians are not "impeccable" by citing acts generally considered to be immoral or improper, suggesting "dissolute."

4. Correct answer: (A)
Earlier the author described how the responses of the British and French towards their treatment of politicians were contrasting, and here he explains why.

5. Correct answer: (E)
The author writes that "The British believe that all problems can be resolved if one works hard enough and long enough to do so," tone (+). He then writes "The French believe that if one leaves a problem alone for long enough, it will eventually diminish and disappear, or become irrelevant and, therefore acceptable," tone (-). Look for the only answer that shifts from (+) to (-).

6. Correct answer: (B)
In this LR the author writes that "the only thing to have been changed since 1789 is that a hereditary head of state (the King) has been replaced by a head of state who is elected every five years (the President)," suggesting not much has changed in the ruling of France.

Single Long Comprehension
9 Questions Total, Pages 84-85

1. Correct answer: (C)
The overall tone of this passage is (+), eliminating (A), (B), and (E). The author's use of the word "I" creates more of a conversational tone rather than a formal one.

2. Correct answer: (B)
The author claims that when he starts to write, he first creates "a long first paragraph, trying to make it striking and invitingly phrased," suggesting that he wants the reader to be intrigued into reading more.

3. Correct answer: (D)
In this LR, the author describes the "show-off stuff" as "unnecessary" which is synonymous with "superfluous."

4. Correct answer: (E)
The tone here is (+), eliminating (A), (B), and (D). The author writes that when he is "behaving like a camera" he is "recording what I see in my mind's eye," suggesting that he is being "candid," or honest, rather than "imaginative."

5. Correct answer: (A)
The author writes that "an honest eye stops me from being too clever for words," meaning that this "honest eye" keeps him from being dishonest. The question asks what the author would consider NOT to be dishonest, eliminating (B), (C), (D), and (E) since they all show examples of dishonesty.

6. Correct answer: (B)
The author writes, "I liked nearly all the classes I used to teach," but then limits this remark by saying, "well, for sure, there were some difficult times," which means he is qualifying his prior statement.

7. Correct answer: (A)
The author writes, "I treated my classes like they were theatre performances…in the theatre you have to work the audience, to engage it, to surprise it, to make the audience want to come back," meaning his teaching and the theatre both "have to captivate the audience."

8. Correct answer: (D)
The first time the author uses the word weapons he writes, "Attack and enthusiasm are the weapons you use," pointing to motivational. The second time he mentions weapons, he writes, "You don't use grades as a weapon to make sure the student is sycophantic," meaning that the teacher should not "threaten" the student with poor grades in order to make the student act more obediently.

P1 - Passage 1   P2 - Passage 2
LR - Line Reference
(+) - Positive
(-) - Negative
All quotes in answer choices can be found in or around the line reference.

9. Correct answer: (E)
The author describes "strictness of quality" as giving students the grade they deserve and giving "a top grade, only when there is nothing further to be said on what the student has produced."

Single Long Comprehension
12 Questions Total, Pages 86-88

1. Correct answer: (D)
Because this is an "in order to" question, the answer will be found around the LR. The author writes that camping was "pretty familiar until, one night…I heard a new sound that…was raw, edgy and, above all, incredibly sensual." In the first sentence of the next paragraph, he writes, "Musically, of course, this was really where the sixties started." The story of the camping trip was an introduction.

2. Correct answer: (C)
The author writes, "Musically, of course, this was really where the sixties started." He then writes that these artists "carried music from Rock 'n' Roll to the development of Hard Rock, by way of Motown and elsewhere." The implication here is that this type of music was never heard before the 1960s, making these artists the "representative figures" who played in these "new musical styles."

3. Correct answer: (E)
The author writes, "no young teenager could afford to miss a chord." Unfortunately, "when the calendar changed to 1960," the author "was no longer a teenager," therefore "most of this excitement passed [him] by." Suggesting that "his involvement" may have been "different…had he been younger."

4. Correct answer: (B)
In this paragraph the author reflects on the fashion of the 60s and writes, "I distinctly remember wearing Cuban heeled boots and long limp-collared and full-sleeved shirts in paisley, not to mention bell-bottom trousers," which means he "exploited the new fashion." He goes on to write, "I tottered down the street, an overweight bear, bulging at every pore," which means that he wore these trends "to the best of his physical ability."

5. Correct answer: (D)
The author describes men's fashion in the 60s as "becoming more adventurous" (eccentric) and that when he wore the fashion of the time he looked "very silly" (awkward).

6. Correct answer: (C)
Given that the author, when looking back, describes himself as looking "very silly" but at the time "thought I looked the 'bees' knees,'" it can be gathered that he was unaware at the time that he looked ridiculous.

7. Correct answer: (A)
Since this is an "in order to" question, the answer will be found around the LR. Before the LR, the author writes, "It was all a bit of fun really," implying that the youth were simply trying to "enjoy themselves" after such "a difficult past."

8. Correct answer: (E)
The author writes that "British films were improving… from the monotone, repressed, repetitive movies of how British stiff upper lips had won the war," meaning that these films "no longer focused on representing" how the British had succeeded in their war efforts.

9. Correct answer: (C)
The author writes that "there really had not been much [fun] since the war ended in 1945," suggesting that there was a lot of "tension" due to the "war years." The author then writes that these "attitudes were replaced by optimism," or "hope for the future."

10. Correct answer: (B)
In this paragraph the author illustrates for the reader this "unforgettable" sketch. The man in the sketch turns off a radio that is about to give an important news announcement. The audience laughs at the depiction of this "disdain for the media," as "that was the usual reaction to such interruptions." After the show, the author learns that the man had turned off an announcement about a presidential assassination, which is "coincidentally" a "major news event."

11. Correct answer: (C)
The author writes that the 60s was a time when "People began to say what they thought." He goes on to say that "satire was popular" and almost everything was mocked. With this attitude as the backdrop of the sketch, the actor, turning off the radio after the news broadcast comes on, would be very in keeping with the attitudes of the society at the time, suggesting that the audience would have "identified and agreed with the actor's response to the news."

12. Correct answer: (B)
Since the author was already 20 years old when the 60s came around, he claims "the excitement passed me by." But he did participate in wearing the fashion of the time as best as he could, even claiming he looked like "an overweight bear, bulging at every pore." He was a "participant," but not a typical one.

Double Long Comprehension
13 Questions Total, Pages 89-91

1. Correct answer: (B)
In this LR, the author uses exaggerated language to make a point about agonizing nature of exam taking. An exaggeration is also known as a "hyperbole."

2. Correct answer: (C)
The tone of this LR is (-), eliminating (A) and (D). In (B), "personal bias" is false and the author is not moving onto "an unrelated topic," eliminating (E).

3. Correct answer: (A)
Following the LR, the author expresses that he feels giving "honorary degrees" to "great actors, and businessmen, and authors, and pop-singers" is in fact "a rather patronizing gesture." "Condescending" and "patronizing" are similar in meaning.

4. Correct answer: (E)
In this LR, the author writes, "We should not feel bullied and dragooned by a system" of exams. He finds this "system" to be "an oppressive practice."

5. Correct answer: (B)
In the LR in which this phrase appears, the author writes that "AYP has become a 'hot button' issue," suggesting that the answer will be about "the AYP debate" and how "factious quarrels have pervaded," or "contention over" this topic has become "widespread."

6. Correct answer: (D)
The support for this answer comes from the first sentence of this LR in which the author writes, "meeting or exceeding AYP objectives is a significant step toward educational reform," pointing to (D).

7. Correct answer: (C)
The LR in which this phrase appears starts with "This"; read up to find out what "this" is. The author writes, "public schools rely on federal funding to operate [therefore] it is imperative that they provide the necessary proof [sufficient AYP results] to secure that money." In other words, "This type of 'education'" is essentially "dictated by the federal funding a school gets."

8. Correct answer: (D)
The tone of this LR is (-), eliminating (B) and (E). In this LR, the author is contemptuously mocking the notion expressed in the previous sentence, the notion that teachers are taking jobs "in more affluent districts" because these districts "can offer higher salaries." Contemptuously mocking something is to be "derisive."

9. Correct answer: (A)
This question is about what Passage 2 focuses on, which eliminates the choices that are only mentioned in Passage 1: (B), (C), (D), and (E), leaving (A). For further support, the reader must consider that Passage 2 is about schools meeting AYP standards, which, according to some, forces teachers to "adjust their lessons plans to prepare their students for standardized exams," also pointing to (A).

10. Correct answer: (B)
Throughout Passage 1, there are many instances in which the author's tone is clearly disdainful, such as in line 1 "littered," line 10 "torture," line 20 "hard luck," line 34 "patronizing," and line 45 "bullied." Whereas the author of Passage 2 writes, "some question whether [focusing on AYP] is merely a superficial quick fix since its aim is to ensure a school's pecuniary stability and not necessarily improve its educational approach." Here the author is showing "skepticism" and "qualifying" this skepticism by writing, "However, meeting or exceeding AYP objectives is a significant step toward educational reform. AYP sets reasonable goals for each school and is a steadfast method for keeping educators accountable."

11. Correct answer: (E)
The author of Passage 2 writes, "[Anna Thompson] believes that there are possible correlations between a school's socioeconomic background and AYP results," pointing to (E).

12. Correct answer: (C)
The reader must note that both concluding sentences utilize the word "we" in order to rouse "collective interest."

13. Correct answer: (B)
The question is asking what is NOT mentioned by BOTH authors. Only choice (B) is mentioned by the author of Passage 2 but not mentioned by the author of Passage 1.

P1 - Passage 1 P2 - Passage 2
LR - Line Reference
(+) - Positive
(-) - Negative
All quotes in answer choices can be found in or around the line reference.

Chapter Seven

Questions 1-7 are based on the following passage.

In this passage, excerpted from a 2013 essay, the author reveals his personal opinions concerning murder mystery novels.

When it comes to a finding a literary genre which will prove to be relatively relaxing and not too taxing to the little grey cells, there is nothing that fits the bill so well as the crime novel. Foul weather outside? Light the log fire, pop the kettle on for tea and curl up on the sofa with a paperback murder mystery. It is the best way to relax. One can always be confident that, eventually, the detective will solve the crime, despite the fact that it takes two or three corpses before the dénouement reveals all.

However, it is probably fair to say that not every detective in this category gives total satisfaction. American detectives are often far too energetic in their pursuit of the killer, forever racing along those mean streets at high speeds, firing off guns erratically and, in periods of less physical exertion, confronting their emotional neuroses. Swedish detectives, at the moment, are extremely fashionable, but unbearably gloomy – not their fault, of course: it is highly difficult to be cheerful and positive when one spends half a year waist deep in snow and darkness. French detectives, also, are subject to moodiness and introspection - possibly because they are so often dealing with corrupt politicians and pressure from their superiors. On the other hand, Italian detectives review corruption with a shrug of the shoulders; but then, apparently, they spend most of their time eyeing up attractive young women and being fed large meals by their mothers.

In truth, the English are the only writers who are masters of this kind of fiction. They ought to be. Despite the claim by the French that they were the first nation to produce a novel that had as its hero a detective with the name of Arsene Lupin, the first detectives to appear in literature were actually English. And with the appearance of Sherlock Holmes in "A Study in Scarlet" in 1887, the English took the lead in the development of this kind of writing. In the early part of the 20th century, English authors dominated the genre, beginning with Dorothy L. Sayers and her rather pretentious amateur detective, Lord Peter Wimsey. It is perhaps surprising that the best writers of the English detective novel have been, for the most part, women. It is perhaps much more surprising then that whichever sex was the novelist, virtually every detective they created was male.

Of course, the arrival of career women in England was a long time coming and for many decades the idea that women might be quite good at working out "who dunnit" was not something that occurred to "the good and the wise" – men, naturally - who were responsible for running the country. So, in detective novels, we had male inspectors heading the various divisions of the police force who were sometimes helped by intelligence such as that possessed by the great male detectives, such as Sherlock Holmes and Hercule Poirot.

Poirot was the creation of Agatha Christie, probably the most famous and successful of all crime writers after Conan Doyle. But another of Christie's detectives, Miss Marple, was the coup de grace against male domination in the solution of crime. She appears in only nine novels and a few short stories, but her impact was - and is - enormous. She is not in the least what you might expect a detective to be. She is a modest, elderly spinster living in the small and typically English village of St. Mary Mead where she knits and gardens and precisely observes human nature. She travels not by Aston Martin* but by Inch's taxi and British Rail when it was still powered by steam. She understands how people act, react and think, and, gently but relentlessly, she always solves the crime which has baffled England's elite crime bureau, Scotland Yard. She embodies the quiet and forceful intelligence of women.

*a British manufacturer of luxury cars popularized by the James Bond series of movies

1. The main purpose of the passage is to

(A) explain why crime novels are so popular today
(B) discuss the progression of the English detective novel
(C) compare and contrast detectives from various cultures
(D) catalogue the greatest fictional detectives in history
(E) question the rise in female authors among a genre

2. The claim that the crime novel is "not too taxing to the little grey cells" (lines 2-3) most nearly means that crime novels

(A) are a good way to keep your brain active
(B) can be physically, as well as mentally, relaxing
(C) will not have a trying effect on the brain
(D) normally will not be very exciting to read
(E) will always have a cathartic effect on readers

3. It can be inferred from lines 7-10 ("One can...all") that

(A) murder mysteries are too therapeutic to have a profound influence
(B) crime novels stereotypically cause the reader to want more
(C) the thriller genre often produces very realistic storylines
(D) crime novels are frequently too violent and predictable
(E) murder mysteries generally leave the reader feeling satisfied

4. In the second paragraph, the author mentions detectives from different cultures in order to

(A) underscore the superiority of the British detective
(B) undermine the belief that British detectives are the best
(C) make a claim about the poor state of the detective novel
(D) emphasize the pros and cons of each culture's detectives
(E) discuss the progression of the murder mystery detective

5. According to the author, the English are the "masters of this kind of fiction" (line 30) because

(A) they solidified the popularity of a fledgling genre
(B) they were the first to develop the detective genre
(C) they brilliantly translated a French detective novel
(D) Sherlock Holmes is the most widely recognized detective
(E) great authors, like Charles Dickens, featured detectives

6. The fourth paragraph (lines 46-56) emphasizes the extent to which

(A) the police force played the most pivotal role in the novels
(B) female authors were the norm among the genre
(C) the murder mystery genre was male dominated
(D) "who dunnits" were difficult to solve for readers
(E) Agatha Christie stood out among her crime-novel peers

7. The author describes Miss Marple as Agatha Christie's "coup de grace" in line 60 because

(A) she was popular enough to cause other writers to change detectives to women characters
(B) she was the first female detective to encourage women to pursue a career in crime fighting
(C) she was meek and timid around the male characters and so played a supporting role
(D) she was a pivotal character in breaking the mold of the stereotypical detective
(E) she was so different from the male detectives that it spawned a new literary genre

Questions 1-8 are based on the following passage.

In this passage from a 2013 essay about film director David Lean, the author considers the impact Lean had on the art of cinematography.

David Lean was born in London in 1908. He started work in a chartered accountant's office, which bored him, so he left and took a temporary job as a tea-boy at Gaumont Studios. He graduated to the role of clapper-boy and from there to the heights of Third Assistant Director. This led to a real promotion: fifteen years, working as an editor. His move into directing came in 1942 when he worked on "In Which We Serve" with Noel Coward. Lean went on to direct fifteen films in the next forty-nine years, often also working on the script, writing and editing. That may seem a surprisingly small number of films, yet he was nominated for an Academy Award as Best Director for seven of his films and won it twice. The British Film Institute in its list of the best British films ever made includes eleven of his films.

A film directed by David Lean has a sense of place whether it be the deserts of Arabia or the workhouses of Dickens' London. Lean makes us understand the effect these places have on the people who inhabit them. It is not just a question of good photography but a sense of how a place can affect and illuminate human response. There is a shot early in "Lawrence of Arabia" that illustrates this clearly. Lawrence is making his first foray on camel into the Arabian Desert. With him is his guide. The camera is at ground level and the two camels enter the shot from behind the camera and move towards the sloping horizon in the middle distance. On each side of the screen steep rocky cliffs frame the shot. As the two move on, Lean allows the camera to rise gently. This tiny movement transforms what could be simply a narrative link or an observation of the dwarfing quality of the desert, into a comment about the central character. Lawrence is entering into his world, calmly and acceptingly. Later in the film, of course, at the water hole is the stunning arrival of Sherif Ali. For almost a minute of screen time, the camera, like Lawrence himself, stares into the shimmering distance as what at first appears to be a mirage steadily comes closer. There is no sound beyond the padding of the camel. Then, a sudden flurry of cuts brings about the death of Lawrence's guide and Lawrence gazing up into the face of Sherif Ali who is practical and unmoved. It is a stunning sequence and prepares us for the ambivalence that lies at the basis of Lawrence's character and the relationship between the Arabs and the British. No other director would have had the courage to hold that entrance for so long.

Lean always trusted his audience's intelligence and imagination. The brutal murder of Nancy by Bill Sykes in "Oliver Twist" is not depicted directly, but through the metaphor of Bill Sykes' pit-bull whimpering, twisting its body and scrabbling frantically at the door to escape the deed. The horror for the audience is achieved. At the very beginning of this film, he uses filmic metaphor rather than narrative to suggest the pain and stress of Oliver's birth with the use of storm and the close up of aggressive thorn branches scraping against one another as his mother struggles to the gates of the Poor House.

His career reached a pinnacle with the spectacular triumphs of "The Bridge over the River Kwai," "Lawrence of Arabia," "Doctor Zhivago," and "A Passage to India." However, his real triumph was a black and white, British film he made in 1945, "Brief Encounter." It is a quiet examination of a married woman and a stranger whom she briefly meets in the refreshment bar of the local station. Her domestic life is shaken to the roots as she struggles to come to terms with this encounter. It is truly a piece of classic cinema, full of silent observation, understatement, and truth.

1. The primary purpose of this passage is to

(A) document an entire body of work by a famous director
(B) present a director through an analysis of his technique
(C) juxtapose varying styles of British cinematography
(D) explore the background of a legendary director
(E) question a director's achievements

2. In the opening sentences ("David Lean...Studios"), all of the following are mentioned EXCEPT

(A) geographical location
(B) specific era
(C) work attitude
(D) job promotion
(E) duties performed

3. In the second paragraph, the author develops his point by

(A) presenting all accepted analyses concerning a directorial technique and then choosing one
(B) stating a globally accepted opinion about a director and then refuting it with examples
(C) illustrating a director's cinematographic style followed by specific examples from his body of work
(D) making a thorough character analysis of the cast of a famous movie
(E) describing a director through a documentation of his lifetime achievements

4. The descriptions of Lawrence and Sherif Ali in lines 25-45 ("Lawrence is...unmoved") serve to

(A) distinguish between the emotional reactions of two characters
(B) illustrate how cinematography is used to highlight human response
(C) analyze the cultural discrepancies between the British and the Arabs
(D) offer an alternate explanation for a directorial decision
(E) refute a claim about a world famous director

5. "This tiny movement" (lines 31-32) is an example of which of the following?

(A) "His move into directing" (lines 7-8)
(B) "often also working on the script, writing and editing" (lines 10-11)
(C) "how place can affect and illuminate human response" (lines 22-23)
(D) "simply a narrative link or an observation" (lines 32-33)
(E) "what at first appears to be a mirage" (line 40)

6. In context, the word "practical" (line 44) most nearly means

(A) realistic
(B) functional
(C) useful
(D) brave
(E) indifferent

7. Which of the following scenes best illustrates the "narrative" in line 57?

(A) A smoking gun reveals the identity of the true murderer.
(B) Crashing waves represent the anger of a central figure.
(C) A wilting flower illustrates the death of a beloved protagonist.
(D) Snow falling outside speaks to the loneliness of the characters.
(E) A great tree is cut down, symbolizing the fall of an empire.

8. Which aspect of Lawrence of Arabia is LEAST likely to be found in "a piece of classic cinema" (lines 71-72)?

(A) "Lean allows the camera to rise gently" (line 31)
(B) "a mirage steadily comes closer" (lines 40-41)
(C) "no sound beyond the padding of the camel" (lines 41-42)
(D) "a sudden flurry of cuts" (line 42)
(E) "gazing up into the face of Sherif Ali" (lines 43-44)

Questions 1-12 are based on the following passage.

This passage explores the difference in impact between irony and sarcasm. It is adapted from an essay written by an English professor in 2013.

We have all been in a situation where we have tried to silence someone with the use of sarcasm. As a decisive blow in an interchange of opinion, it is a pretty blunt instrument and rarely creates a moment of victory. A sarcastic remark invites a similar volley from one's adversary, which, in turn, provokes an answer in kind and the whole thing descends into a sustained rally of taunt and counter-taunt, gibe piling on gibe, until each player's inventory is exhausted and the only thing for each player to do is to retreat from the net with as much dignity as can be mustered, perhaps with an occasional pause to turn and deliver a rather feeble, flailing, final shot. It is an unedifying and relatively futile game in which neither player's prowess has been sustained.

Of course, that has always been the point of sarcasm. The simplest explanation of the word is "to say one thing and to mean exactly the opposite." It comes from the ancient Greek term designed to describe literally the tearing of flesh or the biting of one's lip in rage - which is a vivid description of the facial distortion caused when we sneer. There is no subtlety involved: it is quite clear that the sting in sarcasm is that we mean precisely the opposite of what we say. It is intended to ridicule our opponent as crudely and contemptuously as possible in order to destroy his feeling of superiority. It is not a subtle weapon to use, and, probably, makes the user of sarcasm look as undignified as the person at whom the sarcasm is aimed.

Sarcasm should not be confused with Irony – although, today, that is very often the case. Irony is an infinitely more subtle mode of attack. On the surface, an ironic remark appears to be a perfectly clear comment; yet, there is an ambivalence about it that suggests that there may be other meanings lying beneath its surface. This kind of riposte can seem a far more humiliating form of attack than sarcasm; for, although the recipient of an ironic remark may not fully grasp the undercurrents of meaning implied, others who are present may well be able to grasp those implications, and their reaction adds a sting to the remark for the person to whom it is made – a sting which is all the more unnerving since he cannot be certain of the real meaning of the comment. Irony is double-edged and, therefore, unnerving. There is a difference between what is being said and what lies beneath the surface; or, to put it another way: a difference between "what is" and "what appears to be."

Irony is far more flexible than sarcasm, for it appears in forms other than the use of language. In a play, Dramatic Irony can often be employed. This is when the audience has been given information that is not known to characters in the play. Thus, characters in the play may be pursuing a line of action which the audience knows is doomed to failure. The audience is powerless to intervene and, as a result, a tension is created. In life, we often encounter the Irony of Situation: a course of action which appears to be leading to a point which we want to attain, but, in fact, creates a situation that is very different from what was expected, whether for good or bad.

Irony reminds us that nothing is as it seems. It demands that we use thought and intelligence and the ability to observe and to realize that nothing in life is exactly as it seems on the surface. For example: a business man slipping on a banana skin and landing heavily on the ground is often regarded as funny by passers-by who see it happen, and we laugh at the vision of his dignity being brought low. However, he himself, and those who know him well – his family, perhaps – would have a very different reaction. He, and they, are aware of the pain which we dismiss. The ability to see beyond the surface and the immediate is a pre-requisite in the use of and the appreciation of irony.

Both Sarcasm and Irony can be used as weapons. Sarcasm expresses a visceral reaction to a situation. It is the sensational statement that is made without equivocation. In literature, Dickens used it deliberately to demand an immediate reaction from his readers. Irony does not state: it considers and implies, and the superficial reader will miss the hidden questioning that lies beneath the surface of the text. To scan, rather than ponder, the text of any Jane Austen novel, is to miss not only the accuracy with which she observes the society in which she found herself but also the perceptive inference she cast on all mortal life. Therein lies the power of Irony.

1. In the first paragraph, the author makes use of which rhetorical device to describe a sarcastic conversation?

(A) personification
(B) repetition
(C) metaphor
(D) alliteration
(E) generalization

2. In context, the word "blunt" in line 4 most nearly means

(A) rounded
(B) ineffective
(C) candid
(D) heavy
(E) forceful

3. The phrase in line 9 ("each player's…exhausted") suggests that

(A) the argument has resulted in a clear win for one side
(B) each party has more that they want to say
(C) the conversation is dull and unimaginative
(D) one player has forfeited and is resigning
(E) the people conversing have run out of clever insults

4. The exchange described in lines 5-13 ("A sarcastic…shot") can most closely be characterized as

(A) serious discussion
(B) poor sportsmanship
(C) gratuitous violence
(D) constructive criticism
(E) competitive denigration

5. The statement in lines 19-22 ("It comes…sneer") can best be described as

(A) the etymology of a word
(B) the reality of a situation
(C) a striking illustration
(D) the conversational use of a term
(E) a criticism of language

6. The author views which of the following as an example of a "subtle weapon" (lines 27-28)?

(A) "a decisive blow" (line 3)
(B) "an answer in kind" (lines 6-7)
(C) "the point of sarcasm" (lines 16-17)
(D) "the undercurrents of meaning" (line 40)
(E) "the sensational statement" (line 78)

7. It can be inferred from lines 27-30 ("It is…aimed") that

(A) in sarcasm, irreverence and subtlety go hand in hand
(B) victory goes to he who delivers the greatest humiliation
(C) a volley of sarcasm does not result in a clear victor
(D) the most obvious remarks are often the most damaging
(E) unlike irony, sarcasm is a justifiable form of attack

8. According to lines 33-37 ("On the…surface"), an ironic comment can be misleading because it uses

(A) specific jargon
(B) equivocal language
(C) superfluous diction
(D) clear communication
(E) profound statements

9. In context of lines 37-45 ("This kind…comment"), irony is "far more humiliating" than sarcasm because

(A) the recipient may understand the true intent of sarcastic statements before others but will attempt to laugh them off
(B) most ironic statements are made to reflect the opposite intention of what they state
(C) all of the listeners will form similar interpretations of the remark's intent and will react on that basis
(D) the recipient is unsuspecting of the insult until others realize and react to the ironic statement
(E) the true meaning of sarcastic statements are often explicitly stated by the speaker

10. The fourth paragraph depicts irony as

(A) scathing
(B) adaptable
(C) humorous
(D) absolute
(E) obvious

11. Lines 64-66 ("It demands…surface") serve primarily to

(A) illustrate a point using slapstick comedy
(B) place irony in a anthropological context
(C) conclude that irony is difficult to grasp
(D) muse thoughtfully on life in general
(E) explain what irony reveals about life

12. The tone of the passage can best be described as

(A) informative
(B) sardonic
(C) inquisitive
(D) sanguine
(E) caustic

Questions 1-13 are based on the following passage.

The passages below discuss the viability of sports as a profession. Passage 1 is adapted from a 2012 memoir by an Asian American author. Passage 2 presents the musings of an aspiring athlete.

Passage 1

I've heard that those who grow up to become successful sportsmen were born rich. There are equipment fees, training fees, club fees, tournament fees, travelling fees: paying for all of this for years must amass to a huge amount of money. For someone born into a wealthy family and with parents inclined to raise a promising athlete, this sacrifice may be easily manageable. But for those raised without comfortable wealth, becoming an athlete may seem like the impossible dream.

When I was eleven, my parents sent me to a very expensive, specialized school in China for table tennis, where I'd join other kids to train for four hours a day, six days a week. After the first few days, my temporary interest as the "American girl" wore off. I was smoothly tossed aside by all the coaches and other students. I ranked as one of the worst players there and soon the only words I exchanged with the coach were translations for the other, *better* foreign students who had arrived. I slugged my way through the next few weeks there as an invisible girl, not worthy of attention and without the promising potential of the other kids.

The last week of my stay, my dad came to visit and watch my training session. Without warning or reason, I was promoted to the better group and allowed to train with the kids who were to become professionals. For the next four hours, the coach came to me every few minutes to point out and adjust my weaknesses. When I won a match, I was lavishly praised. When I lost, the coach shrugged and patted me on the back. I was bewildered, but pleased. When my father left, I was sent back to the drop-out group.

They were courting my father's money. I later found that, in many sports clubs, having good connections and bribing the coaches is a common way to guarantee better training for your children. There are thousands of kids who want the training, but only so many coaches to provide for them. So instead of giving each child equal attention and focus, they pick and choose based on the willingness of their parents' wallets; why not, if it's a better deal for them?

Becoming an athlete is neither easy nor cheap. Those with the heavy pockets and velvet-tongued parents have an immeasurable advantage over those who can't afford to pay for everything an athlete needs. Even those bursting with talent will find it difficult without certain means. Especially for the more obscure sports, where scouting rarely occurs, motivation and raw talent are only as good as the money to back them up.

Passage 2

Becoming an athlete requires a tremendous amount of sacrifice. You have to trade the time you could have spent doing schoolwork, playing, or simply relaxing to practice and improve your skills. Some say only the affluent will become our greatest competitors. But claiming that only children from wealthy households can become successful athletes is like saying any bird that is not exceedingly early will never be able to catch any worms!

Talent isn't something that can be bought, no matter how much money you have; the same goes for love and passion. Rather, the athletic ability that can be seen in every famous athlete is intrinsic. This doesn't mean that they could have gotten where they are today without practice, of course, but not any person could achieve so much with routine practice alone.

With so many children clambering to improve, it's impossible for the coaches and trainers to turn them all into champions. Some children just don't have either the talent or the motivation to cross the hurdles that will block their way in becoming a professional athlete. It's natural for the coaches to focus their attention on those who show that they are capable of going through the hardships of defeat and injury in the future and are still able to pick themselves up and work even harder.

Stating that money makes a successful athlete is both insulting and inaccurate. There have been hundreds of athletes who have come from humble beginnings and made their own way to the top. Olympic gymnastics gold-medalist Gabby Douglas admitted that among the hurdles she had to clear included being homeless at one point. Gabby was raised by a single mother, who struggled through financial issues for years and provided Gabby with the best training she could. Her story of gain after loss is one among many that shows us money doesn't define ability.

While money does factor into the education of an athlete, it is more a testament to how much you're willing to sacrifice to follow your dream than a lever towards success. No matter how much money you pour into hunting down the best coaches, the best environment, and the best equipment, if you don't have the skills or passion for the sport, your efforts will never bear fruit. As master of Tae Kwon Do Kerry Roy puts it, "If you really want something bad enough, you'll find a way to get it." Money is just another hurdle that every athlete has to overcome, not a barrier that prevents them from ever crossing the finish line.

1. Both authors would most likely agree that wealth is

(A) a direct result of inherent talent
(B) integral to the success of an athlete
(C) a boon for those with athletic talent
(D) the cause of talent in most athletes
(E) a deterrent in the lives of athletes

2. The author of Passage 2 would most likely respond to the last paragraph of Passage 1 by asserting that

(A) the author of Passage 1 focuses too much on specialized sports
(B) money is not an unsurpassable barrier for budding athletes
(C) most athletes will become wealthy as a result of playing their sport
(D) affluence will eventually stunt an athlete's training without talent
(E) the pressures of poverty do not only affect athletes in training

3. The author of Passage 1 cites the "equipment fees… travelling fees" (lines 3-4) as obstacles that

(A) many athletes-in-training will require federal funding for
(B) would be impossible to overcome for those facing financial difficulty
(C) are only a concern of the wealthiest athletic coaches and trainers
(D) are easy to overcome when considering a lifelong participation in sports
(E) are unnecessary when dedicating a child to a life of athleticism

4. In context of the passage, the author italicizes the word "better" in line 19 in order to

(A) claim that the other students were lacking in talent
(B) cast doubt on her own talent as a table tennis player
(C) imply that the students were wealthier than she was
(D) shift focus from the Chinese students to the Americans
(E) assume their skill level based on their nationality

5. In context, the author believes the coaches promoted her to the better group in the third paragaph (lines 24-33) in order to

(A) convince her father that he should take her home early
(B) ingratiate themselves with her distinguished father
(C) prove that she has what it takes to play professionally
(D) solicit more monetary incentive from her father
(E) show her father that she was not advancing in the sport

6. In context of the first passage, the "means" mentioned in line 48 are most likely related to

(A) free time
(B) advanced education
(C) self-discipine
(D) parental duties
(E) social class

7. Which of the following, if true, would detract MOST from the argument presented in the first passage?

(A) Most of the top athletic programs in the United States are funded and thus free.
(B) Affluent athletes have a very high chance of dominating their particular sport.
(C) International training camps cost more than those in the United States.
(D) Most sports require a large financial obligation before becoming lucrative.
(E) A competitive market drives many sports to maintain their high standing.

8. The tone of the sentence in lines 57-60 ("But claiming…worms") can best be described as

(A) prudent
(B) jovial
(C) enervated
(D) emphatic
(E) acerbic

9. According to the second paragraph of Passage 2, the author claims that

(A) wealth directly correlates with ability
(B) great athleticism comes from training
(C) training will impede athletes with raw talent
(D) enthusiasm is more important than talent
(E) the athletic ability is primarily inherent

10. According to the third paragraph of Passage 2 (lines 68-77), an athlete's failure can be LEAST attributable to

(A) little desire to work
(B) no inherent talent
(C) lack of financial funding
(D) inability to endure hardships
(E) too much competition

11. The author of Passage 1 would most likely regard Gabby Douglas in lines 82-88 as

(A) an extreme anomaly
(B) the epitome of athleticism
(C) an unnatural athlete
(D) the embodiment of success
(E) an industry standard

12. Compared to the author of Passage 1, the author of Passage 2 considers "money" (line 89) to be

(A) a catalyst to finding inherent talent
(B) as important as training to success
(C) the most important element to success
(D) secondary to innate skill
(E) instrumental in becoming a trainer

13. In contrast to that of Passage 1, the tone of Passage 2 is more

(A) critical
(B) optimistic
(C) absolute
(D) didactic
(E) elitist

Self Evaluation

Self Evaluation is important if you want to see an improvement on your next comprehension passage. Each passage has a set of possible reasons for errors. Place a check mark next to the ones that pertain to you, and write your own on the blank line provided. Use this form to better analyze your performance by filling it out regularly and accurately so you can recognize the pattern of your most common mistakes.

If you don't understand why you have made mistakes, there is no way you can correct them!

1st Long Reading Comprehension: # Correct:____ # Wrong:____ # Unanswered:____

- ○ Did not understand the question, line reference, or answers
- ○ Did not underline the line reference
- ○ Read too much or too little around the line reference
- ○ Summarized the line reference instead of answering the question
- ○ Couldn't find the false words
- ○ Couldn't choose between two possible answers
- ○ Did not use tone to help eliminate answers
- ○ When stuck between two answers, guessed instead of looking for additional facts
- ○ Couldn't finish in time
- ○ Other:____

2nd Long Reading Comprehension: # Correct:____ # Wrong:____ # Unanswered:____

- ○ Did not understand the question, line reference, or answers
- ○ Did not underline the line reference
- ○ Read too much or too little around the line reference
- ○ Summarized the line reference instead of answering the question
- ○ Couldn't find the false words
- ○ Couldn't choose between two possible answers
- ○ Did not use tone to help eliminate answers
- ○ When stuck between two answers, guessed instead of looking for additional facts
- ○ Couldn't finish in time
- ○ Other:____

3rd Long Reading Comprehension: # Correct:____ # Wrong:____ # Unanswered:____

- ○ Did not understand the question, line reference, or answers
- ○ Did not underline the line reference
- ○ Read too much or too little around the line reference
- ○ Summarized the line reference instead of answering the question
- ○ Couldn't find the false words
- ○ Couldn't choose between two possible answers
- ○ Did not use tone to help eliminate answers
- ○ When stuck between two answers, guessed instead of looking for additional facts
- ○ Couldn't finish in time
- ○ Other:____

4th Long Reading Comprehension: # Correct:____ # Wrong:____ # Unanswered:____

- ○ Did not understand the question, line reference, or answers
- ○ Did not underline the line reference
- ○ Read too much or too little around the line reference
- ○ Summarized the line reference instead of answering the question
- ○ Couldn't find the false words
- ○ Couldn't choose between two possible answers
- ○ Did not use tone to help eliminate answers
- ○ When stuck between two answers, guessed instead of looking for additional facts
- ○ Couldn't finish in time
- ○ Other:____

Single Long Comprehension
7 Questions Total, Pages 98-99

1. Correct answer: (B)
The author relates stories about the advancement of murder mystery novels and the changes in the authors. To eliminate the others, look for false words: in (A), cross out "popular today." In (C), the author discusses cultures in just one paragraph. In (D), cross out "in history," and in (E), cross out "question."

2. Correct answer: (C)
In the LR, before the author writes "not too…cells," he writes "will prove to be relatively relaxing." (A) is the opposite of this statement. In (B), "physically" is false. In (D), relaxing can still be exciting. And in E, "cathartic" is false.

3. Correct answer: (E)
This LR states that murder mysteries are generally not open ended; they do not leave the reader with lingering, unanswered questions. One can infer that the reader of a murder mystery will be left "feeling satisfied." In (A), "too therapeutic" is false. (B) is the opposite of the inference. And the author provides no support for (C) or (D).

4. Correct answer: (A)
In an "in order to" question, the reader must read above or below the LR to find the answer. In this case, below the LR, the author states "In truth, the English are the only writers who are masters of this kind of fiction." This is why he first points out the flaws in the detectives of other cultures.

5. Correct answer: (B)
The author writes that the English "ought to be" the best in this field because "the first detectives to appear in literature were actually English."

6. Correct answer: (C)
The author writes that "the arrival of career women in England was a long time coming" and that "in detective novels, we had male inspectors" and "great male detectives."

7. Correct answer: (D)
The author writes that Miss Marple "was the coup de grace against male domination in the solution of crime," which, put simply, means she broke the stereotype of a male-only detective.

Single Long Comprehension
8 Questions Total, Pages 100-101

1. Correct answer: (B)
This passage is about David Lean, as we can learn from the blurb in italics, which eliminates (C). Furthermore, the blurb tells us that "the author considers the impact Lean had on the art of cinematography," eliminating (D), which is about the director's background, and (E), which is about questioning his achievements, and (A), which is about simply documenting all of Lean's work.

2. Correct answer: (D)
The author writes, "born in London in 1908," eliminating (A) and (B). In the next sentence the author writes, "which bored him, so he left and took a temporary job as a tea-boy," eliminating (C) and (E).

3. Correct answer: (C)
In the very beginning of the paragraph the author writes, "A film directed by David Lean has a sense of place whether it be the deserts of Arabia or the workhouses of Dickens' London. Lean makes us understand the effect these places have on the people who inhabit them." In these two sentences the author explains Lean's cinematographic style and alludes to two of his films, the first one being "Lawrence of Arabia" and the other based on a Dickens novel, pointing to (C).

4. Correct answer: (B)
In the two sentences prior to the LR, the author writes, "It is not just a question of good photography but a sense of how a place can affect and illuminate human response. There is a shot early in "Lawrence of Arabia" that illustrates this clearly." Therefore, the "descriptions" referred to in the LR "serve to" show how Lean's sense of cinematography "highlights human response."

5. Correct answer: (C)
The author writes that this "movement transforms what could be…an observation of the dwarfing quality of the desert into a comment about the central character," pointing to (C).

6. Correct answer: (E)
In the context of the sentence, the word "practical" is used in a way that means "unmoved" which is synonymous with "indifferent."

7. Correct answer: (A)
The author claims that Lean "uses filmic metaphor rather than narrative to suggest the pain and stress," suggesting that the narrative cannot be made using metaphor, eliminating all representations (B), illustrations (C), subtle scenes (D), and symbols (E).

8. Correct answer: (D)
According to the author "classic cinema" is "full of silent observation, understatement, and truth." (B) and (E) depict "observation." (A) and (C) depict "understatement," leaving (D), an action shot shown through a montage.

Single Long Comprehension
12 Questions Total, Pages 102-103

1. Correct answer: (C)
In this paragraph, the author describes how similar this "interchange of opinion" is to a sporting match in which both "players" are competing to win the "interchange," using metaphor.

2. Correct answer: (B)
The author states that "as a decisive blow," sarcasm "rarely creates a moment of victory" suggesting that it is an ineffective tool in winning this "interchange of opinion."

3. Correct answer: (E)
The author states that this "interchange of opinion" turns into a "sustained rally of taunt and counter-taunt" ending with each player retreating "from the net." This suggests that both "players" have run out of sarcastic remarks.

4. Correct answer: (E)
The author compares this "interchange of opinion" to a sporting match. We can infer that there is competition between the two "players." Furthermore, the author states that "the whole thing descends into a sustained rally of taunt and counter-taunt, gibe piling on gibe," pointing to the "denigration" – or damaging with words, attacking character.

5. Correct answer: (A)
The author states that the word sarcasm "comes from the ancient Greek term…" This sort of description is called the etymology, or history and origins, of a word.

6. Correct answer: (D)
The "undercurrents of meaning" must be implied but not said, or subtle. Eliminate (A) because a decisive blow cannot be subtle. (B), (C), and (E) all describe sarcasm, which the author claims "is not a subtle weapon" (lines 27-28).

7. Correct answer: (C)
The author states that sarcasm "is intended to ridicule our opponent… in order to destroy his feeling of superiority." But what results is that it "makes the user of sarcasm look as undignified as the person at whom the sarcasm is aimed." We can infer that in the end, neither person comes out on top.

8. Correct answer: (B)
The author states that while sarcasm "appears to be a perfectly clear comment…there is an ambivalence about it that suggests that there may be other meanings lying beneath its surface." This "ambivalence" points to choice (B), as "equivocal" means misleading.

9. Correct answer: (D)
The author states that "although the recipient of an ironic remark may not fully grasp the undercurrents of meaning inferred, others who are present may well be able to grasp those inferences, and their reaction adds a sting to the remark for the person to whom it is made."

10. Correct answer: (B)
In the first sentence of the paragraph the author states that "Irony is far more flexible than sarcasm." Remember, adaptable means irony can change for different situations.

11. Correct answer: (E)
Because the LR begins with a pronoun (it), we should read the previous sentence. The author states that "Irony reminds us that nothing is as it seems." He goes on to say that "It demands that we…realize that nothing in life is exactly as it seems on the surface." Here, according to the author, irony tells us about life.

12. Correct answer: (A)
In this passage, the author describes for the reader the difference between sarcasm and irony, therefore the tone could best be called descriptive, or "informative."

P1 - Passage 1 P2 - Passage 2
LR - Line Reference
(+) - Positive
(-) - Negative
All quotes in answer choices can be found in or around the line reference.

Single Long Comprehension
13 Questions Total, Pages 104-106

1. Correct answer: (C)
The author of P1 writes, "Those with the heavy pockets and velvet-tongued parents have an immeasurable advantage …" Similarly, the author of P2 writes, "While money does factor into the education of an athlete, it is more a testament to how much you're willing to sacrifice to follow your dream than a lever towards success." Both authors would agree that having financial backing is "a boon for those" who are athletically talented.

2. Correct answer: (B)
The author of P2 writes, "Money is just another hurdle that every athlete has to overcome, not a barrier that prevents them from ever crossing the finish line," meaning that an athlete can achieve success without financial wealth.

3. Correct answer: (B)
After listing the expenses of an athlete, the author goes on to write that "for those raised without comfortable wealth, becoming an athlete may seem like the impossible dream."

4. Correct answer: (C)
In the context of P1, the author implies that the "better" students were in fact the "wealthier" students. The author writes, "I was smoothly tossed aside…for the other, better foreign students." The author later explains why this had happened by writing, "they pick and choose based on the willingness of their parents' wallets."

5. Correct answer: (D)
The author explains how much attention she was paid by the instructors when her father was present. The author then explains why she thinks this happened by writing, "They were courting my father's money."

6. Correct answer: (E)
In the context of P1, the "means" that the author thinks an athlete needs to get ahead are "comfortable wealth" (line 9) and "good connections" (lines 35-36), which point to a high "social class."

7. Correct answer: (A)
The argument presented in P1 can be summed up in the last paragraph. To be a successful athlete, one must have not only "motivation and raw talent" but also "the money to back" those things up. A statement suggesting that one can be a talented and well-trained athlete without any financial backing would undermine this argument, pointing to (A), in which the "top athletic programs…are funded and thus free."

8. Correct answer: (D)
The clue here is the exclamation mark, which points to "emphatic."

9. Correct answer: (E)
The author writes, "athletic ability…is intrinsic." "Intrinsic" is synonymous with "inherent."

10. Correct answer: (C)
The author writes, "With so many children clambering to improve, it's impossible for the coaches and trainers to turn them all into champions. Some children just don't have either the talent or the motivation to cross the hurdles that will block their way in becoming a professional athlete," eliminating (A), (B), (D), and (E).

11. Correct answer: (A)
Given that the author of P1 feels "comfortable wealth" is a requirement to becoming "successful sportsmen," she would feel that anyone who attained that dream without "the money to back [the talent] up" would be considered an "anomaly" or inconsistent with the norm.

12. Correct answer: (D)
The author of P2 writes, "No matter how much money you pour into hunting down the best coaches, the best environment, and the best equipment, if you don't have the skills or passion for the sport, your efforts will never bear fruit," meaning that "innate skill" is more important than "money."

13. Correct answer: (B)
The tone of P2 is more (+) than that of P1, eliminating (A) and (E). Since the author of P2 concedes (to an extent) that "money does factor into the education of an athlete," the tone cannot be "absolute," (C). Lastly, the author is not being instructive, eliminating (D).

Chapter Eight

Questions 1-6 are based on the following passage.

In this passage, the author discusses the role of reason and logic as a serious, philosophical lifestyle during the reign of the Greek empire.

The cultures of the classical world, around the 6th century B.C.E., leaned heavily on belief in gods. The resurgence of Hinduism in India with the Vedic sagas of gods and heroes was in full force; Zoroastrianism was stressing a belief in one omnipotent, benevolent god fighting a pervasive evil spirit in Persia; Buddhism and Daoism had not yet completely overtaken the folk mythologies of their respective regions—and in the midst of it all, the Greeks were heading in a different direction. After years of telling themselves that the storms and the sunshine and the seas were the gods' doing, some Greek philosophers decided that the forces of nature were no more divine than the forces of man. They began to hypothesize based on empirical data, no longer believing that they were golden and prosperous because of a god's favor. The Greeks accepted that they were prosperous because of their own merits. The Greeks, contradicting all other major cultural religious traditions of the time, decided to pursue reason.

The incentive for such a change was obvious: Athens was beaming in its art and economy after its recent victory over the Persians; Sparta was well known for its military might and moral honor. It was the perfect time for Democritus of Abdera and Pythagoras of Samos to join math and science and fuel an entire society with the tenets of reason. All of a sudden, Empedicles forged the first thoughts on natural selection as Plato brewed up new ideas for a society of equal education. The Greeks wanted the world to be understood, to have order, and this order needed to transcend myths of ancestors and gods; nature, they found, operated under immutable laws and forces rather than the whims and caprice of the divine.

Perhaps this was radical thinking, and perhaps this was questioned by some, yet the rest of world supported, or even downright envied, the Greeks. The Greek alliance was the principal power of the Mediterranean after the Persian Wars—and power over the Mediterranean was power over the whole of Western Europe. The Eastern world could not comprehend the effectiveness of Greece's form of government based on rival city-states. How could an entire civilization be so decentralized in daily life, yet so unified when threatened by outside forces? The simple answer was that the Greeks were the only classical civilization to pursue reason and logic, so, regardless of their differences, they would find a way to unify themselves in a crisis.

As a result of the unifying strength of reason, when philosophy took hold on education and government, and the humanities began to influence each citizen across their hierarchy, it was hardly a shock to the Greeks themselves. In the words of Plato, "philosophy begins when you learn to doubt," and doubt they did. Within this birth of logic, within this revolution of philosophy, and within this attention to aesthetics, there were those who assumed this lust for reason was fiscally driven.

Perhaps, the Easterns said, the Greeks needed to retain control over the Mediterranean, so the Greeks "reasoned" out why they deserved it. Logically speaking, the "reasonable" ones are the deserving ones. Logically speaking, to keep such commerce and trade alive, the Greek people needed in them a trigger, a belief that they were on top of the world because they were the smarter people, the "philosophic" people. But, in reality, how can one logically conclude that the entire materialization of philosophy was based on a mere hunger for money?

1. The primary purpose of the passage is to

(A) question the role of the gods in everyday Greek society
(B) consider the motivations behind the birth of reason
(C) condemn the Greeks for losing sight of their religion
(D) determine the role of philosophy and art in religion
(E) prove a point about the downfall of Greek culture

2. The first paragraph relates a contrast between

(A) classical religion and Greek mythology
(B) religious conviction and academic controversy
(C) spiritual enlightenment and observational theories
(D) indisputable logic and personal anecdote
(E) strict monotheism and widespread polytheism

3. In line 27, "fuel" most nearly means

(A) rouse
(B) shove
(C) fill up
(D) instigate
(E) burn

4. The author states in line 33 that the Greeks embraced the idea that nature "operated under immutable laws" because

(A) art, math and science were considered to stretch beyond the natural order
(B) their society had been modeled after the hierarchies they observed in nature
(C) nature proved to be a fearsome contestant with whom the Greeks often fought
(D) they desired stable explanations of events that wouldn't change on a god's whim
(E) nature's wrath had a destructive effect on every classical society except the Greeks

5. According to the author, some outsiders believed that the Greek reasoning "revolution" (line 57) was catalyzed by

(A) logical nature
(B) dubious philosophy
(C) economic growth
(D) belligerent civilization
(E) aesthetic desire

6. The author repeats the phrase "logically speaking" in the fifth paragraph (lines 60-70) primarily to

(A) sarcastically attack the Greeks for their flawed and selfish reasoning
(B) inject the essay with a dose of purposeful levity through flair
(C) emphasize the thought process that led to global Greek dominance
(D) contend that all civilizations will fall without reason and logic
(E) show contempt for an attitude through deliberate repetition

Questions 1-9 are based on the following passage.

The following passage discuss theatre. The first looks into British Pantomime, while the second focuses on American Vaudeville.

Passage 1

It is quite difficult to explain to anyone who is not British what Pantomime exactly is. Foreigners are bemused by this particular theatrical genre, which appears annually from Christmas to March. Clearly it is popular: it plays to packed houses. Going to see "Panto" at Christmas has often been the first (and, in many cases, the only) time a child is ever taken to the theater. The whole family goes, for a Christmas treat, so there has to be something that will appeal to every member of the family. The theme is always about the poor and good hero making his way to success and riches against all odds. An element of magic is important since it allows for a "transformation" scene, which is always the magical, sparkling climax to the first half of the Pantomime. Children (and very often adults) sit agape when this happens before their eyes on stage.

A proper "Panto" is an eclectic affair: something for everyone means the inclusion of acrobatics, dancing, music, and, above all, glamour and comedy. These two last elements are created through cross-dressing and role reversal—probably a likely source of dubious glances from foreigners. The Hero creates the glamour: "he" is always played by a woman, quite clearly striding across the stage dressed as a man. The comedy is provided by the role of the Dame, always played by a man in a big wig, big costume, exaggerated makeup and a very deep voice. This role reversal is one of the ways in which the Pantomime takes on the surrealism of a dream and motivates the audience's suspension of disbelief.

The most extraordinary element of Pantomime is the participation of the audience, encouraged to sing along with the cast, call out when the hero is in danger, join in the moments of slapstick comedy on stage, boo the villain and sigh contentedly when the hero finally wins the heroine. A tremendous sense of relationship builds up between the characters on the stage and the real life of the audience: topical jokes, double-entendres, characters coming down from the stage and mixing with the audience. The final moments of Pantomime bring this element to a climax. The Dame appears in front of the curtain. The song sheet descends. The Dame and the audience work together, chatting, interacting and singing the song together lustily. Then, with a drum roll, those onstage return to their seats. The Dame exits, and the curtains part to reveal the final scene, where the villains are thwarted and the hero and heroine are united, rich at last. All is glitter and brightness and warmth and happiness.

Passage 2

Vaudeville, an American theatrical pastime, still exists today as the more commonly known "variety show." This form of theatre began in the late 1800s before reaching the peak of its popularity around 1910. Clearly, Americans at this time needed escape from the pangs and tribulations of the economic strife that would eventually lead to the Great Depression of 1929. Vaudeville's audiences were mostly adult because of its burlesque set pieces, which featured scantily clad female performers. However, because of the impending economic collapse, Vaudeville eventually evolved into a more genteel version better known as "Polite Vaudeville."

This form of Vaudeville did not have any uniform structure other than an eclectic set of acts mashed under one playbill. Performances included musicians, singers, dancers, set-piece comedians, magicians, male and female impersonators, acrobats, jugglers, and occasionally one-act plays. Most of these forms were interactive in nature, often provoking the audience to cheer or sneer at the performances and the performers. Most importantly, Polite Vaudeville centralized on family entertainment as a marketing ploy to sell more tickets. The American family became the sole concern for Polite Vaudeville. And with that change, this form of theatre also changed its focus.

As the audience transitioned into parents with children, many performances instead became about the lionization of the American Dream. This theme, the motif of a "city upon a hill," was continuously met with harsh scrupulousness and in some respects, animadversion, because of the unattainable quality of life that permeated from this idea that has defined America even today. Upward mobility through individual thrift meant that most set pieces for Polite Vaudeville had to be "peppy" with an often superficial struggle of a protagonist overcoming all odds. The hero rises to the occasion and saves his family, saves the farm, or some other arbitrary pecuniary obstacle. But, in some rare pieces, the role-reversal of genders, particularly when a woman would play the husband or father character, was a derisive jab at the institutions that perpetuated the American Dream. These pieces were political.

But all that would change. Some dramaturges, or theatre pundits, suggest that as cinema's popularity promulgated, the interactive nature of performances like those in Polite Vaudeville declined. This theatrical ebb led to a discord between the audience and the performance, between Americans and politics, between a citizen and his government - relegating what was once engaging political satire to passive and rote drollery on a celluloid screen.

1. The unifying theme of both Panto and Polite Vaudeville is

(A) the antagonist is vanquished and the people rejoice
(B) the protagonist overcomes all hardships and prevails
(C) that the ancillary characters help the protagonist
(D) the belief that magic can be a very powerful tool
(E) that good family values equate to financial success

2. The author of Passage 1 describes Pantomime as a

(A) heartening and enjoyable family affair
(B) politically motivated art piece
(C) form of witchcraft and medieval magic
(D) play made for only children to enjoy
(E) controversial holiday extravaganza

3. The author of Passage 1 calls Pantomime an "eclectic affair" (line 17) because

(A) it incorporates both cross-dressing and role reversal
(B) it seamlessly mixes both art and science in one production
(C) it is an amalgamation of acts that people of all ages can enjoy
(D) of Pantomime's surrealistic depiction of a dreamlike state
(E) of its versatility to remain pertinent in all seasons of the year

4. According to the author of Passage 1, "The most extraordinary element of Pantomime" (lines 31-32) is the

(A) mix of various acts that create an affair for members of the whole family to enjoy
(B) humor utilized by the actors to create a sense of camaraderie between the characters and the audience
(C) sense of climax reached at the end of the play through the elements of suspense and audience participation
(D) meaningful relationship that develops between the characters and the audience through mutual interaction
(E) commentary made on gender roles through the use of cross-dressing and role reversal

5. According to the first paragraph of Passage 2, the transformation of Vaudeville closely follows

(A) the progression of American ethics
(B) fluctuations in the financial environment
(C) increased opportunities for theatre profits
(D) changes in national demographics
(E) the evolution of contemporary entertainment

6. The sentence in lines 78-80 ("As the...Dream") primarily serves to

(A) poke fun at the establishments that encouraged unattainable dreams
(B) transition from the original Vaudeville to what is considered Polite Vaudeville
(C) explain the uniform structure of all Vaudeville performances
(D) shed light on the political motivations of Vaudeville actors
(E) implicate that the new Vaudeville became a way to propagate American ideals

7. The phrase "These pieces" in line 95 refers to

(A) an ideology that promotes the working class American Dream
(B) Vaudeville's inability to thrust a political agenda into mainstream view
(C) a motif that downplays the ideals behind the industrialization of America
(D) how theater can subtly undermine an institution while being seemingly benign
(E) strategically poking fun at failing political policies

8. Unlike Passage 1, Passage 2 mentions

(A) appeal to family
(B) gender role reversal
(C) a hero's perseverence
(D) audience participation
(E) political satire

9. According to both passages, Panto and Vaudeville require the audience to

(A) partake in gendered role reversal
(B) pay exorbitant ticket prices
(C) interact with what unfolds on stage
(D) participate on stage with the actors
(E) sit in silence for the duration of the show

Questions 1-12 are based on the following passage.

In the following passage, the author relates his experience leaving his hometown of Domfront, in rural France, in order to travel to New York City and meet some friends.

I live in France, in the area known as Lower Normandy. This is rural France, full of dairy farms that provide the milk for the making of such cheeses as Camembert and Brie, and orchards of apple and pear. It is a gentle, forested countryside with slow, lazy rivers winding their way to join the greater rivers of the Seine to the North or the Loire to the South. To the West lie Brittany and La Manche with its Channel ports of Le Havre and Caen. To the West is an escarpment that thrusts abruptly as the beginning of an area which is known as Suisse Normandie. My town stands on this height. It is called Domfront. It dates back to the eleventh century and has a ruined castle, the foundations of which were set by William the Conqueror. As the visitor approaches the town from the east, long before he sees the protective, stern stone ramparts of the Old Town, he is aware of the towering spire of the church of St. Julien that dominates the land below.

Domfront was once an important center of mediaeval politics, the home of Henry II and Aelinor of Aquitaine, visited regularly by Thomas Beckett, fought over by English and French troops. Today, it has a population of just over two thousand, a number which is gently swollen by tourists in the summer months. Nothing much happens here apart from a tiny market on Friday mornings. The cobbled streets of the old town are empty from six o'clock at night until the next morning at nine, and, of course, again between noon and two o'clock when everything stops for lunch. For the rest of the day, one can hardly describe them as seething with activity. Yet it is a comfortable and comforting home town.

So, when, recently, I was invited to New York for a week, it was with some trepidation that I made my way to Charles de Gaulle Airport in Paris and mounted the steps of the Delta airliner that would hurtle me across the Atlantic and dump me in JFK at an hour that was six hours ahead of the time as I knew it in France. Of course, I had been to New York before, but that was in my youth when I was up for any experience. I remembered that, in those days, it had branded itself as "the city that never slept," which had proved to be an accurate soubriquet. Now, as a senior citizen, I was not so certain that I could sustain a week of such constant and electric hustle and perturbation.

The progress from the airport to the hotel did little to dispel my sense of unease. The density and speed of the traffic reminded me of the "péripherique" in Paris, although I did note that American drivers appeared to be far more responsible and orderly than their French equivalents - a Parisian sees his car as an extension of his ego: an American sees his transport as an essential cog working with others to achieve overall progression. We arrived at a hotel which towered above Sixth Avenue: its forecourt seemed to be a hive of constant motion and a cacophony of shouts, whistles and revving engines. Its lobby, about as large as the Place St Julien, was filled with more guests than there were townsfolk in Domfront. For a moment, I felt panic. Then I took a deep breath, muttered the mantra "You can do this" and strode towards the front desk and asked for my key with what I hoped appeared to be an air of nonchalance and familiarity with the scene. I felt that I was fooling no-one. Had I really grown so old and out of touch?

That evening, I found myself at a pier, with friends, setting off to sail around the lower part of Manhattan Island. Gently the boat set forward and took to the middle channel. The sounds of the city faded, the sun glowed on the skyscrapers which glittered as we moved down the Hudson River and past the Statue of Liberty. I looked at her and remembered that she was the first view all those immigrants had of this "promised land" of America. What emotions had flowed through them at the moment, I wondered. A little as I had felt earlier in the day, perhaps?

I turned and looked at the city. The pounding sounds were not audible here on the water, although one could dimly view the traffic passing along the distant water's edge. The skyscrapers shone, towered along the shore, reaching upwards, a barrier between the sea and the land beyond...and the view felt, somehow, reassuring. Here was the modern equivalent of those mediaeval ramparts home at Domfront, protective and sheltering the city within.

My anxieties fell from me. I had a lovely week in New York.

1. The principal function of the opening paragraph is to

(A) situate the author in a town famous for its architecture
(B) locate and describe the author's birthplace
(C) provide historical and geographical exposition
(D) encapsulate the author's motivation to live in Domfront
(E) contrast modern-day Domfront to its historical roots

2. The reference to the "visitor" in line 15 is best characterized as

(A) a rhetorical device used by the author to delve into the history of Domfront
(B) an anonymous outsider used by the author to represent a newcomer's perspective
(C) an allusion to the historical figures who have visited Domfront in the past
(D) the epitome of a stereotypical visitor to the rural French countryside
(E) a whimsical retelling of the author's first time visiting Domfront alone

3. According to the second paragraph, modern Domfront (line 20) can best be described as

(A) a town characterized by contention and laziness
(B) a center of sociopolitical activity
(C) a bustling tourist destination
(D) a meeting place for the small businessman
(E) a small town characterized by tranquility

4. In context of the passage as a whole, the author's use of the words "hurtle" and "dump" in line 38 conveys his feeling of

(A) hostility and frustration
(B) anxiety and helplessness
(C) dread and sadness
(D) nostalgia and sentimentality
(E) exhaustion and debilitation

5. The author's remark in lines 50-52 ("although I... equivalents") serves to

(A) qualify an earlier negative sentiment
(B) reinforce an already-entrenched idea
(C) discuss an international stereotype
(D) question the traditions of his hometown
(E) comment on the egoism of Americans

6. The observation in lines 53-55 ("an American... progression") portrays American drivers as

(A) mostly unemotional
(B) reliably diligent
(C) unflinchingly rigid
(D) efficiently cooperative
(E) interminably busy

7. Ultimately, the author views his "nonchalance" (line 64) as

(A) authentic
(B) conspicuous
(C) spurious
(D) innate
(E) auspicious

8. According to the passage, the author feels that he has "grown so old and out of touch" (lines 65-66) because

(A) his current mentality was that of a man much older than he is now
(B) his younger self was quicker to adapt to modern technology
(C) his hometown of Domfront had few of the modern conveniences of New York
(D) his lifestyle had stayed consistent throughout the decades of his life
(E) his attitude toward travel has drastically changed since his youth

9. In context, the author states that the "immigrants" in line 74 most likely felt

(A) as though they were entering a hostile environment
(B) similar to the author at landing in New York City
(C) the beauty of New York City was outweighed by its grittiness
(D) the New York City harbor was more impressive than the city
(E) the opposite of what the author had felt in the city

10. Based on the information in lines 78-86 ("I turned...within"), the author would most likely agree with which of the following statements?

(A) The main reason the author felt uncomfortable in New York City was the noise.
(B) Modern skyscrapers were likely to have been modeled after castles and churches.
(C) The town of Domfront is more contemporary than the author initially thought.
(D) New York City evoked in him many of the same feelings as does Domfront.
(E) The buildings lining the water's edge in New York City are likely to be very old.

11. In the last sentence, the author's attitude toward New York City had changed from

(A) apprehension to contentment
(B) unease to complacency
(C) familiarity to trepidation
(D) consternation to obsession
(E) fear to disquiet

12. The change in the author's attitude towards New York City can best be attributed to

(A) his sense of awe at the majesty of the skyscrapers
(B) the friends that accompanied him in the city
(C) his proclivity for maritime activities
(D) aspects of the city that evoked a sense of familiarity
(E) his identification with the immigrants' experience

Questions 1-13 are based on the following passage.

This passage was adapted from a book released in the early 1900s about an author's respect for nature and disdain for the way humanity treats it.

I do not know of any poetry to quote which adequately expresses my yearning for the Wild. Approached from this side, the best poetry is tame. I do not know where to find in any literature, ancient or modern, any account which contents me of that Nature with which even I am acquainted. You will perceive that I demand something which no Augustan nor Elizabethan age, which no culture, in short, can give. Mythology comes nearer to it than anything. How much more fertile a Nature, at least, has Grecian mythology its root in than English literature! Mythology is the crop which the Old World bore before its soil was exhausted, before the fancy and imagination were affected with blight; and which it still bears, wherever its pristine vigor is unabated. All other literatures endure only as the elms which overshadow our houses; but my Nature is like the great dragon-tree of the Western Isles, as old as mankind, and, whether that does or not, will endure as long; for the decay of other literatures makes the soil in which it thrives. My Nature lies not in books, but in the stories told by old civilization.

Worse yet are the laws of modern man. While almost all men feel an attraction drawing them to society, few are attracted strongly to Nature. How little appreciation of the beauty of the landscape there is among us! In their reaction to Nature, men appear to me for the most part, notwithstanding their arts, lower than the animals. It is not often a beautiful relation, as in the case of the animals. We have to be told that the Greeks called the world Beauty, or Order. Live free, child of the mist—and with respect to natural knowledge we are all children of the mist. The man who takes the liberty to live is superior to all the laws, by virtue of his relation to the lawmaker. "That is active duty," says the Vishnu Purana, "which is not for our bondage; that is knowledge which is for our liberation in nature: all other duty is good only unto weariness; all other knowledge is only the cleverness of an artist, not Mother Earth herself."

For my part, I feel that with regard to Nature I live a sort of border life, on the confines of a world into which I make occasional and transient forays only, and my patriotism and allegiance to the state into whose territories I seem to retreat are those of a moss-trooper. Unto a life which I call natural I would gladly follow even a will-o'-the-wisp[1] through bogs and sloughs unimaginable, but no moon nor firefly has shown me the causeway to it. Nature is a personality so vast and universal that we have never seen one of her features. The walker in the familiar fields which stretch around my native town of Concord sometimes finds himself in another land than is described in their owners' deeds, as it were in some faraway field on the confines of the actual Concord, the wild nature, where the city's jurisdiction ceases, and the idea which the word "Concord" suggests ceases to be suggested.

And we are landbound. We hug the earth—how rarely we mount! Methinks we might elevate ourselves a little more. We might scale a tree, at least. I found my account in scaling a tree once. It was a tall white pine, on the top of a hill; and though I got well pitched, I was well paid for it, for I discovered new mountains in the horizon which I had never seen before—so much more of the earth and the heavens. I might have walked about the foot of the tree for threescore years and ten, and yet I certainly should never have seen them. But, above all, I discovered around me—it was near the end of June—on the ends of the topmost branches only, a few minute and delicate red conelike blossoms, the fertile flower of the white pine looking heavenward. I carried straightway to the village the topmost spire, and showed it to stranger jurymen who walked the streets—for it was court week—and to farmers and lumber-dealers and woodchoppers and hunters, and not one had ever seen the like before, but they wondered as at a star dropped down. Tell of ancient architects finishing their works on the tops of columns as perfectly as on the lower and more visible parts! Nature has from the first expanded the minute blossoms of the forest only toward the heavens, above men's heads and unobserved by them. We see only the flowers that are under our feet in the meadows. The pines have developed their delicate blossoms on the highest twigs of the wood every summer for ages, as well over the heads of Nature's red children as of her white ones; yet scarcely a farmer or hunter in the land has ever seen them.

1: A will-o'-the-wisp is a ghost thought to lead travelers deep into the woods.

1. The primary purpose of the passage is to show how the author

(A) doesn't think humans are a part of nature
(B) wants to live outside of society
(C) feels about our connection to nature
(D) has lost his way by ignoring nature
(E) finds human progress superior to nature

2. In context, the phrase "the best poetry is tame" (line 3) helps to suggest that

(A) writing cannot effectively communicate the power of nature
(B) poets have stopped taking chances with their writing
(C) poetry must be easy to understand to be considered good
(D) very few writers in history were considered naturalists
(E) stimulating poetry cannot express what nature is about

3. Based on the information in lines 9-11 ("Mythology comes…literature!"), which of the following would the author be most likely to read?

(A) Science fiction about the future of Earth
(B) A folk tale about the strength of nature
(C) An ancient tale of Roman war and strife
(D) A comedy about bandits in the woods
(E) A Shakespearean play on forest spirits

4. When the author talks about the soil being "exhausted" (line 13), he makes use of which of the following?

(A) exaggeration
(B) citation
(C) metaphor
(D) repetition
(E) qualification

5. According the first paragraph, the "laws of modern man" are "worse" (line 23) than

(A) archaic oral tradition
(B) modern spiritual texts
(C) contemporary comedy
(D) past and present literature
(E) fanciful urban legends

6. In lines 25-29 ("How little…animals"), the author implies that animals

(A) obey their own set of natural laws
(B) are oblivious to the nature around them
(C) help us understand nature's beauty
(D) are not attracted strongly to nature
(E) appreciate nature unconditionally

7. In line 28, the "arts" represent

(A) a skill possessed singularly by humans
(B) something that is reserved for animals
(C) what the Greeks before us called "Order"
(D) one way in which humans do connect to nature
(E) the landscape found within a forest

8. According to the second paragraph, the author most likely quotes "Vishnu Purana" (line 36) in order to point out that

(A) an intimate knowledge of nature is in direct correlation to real freedom
(B) the man who lives without law in his life is the most free of all men
(C) members of government who can connect with nature will be powerful
(D) individuals escaping capture should try hiding deep in the forests
(E) active duty is shirking the responsibility of society and living alone in nature

9. The view of the natural life in lines 46-49 ("Unto a…it") can best be described as

(A) ubiquitous
(B) pragmatic
(C) accessible
(D) trite
(E) magical

10. The author uses "The walker" in lines 51-57 ("The walker...suggested") to make which point about nature and Concord?

(A) The boundary between man and nature is hazy at best.
(B) All of nature belongs to man at some point or another.
(C) The citizens of Concord often find trespassers on their land.
(D) City names are never used to describe natural habitats.
(E) Criminals can find respite in the nature surrounding cities.

11. In context, the word "mount" (line 59) most nearly means

(A) straddle
(B) climb
(C) ride
(D) hike
(E) attack

12. It can be inferred from lines 80-82 ("Nature has... them") that the author believes that

(A) humans are a necessary part of nature
(B) nature proves the existence of heavenly beings
(C) nature does not purposefully grow for human enjoyment
(D) humans can cultivate nature for their own needs
(E) humans and nature cannot truly coexist

13. The author's perspective on nature reveals that, in general, he views his contemporary society as

(A) adequately in tune with their surroundings
(B) too concerned with everyday business
(C) decent, hardworking people
(D) disconnected from a pristine environment
(E) devout patriots of Mother Earth

Self Evaluation

Self Evaluation is important if you want to see an improvement on your next comprehension passage. Each passage has a set of possible reasons for errors. Place a check mark next to the ones that pertain to you, and write your own on the blank line provided. Use this form to better analyze your performance by filling it out regularly and accurately so you can recognize the pattern of your most common mistakes.

If you don't understand why you have made mistakes, there is no way you can correct them!

1st Long Reading Comprehension: # Correct:____ # Wrong:____ # Unanswered:____

- ○ Did not understand the question, line reference, or answers
- ○ Did not underline the line reference
- ○ Read too much or too little around the line reference
- ○ Summarized the line reference instead of answering the question
- ○ Couldn't find the false words
- ○ Couldn't choose between two possible answers
- ○ Did not use tone to help eliminate answers
- ○ When stuck between two answers, guessed instead of looking for additional facts
- ○ Couldn't finish in time
- ○ Other:____

2nd Long Reading Comprehension: # Correct:____ # Wrong:____ # Unanswered:____

- ○ Did not understand the question, line reference, or answers
- ○ Did not underline the line reference
- ○ Read too much or too little around the line reference
- ○ Summarized the line reference instead of answering the question
- ○ Couldn't find the false words
- ○ Couldn't choose between two possible answers
- ○ Did not use tone to help eliminate answers
- ○ When stuck between two answers, guessed instead of looking for additional facts
- ○ Couldn't finish in time
- ○ Other:____

3rd Long Reading Comprehension: # Correct:____ # Wrong:____ # Unanswered:____

- ○ Did not understand the question, line reference, or answers
- ○ Did not underline the line reference
- ○ Read too much or too little around the line reference
- ○ Summarized the line reference instead of answering the question
- ○ Couldn't find the false words
- ○ Couldn't choose between two possible answers
- ○ Did not use tone to help eliminate answers
- ○ When stuck between two answers, guessed instead of looking for additional facts
- ○ Couldn't finish in time
- ○ Other:____

4th Long Reading Comprehension: # Correct:____ # Wrong:____ # Unanswered:____

- ○ Did not understand the question, line reference, or answers
- ○ Did not underline the line reference
- ○ Read too much or too little around the line reference
- ○ Summarized the line reference instead of answering the question
- ○ Couldn't find the false words
- ○ Couldn't choose between two possible answers
- ○ Did not use tone to help eliminate answers
- ○ When stuck between two answers, guessed instead of looking for additional facts
- ○ Couldn't finish in time
- ○ Other:____

Single Long Comprehension
6 Questions Total, Pages 112-113

1. Correct answer: (B)
The author writes, "some Greek philosophers decided that the forces of nature were no more divine than the forces of man." The author then sums up the main idea in the last sentence of the introduction, writing, "The Greeks, contradicting all other major cultural religious traditions of the time, decided to pursue reason."

2. Correct answer: (C)
The author begins by writing, "The cultures of the classical world...leaned heavily on belief in gods." Then the focus shifts to the Greeks and their change in thinking, as "They began to hypothesize based on empirical data, no longer believing that they were golden and prosperous because of a gods' favor." The contrast is a "belief in gods" (spiritual enlightenment) to "empirical data" (observational theories).

3. Correct answer: (A)
The tone of this word is (+), eliminating (B), (D), and (E). The author isn't discussing physical fuel, eliminating (C).

4. Correct answer: (D)
The author writes, "The Greeks wanted the world to be understood, to have order, and this order needed to transcend myths of ancestors and gods." They preferred this order to understanding the world through "the whims and caprice of the divine."

5. Correct answer: (C)
The author writes, "there were those who assumed this lust for reason was fiscally driven," or driven by "economic growth." In the following paragraph, the author explains this in more depth.

6. Correct answer: (E)
The author writes "Logically speaking" twice to illustrate the thought process of "the Easterns." Then, "But, in reality, how can one logically conclude…" suggesting disagreement with this logic and contempt for such an attitude.

Double Long Comprehension
9 Questions Total, Pages 114-115

1. Correct Answer: (B)
The author of P1 describes Panto's theme as "the good hero…against all odds" (lines10-12) and the author of P2 describes Polite Vaudeville's protagonist as "overcoming all odds" (line 89). The themes' focuses are not about the antagonists (A) or the ancillary (supporting) characters (C). Magic is only stated in P1 (D). Neither passage discusses family values (E).

2. Correct Answer: (A)
The author of P1 refers to Pantomime as something for "the whole family" in the first paragraph, not discussing politics (B), witchcraft (C), or the controversy (E) of Pantomime. (D) is wrong because Pantomime was for the entire family, not just children.

3. Correct Answer: (C)
The author of P1 uses several examples to explain how Panto is "eclectic," or diverse, by stating its many elements such as "acrobatics, dancing, music… glamour and comedy" (lines 19-20). (A) only refers to glamour and comedy, not the entire Panto. (B) There is no mention of science in P1. (D) The surrealist depiction is due to only role reversal, not the "eclectic" mix. (E) In paragraph 1, Panto is only celebrated from Christmas to March, not all seasons of the year.

4. Correct Answer: (D)
The author of P1 states that that "participation of the audience" (line 32) is the most important characteristic of Panto. (A), (B), and (C) each refer solely to one element of Panto, not its most "extraordinary one." (E) refers to P2 and its commentary on role reversal.

5. Correct answer: (B)
According to the author of P1, "because of the impending economic collapse, Vaudeville eventually evolved into a more genteel version better known as 'Polite Vaudeville.'" This means that the "evolution" of Vaudeville "closely follows" the "fluctuations in the financial environment," choice (B).

6. Correct Answer: (E)
In the context of the question, consider what the LR is doing, not its content. The sentence introduces the author's idea, discussed further in the third paragraph, that Polite Vaudeville became a way to discuss politics, particularly perpetuating the American Dream and its principles. To eliminate the others, consider that (A) "poke fun" refers only to the "derisive jab" (line 94) from role-reversals which were only used "in some pieces" (line 91). The transition in (B) occurred in the previous paragraph. (C) Vaudeville did not have a uniform structure. (D) The political motivations from Polite Vaudeville encompassed more than just actors.

P1 - Passage 1　　P2 - Passage 2
LR - Line Reference
(+) - Positive
(-) - Negative
All quotes in answer choices can be found in or around the line reference.

7. Correct Answer: (D)
"These pieces" (line 95) refer to the specific "derisive jab[s] at the institutions that perpetuated the American Dream" (line 94). (A) suggests that the pieces encouraged the American dream. (B) these pieces did thrust a political agenda (C) these pieces do not refer to America's industry. (E) these pieces mocked a prevalent institution, not a failing one.

8. Correct answer: (E)
The author of P1 writes, "The whole family goes, for a Christmas treat, so there has to be something that will appeal to every member of the family," eliminating (A). Then, "These two last elements are created through cross-dressing and role reversal," eliminating (B). Later, "The theme is always about the poor and good hero making his way to success and riches against all odds," eliminating (C). Finally, "The most extraordinary element of Pantomime is the participation of the audience," eliminating (D).

9. Correct Answer: (C)
Both authors discuss the interactive nature of their genres: "participation of the audience" (line 32, P1) and "interactive in nature" (line 70, P2). (A) only refers to P1. (B) and (E) do not occur in either passage. (D) There is no evidence from either passage that the audience had to be on stage with the actors.

Single Long Comprehension
12 Questions Total, Pages 116-118

1. Correct answer: (C)
The first paragraph describes where the author currently lives. But it's not "famous for its architecture," eliminating (A). In (B), "birthplace" is a false word. To eliminate (D), cross out the word "motivation," and there is no contrast, eliminating (E).

2. Correct answer: (B)
The visitor is used to describe a person's first experience of Domfront. To eliminate the others, focus on false words: In (A), cross out "the history of Domfront." In (C), cross out "historical figures." In (D), cross out "stereotypical visitor," because the author tells us nothing about the visitor. And in (E), cross out "whimsical retelling."

3. Correct answer: (E)
In the second paragraph, the author describes Domfront as peaceful and quiet, using such phrases and language as: "Nothing much happens here," "streets of the old town are empty," and "it is a comfortable and comforting home town."

4. Correct answer: (B)
The author states that he feels "trepidation" as he begins his travels and later uses the word "perturbation." Trepidation and perturbation are both defined as a state of anxiety and unease; a definition choice (B) supports.

5. Correct answer: (A)
In the sentence containing the LR, the author states that "the density and speed of the traffic reminded" him of that in Paris. But then, he limits the scope of that statement by giving his perception of American drivers versus what he thinks of Parisian drivers, qualifying his original statement.

6. Correct answer: (D)
In the LR, the author describes American drivers as part of a whole working towards the same collective goal, or being "efficiently cooperative."

7. Correct answer: (C)
In the following sentence the author states that he "was fooling no-one" which means that the "air of nonchalance and familiarity" was in fact not genuine, pointing to "spurious," which means inauthentic.

8. Correct answer: (E)
This question tells the reader to look "in context" of what is written. In the third and fourth paragraphs, the author states that when he visited New York City in his youth he was "up for any experience" but now, after seeing and experiencing the hustle and bustle of New York City again, he "felt panic."

9. Correct answer: (B)
As the author moves past the Statue of Liberty, he thinks of the "immigrants" and concludes they must have felt the way the author "had felt earlier in the day" when he first got to New York City.

10. Correct answer: (D)
In this LR, the author states that the view of NYC felt "reassuring." He then goes on to say that the skyscrapers of NYC were "the modern equivalent of those mediaeval ramparts home at Domfront," suggesting that NYC "evoked in him many of the same feelings" as Domfront.

11. Correct answer: (A)
The author states that he was no longer anxious and ended up having "a lovely week in New York." This means the tone went from (-) to (+), eliminating every choice except (A).

12. Correct answer: (D)
The author feels uneasy about his visit to NYC until the paragraph beginning in line 47. Here he relates the similarities between NYC and Domfront, and suddenly his "anxieties fell from" him. We can conclude that it was this realization that changed his attitude. While he did feel awe (A), it wasn't what changed his outlook. There is no support for the other answer choices.

Single Long Comprehension
13 Questions Total, Pages 119-121

1. Correct answer: (C)
In the first two paragraphs, the author laments how weak humans are at describing and relating to nature, before moving in the final two paragraphs to a discussion about how humans have built walls and borders, effectively distancing ourselves from Nature. In summation from the last sentence, "The pines have developed their delicate blossoms on the highest twigs…yet scarcely a farmer or hunter in the land has ever seen them."

2. Correct answer: (A)
In the sentence before the LR, the author writes, "I do not know of any poetry to quote which adequately expresses my yearning for the Wild," meaning no poetry can match Nature in the eyes of the author.

3. Correct answer: (B)
The author appreciates "Grecian mythology" and would thus prefer a traditional story about Nature.

4. Correct answer: (C)
The author claims that "Mythology is the crop" that grew in the "soil" before the soil became "exhausted." Given that mythology is not a crop, the reader can assume the author is comparing it to a crop, which means the soil becoming exhausted is simply an extension of this metaphor. The soil is not literally exhausted.

5. Correct answer: (D)
In the line prior to the LR, the author claims that "My Nature lies not in books, but in the stories told by old civilization." So, worse than the "laws of modern man" are the books, or literature.

6. Correct answer: (E)
According to the author, "In their reaction to Nature, men appear to me…lower than the animals." This reaction is that men have "little appreciation of the beauty of the landscape," which in turn means animals do "appreciate nature."

7. Correct answer: (D)
We know that "In their reaction to Nature," humans are unappreciative. But in this LR, the author qualifies his claim by stating, "notwithstanding their arts," meaning that the "arts" is the one area where humans "do connect to nature."

8. Correct answer: (B)
In lines 35-40, Vishnu Purana claims that living without the laws of mankind "is knowledge which is for our liberation in nature," and that following laws "is good only unto weariness." So, by refusing to live by law alone, we can set ourselves free.

9. Correct answer: (E)
In order to follow "a life which I call natural," the author would follow will-o-wisps (ghosts) and fireflies, which is a supernatural, or magical, way of thinking.

10. Correct answer: (A)
The author claims that the walker "sometimes finds himself in another land than is described in their owners' deeds," which is a fanciful way of saying that land that is "owned" can sometimes still be wild, blurring the boundaries between civilization and Nature.

11. Correct answer: (B)
In the sentence prior to the LR, the author claims that "we are landbound." And so, to mount must be to get up off of the land, or to climb.

12. Correct answer: (C)
The author claims that Nature shows its flowers "only toward the heavens, above men's heads and unobserved by them." This means that we have to work to enjoy natural beauty, and that beauty is for the heavens.

13. Correct answer: (D)
Throughout the passage, the author praises Nature as being supremely (+) and dismisses humans as (-). The author does not believe humans love Nature, eliminating (A) and (E). Answer choice (B) is only one small piece of the problem, not the thesis, and (C) is not concerning the passage.

P1 - Passage 1 P2 - Passage 2
LR - Line Reference
(+) - Positive
(-) - Negative
All quotes in answer choices can be found in or around the line reference.

Chapter Nine

Questions 1-7 are based on the following passage.

The passage is adapted from a 2013 essay comparing international television.

One of the advantages of living in that part of France which edges the English Channel is that I can get not only the TV channels of France, but also those of the UK. I should like to be able to say that I switch energetically between the two, thus enjoying two very different views of how the world is turning. Sadly, the truth is that I have neither the ability nor the patience to follow French programs.

French television is placid, urbane, patronizing and boring. It is also misogynistic. Of course, women do appear, but rarely as central performers in a program. In early evening chat shows, they are always supporters to the central male "star of the show," a rather avuncular gigolo who flashes a smile that does not reach his eyes from time to time: he clearly thinks that he is irresistible. They laugh a great deal and he talks, interminably. French News Bulletins are invariably presented by men and present a view of the world that is centered completely on Paris, as if the rest of France did not exist. Politicians are treated with deference and, unlike the BBC, ITV or Sky News channel in the UK, never questioned aggressively. The major evening program is inevitably a movie, preferably French but if an American or English film, poorly dubbed. There is no variation throughout the week, except on Saturday nights when the film is replaced with an endless cabaret featuring very old French singers who have long passed their sell-by date.

British news programs, on the other hand, are aggressive, investigative, critical of politics, and wide-ranging in their attempts to provoke, infuriate and entertain their viewers. No matter which news channel one watches, the reporters from war zones or other dangerous situations are as likely to be female as well as male. They will also be of different origins. What the viewer sees on television reflects the full spectrum of UK society. The accents of those who present television range from Northern Irish to West Indian to Asian. As a result, television is a much more important element in the society of the UK: in France, it is, by and large, ignored.

This is not to say that my evenings are replete with watching the news. It is ironic that even with such a plethora of choice, there are some evenings when I look through the TV schedules and declare that there is nothing new worth watching. On nights like that, there is only one thing to do: give way to my guilty TV pleasure. There is a channel which only shows endless repeats of shows from the past. There I find my favorite program when the news is not on. It is neither British nor French. It is an old American TV series and it ran for over ten years in the States.

"Murder, She Wrote" features an amateur detective, loosely based on Agatha Christie's Miss Marple but transformed into an American writer of detective novels. Her name is Jessica Fletcher and she lives in Cabot Cove in New England. But no matter where she is, her appearance in any town means that very shortly at least one murder will occur. Sadly, the police are quite incapable of solving the crime and are determined to imprison the innocent. Happily, in between finishing the latest novel in time for its publication deadline, giving lectures at various academic institutions, staying at the homes of her rich and famous friends, Jessica is able to sort things out to the admiration of the professionals and the gratitude of the falsely accused - and all in forty-five minutes! The show is total nonsense: absurd plots, mechanical acting, and appalling scripts. However, from the moment the opening bars of the show's opening theme are sounded, I am hooked. As the credits roll, there is Jessica, typing furiously: always the same paragraph, "Arnold raced through the door..."

1. The primary purpose of the passage is to

(A) analyze the TV viewing habits of a stereotypical European viewer
(B) describe an individual's reactions to the variety of TV shows available to him
(C) document the role of TV in both British and French societies
(D) suggest improvements to the TV programs offered in France and the UK
(E) introduce the author's favorite famous television character

2. According to the second paragraph, the author views French TV as "misogynistic" (line 10) because

(A) women are never given leading roles in popular French movies
(B) women are utilized only to highlight the qualities of their male colleagues
(C) women are systematically objectified and degraded on French talk shows
(D) women's political views are always rejected in favor of men's
(E) women presenters are instructed to laugh, but never to speak

3. The phrase "a smile that does not reach his eyes" (lines 14-15) refers back to a

(A) conceited show host
(B) charismatic model
(C) serious news anchor
(D) boring interviewer
(E) attractive comedian

4. The author characterizes French television as all of the following EXCEPT

(A) temperate
(B) monotonous
(C) condescending
(D) mannered
(E) depraved

5. According to the second and third paragraphs, British TV differs from French TV primarily by the

(A) variety of programs available to the viewer
(B) popularity among their specific audiences
(C) representation of their respective societies
(D) frequency with which the news is presented
(E) amount of reruns that are shown nightly

6. The author uses the word "However" in line 69 primarily in order to

(A) praise the high production value of a popular American mystery program
(B) discredit the show for having unrealistic premises
(C) suggest practical ways to improve the show's plotline
(D) demonstrate the inherent flaws in the show
(E) juxtapose the show's lack of merit and his feelings about it

7. It can be inferred from the passage that the author would most likely choose to watch

(A) the urbane style of the French talk shows and news programs
(B) any program, whether it be American, British, or French
(C) television only if there is nothing else to do on that day
(D) a program that realistically depicts the society in which it airs
(E) the reruns from an old American news broadcast

Questions 1-8 are based on the following passage.

In this passage, the author describes the phenomenon of 3D films, discussing their prominence in the movie theatres as well as the likeliness that they will continue to exist.

Whenever a family friend declines an invitation to the movies using the excuse of "it's too expensive for a waste of time," my mom always likes to turn to me with arched eyebrows and tut, "the movies are the cheapest form of entertainment!" There's an indubitable truth in her statement, for when compared to other forms of entertainment like operas, concerts, and plays, a movie is relaxed, informal, and cheap with just as much excitement. Throughout the years, films have developed from the quaint, silent, black-and-white reels of the early nineteenth century to the colorful, action-packed movies shown in wide theaters with surrounding sound effects afforded by advanced technology. And today, the latest fad makes its way into theaters: 3D.

Contrary to the common misconception, 3D films really aren't something new created with the most up-to-date technology—in fact, 3D film has existed for nearly a century now. But why the overnight fame? If you walk into a cinema today, at least half of the showings are 3D. It doesn't matter what genre of movie it is, whether it's animated or filmed with red carpet actors; if a film wants to join the "it" crowd, it has the 3D label next to it.

Joining in with the astounding technological age of today, perhaps the most obvious and logical influx of 3D films is the capital allure. Because you are provided with a pair of flimsy 3D glasses wrapped in a plastic bag, the movie dealers reason that you should be willing to pull out a few more bills. But it isn't just the extra cost for the glasses: viewers are given the latest technological feat and the added spice to special effects, so it's only to be expected that they pay a little more.

Recent statistics show that 3D showings have boosted cinema revenues significantly. Comparing average revenues for the same movie shown in 3D and 2D shows that, in almost every scenario, the 3D version out-markets the 2D by hundreds of thousands of dollars. Moreover, the number of 3D screen installations in theaters around the country more than doubled in 2011 according to *Box Office Pro Magazine*. Not only do the people seem to flock to the concept of 3D film, but directors also see this fad as a chance to cash in. Now, not only can they create new films, but they can also re-release timeless (and finished!) films in the latest fashion. The only thing better than the tearjerking *Titanic*? A tearjerking *Titanic* in 3D!

Philip Bowcock, Cineworld financial director, dubs 3D films as "a fad with legs… The right films will do well. 3D will keep going." However, the most recent surveys of the rising generation may prove otherwise. After the initial novelty of 3D, the more technologically savvy current generation isn't as easily impressed. 3D film has become prosaic, so viewers are more wont to complain about the resulting motion sickness. With new technological breakthroughs appearing every day, the people demand higher stakes to be impressed than just slightly three-dimensional effects.

Besides the headache, though, the overwhelming cry from the opposition, according to a media researcher, is that "a 3D film may look pretty, but it needs substance, too, if it is to revive cinema's fortunes." Basically, once the preliminary awe for 3D wears off, the viewers go back to square one: the actual movie plot. Most viewers see the rise of 3D for every movie as attempts to cover up poorly written screenplays. Who cares if the story itself isn't as exciting? The visual effects will surely make up for that!

In this day and age, no technological innovation can stay fresh forever; however, 3D cinema may yet hang on. Despite the higher ticket price of 3D films, movies in general are still cheaper and more convenient than live entertainment. Furthermore, scientists are working on adding new perks to the idea of 3D viewing. According to CNN, South Korean researchers are developing a method to create the 3D environment without glasses. There are even rumors of being able to enjoy a 3D film on a couch in a living room in a few years. Steven Spielberg, a world-renowned film director, remarked, "I'm certainly hoping that 3D gets to the point where people do not notice it, because then it becomes another tool." If the production of 3D cinema can continue to improve without significantly increasing prices, one day it may no longer just be a fad.

1. The primary purpose of this passage is to

(A) discuss increased research in entertainment technologies
(B) argue in favor of cheaper tickets at the movies
(C) relate a personal experience about a phenomenon
(D) analyze the future prospects of a trend in film
(E) account for the inevitable fall of 3D cinema

2. In the context of the first paragraph, the author views movies as

(A) frivolous and exciting
(B) affordable and thrilling
(C) soothing and casual
(D) prohibitive and ceremonial
(E) old-fashioned and picturesque

3. The author claims that the "common misconception" (line 16) relates to

(A) the recent rise in 3D popularity
(B) the underlying causes of the 3D fad
(C) the longevity of 3D technology
(D) the prevalence of 3D technology
(E) the prejudices surrounding 3D movies

4. In context, the phrase "red carpet" (line 23) most nearly means

(A) ordinary
(B) fashionable
(C) live
(D) famous
(E) relevant

5. According to the third paragraph, the "capital allure" (line 27) refers to

(A) the justification used by the movie industry to charge higher prices for 3D movies
(B) the additional merchandise that is sold in tandem with 3D films
(C) the sudden rise in investments for film production
(D) the increase in special effects afforded by the increased revenues
(E) price gouging by movie dealers selling movies to the theatres

6. According to the fourth paragraph, movie directors might favor shooting in 3D for any of the following reasons EXCEPT

(A) the chance to remake a classic movie
(B) the increased availability of 3D movie theaters
(C) a higher rate of financial return on a movie
(D) the increased popularity of three dimensional movies
(E) an improvement in the quality of the cast

7. It can be inferred from the final paragraph that

(A) technology is inherently prone to obsolescence, enhancing 3D's prospects
(B) the 3D industry will continue to prosper if it can remain progressive
(C) reflecting industry trends, constant renewal will hinder 3D films
(D) 3D movies have sufficient allure to make up for weak story lines
(E) audiences will become more accepting of 3D movies sooner than later

8. The structure of this passage can best be described as

(A) a general description of an industry followed by specific examples
(B) a personal anecdote supported by scientific data
(C) an analysis of a fad followed by its negative and positive aspects
(D) a lighthearted musing followed by a scholarly inquiry
(E) a strong argument ending with an unorthodox viewpoint

Questions 1-12 are based on the following passage.

This passage is taken from the introduction to a 2013 essay concerning the evolution of travel.

"To travel hopefully is a better thing than to arrive." wrote Robert Louis Stevenson. Of course, he was referring to the nineteenth century when the idea of moving freely about the country or even the world was a rather new and wondrous thing. Before 1800, if you wanted to get from one place to another, then you walked along muddy tracks if you were poor, or, if you were wealthy, you rode on horseback or in a coach pulled by horses. It did not much matter which mode you used: the journey was excruciatingly long, exhausting and uncomfortable. It was certainly a hazard to health. It was prone to accidents and robbery. Highwaymen were common and unromantic: bands of thieves, predatory and vicious. The inns along the road charged as high a price as they could. The countryside was dangerous and unlit: the city, relatively safe, was equally unlit. Little wonder that the traveler needed hope for the journey: arrival must have seemed a miraculous relief.

It was the Industrial Revolution that altered everything. The whole pattern of living was changed by the need of people to move out of the countryside with its agricultural attitudes and into the growing cities with their mills and factories and hopeful promise of a better standard of living. Robert Macadam set about creating improvements to roads, something that had not been achieved since the days of the Roman Empire, and Robert Stephenson set about creating his Rocket, which introduced the idea of steam rail traffic and increased the speed with which the distance between towns and cities could be achieved. It had become imperative to be able to move smoothly and safely from factory to city to port. Market forces were already at work.

The new inventions were not confined to the land. Port to port traffic of goods and workers and administrators was aided by the new steam-driven vessels. The need for worldwide trade between producers on the other side of the world and consumers in Europe became a major driving force for governments. Inevitably, if not naturally, the idea of empire–building followed. Equally inevitably, if not unnaturally, empires had to give way eventually to new, independent states. This probably explains why, if the nineteenth century can be regarded as a century of industry and progression, the twentieth century can be regarded as a century of destruction and war. Certainly all those European hopes of world trade domination appeared deflated by the halfway point of the twentieth century.

Yet the wars of the twentieth century led to the development of the aeroplane. The jet age arrived, ensuring that travel between countries – indeed, between continents – was achieved in the shortest time possible: lunch in Paris and see a show on Broadway that evening. The flight time from Paris to New York is now approximately six hours. Robert Stephenson must be spinning in his grave.

Or possibly not. Speed in the air is one thing: speed on the ground is another. To move from Paris to New York takes a considerably longer time. The passenger is advised to be at the airport three hours before the flight takes off. This time is taken up with examination of baggage, followed by the removal of your coat, shoes, belt, any metal objects in your pockets, before you are passed through a detector that scans your entire body - you might as well be naked. You shuffle back into your now somewhat dishevelled clothing and move on to passport control, where your identity is perused and noted, and you are contemptuously dismissed to wander into the departure hall where such items as a cup of coffee or a croissant may be obtained at a price three or four times more than you would pay outside the airport terminal. The modern version of the highwayman will proceed to denude your purse by offering to change your money at a rate which has nothing to do with reality and everything to do with profiteering. Finally, exhausted, you will be allowed to mount the plane. Arriving at your destination is no better. You will walk several miles to passport control where you will join a queue that shuffles interminably towards the booth where a bored controller will examine and scan your passport, demand how long you intend to stay in New York, where will you stay in New York, when you intend to leave New York and go home, before dismissing you with a shrug and a somewhat ironic wish that you enjoy your stay. You will then walk a further marathon to collect your luggage. Time taken for all this? Anything up to three hours.

Oh yes, how the possibilities of travel have advanced and developed; but what chaos there is at the point to which it has arrived!

1. Lines 2-5 ("Of course … thing") are primarily intended to

(A) foreshadow a topic
(B) reiterate a sentiment
(C) qualify a statement
(D) reject an idea
(E) correct a mistake

2. In the first paragraph, the highwaymen are referred to as "unromantic" (line 14) because they were

(A) antagonists of the thieves
(B) generally base and cruel
(C) complex and territorial
(D) common travelers
(E) the lesser of the dangers

3. In lines 17-19 ("Little wonder...relief"), the author's comment about "arrival" suggests that

(A) some travelers eventually became highwaymen
(B) most travelers were religious followers
(C) people had a carefree attitude towards life
(D) villagers made a point to travel infrequently
(E) the journey was grueling and perilous

4. According to the first two paragraphs, the "Industrial Revolution" (line 20) marks a shift in travel from

(A) carelessness to caution
(B) exposure to assurance
(C) anxiety to hopelessness
(D) safety to jeopardy
(E) romance to realism

5. In lines 25-32 ("Robert Macadam … achieved"), the author describes Robert Macadam and Robert Stephenson as

(A) innovators during the Industrial Revolution
(B) early environmental scientists
(C) civil engineers of the Roman empire
(D) farmers who abandoned their farms for city life
(E) industrialists at the forefront of agricultural reform

6. Ultimately, the "Market forces" in line 34 would best be described as

(A) unrestrained travel
(B) international banking
(C) small town bartering
(D) commercial business
(E) national politics

7. The result of the "traffic of goods" in line 36 would be

(A) a decrease in international relations
(B) a single, unstoppable empire
(C) the burgeoning of empires
(D) the formation of a global government
(E) an increase in domestic civil war

8. According to the information presented in the third paragraph, the Europeans were "deflated" (line 49) most likely because

(A) they had anticipated inventing the aeroplane themselves
(B) their international trade was becoming too popular
(C) the British empire was facing a serious revolution
(D) a period of progress was followed by a period of war
(E) travel between continents took an excessively long time

9. The first sentences of both the fourth and fifth paragraphs primarily serve to

(A) contrast ancient travel with modern travel
(B) introduce a digression from the topic
(C) state exceptions to previous arguments
(D) set qualifications for his primary thesis
(E) justify an unpopular opinion

10. In context of the passage, the purpose of lines 56-57 ("The flight … hours") is to

(A) deter travellers from what is a harrowing process
(B) exemplify an unfortunate outcome of war
(C) promote good international relations concerning art
(D) suggest that flight times are excessively lengthy
(E) underscore the progress that has been made in travel

11. The tone of the fifth paragraph (lines 59-90) can best be described as one of

(A) concern
(B) trepidation
(C) reverence
(D) exasperation
(E) perplexity

12. The use of the term "highwayman" in line 75 is intended to

(A) parallel a character discussed earlier in the passage
(B) colloquially rename a specific profession
(C) highlight the inherent danger in travel
(D) describe the airline passengers as thieves
(E) introduce an innovative idea about modern travel

Questions 1-13 are based on the following passage.

The following passages are written about owls. The first passage is written by an anthropologist and bird enthusiast. The second passage reflects on a childhood experience.

Passage 1

The war goddess Pallas Athena is often depicted bearing an Owl on her arm, and, through the ages, that bird's reputation has reflected her ambiguity. Owls have been regarded as symbols of wisdom: they have been seen also as harbingers of death and ill fortune. In many African and Arab countries, they are regarded as prone to bring bad luck, ill health and death. In Europe, they are associated with sorcery and dark ideas. Even Shakespeare, in "Julius Caesar," he refers to a legend that an owl was seen, perched in the Forum of Rome, prognosticating the assassination, in full daylight.

Owls are one of the few nocturnal birds of prey. Silent and deadly, they glide, hunting small rodents and birds in the darker hours. Because of this association, Kenyans and Native Americans consider that a large owl perched outside of someone's home indicates that the owner practices dark magic and can possibly be a shaman. They believe that the owl carries messages back and forth from the spirit world, from which a shaman is believed to procure his baneful power. In a certain respect, the owl perched outside of one's home may act as a warning, steering away those afraid of evil sorcery. In Cameroon, the owl has no official name. Rather, it is referred to as "the bird that makes you afraid." In some regions of Malaya, or the Malaysian islands, owls are believed to eat new-born babies and bring sickness to children. To skeptics, these cultural myths may seem to be only that – myths.

But there is some substance to these sociocultural beliefs. This is not to say that owls have some mystical or fanciful properties. After all, such associations were usually birthed from a misunderstanding or fear of the environment. Similar to owls, snakes have had symbolic significance in many cultures as omens for death and sin but also for power. But, it is perhaps an interesting, universal phenomenon that so many cultures, indigenous or otherwise, share very similar sentiments toward a singular creature. What does this suggest about humans and their fear of the unknown?

Well consider for a moment that you are confronted by that unknown presence in the middle of the night. It can be unnerving: the steady, unmoving gaze of their glaucous eyes and the turning of their heads in almost a full circle, like a clockwork toy. Their eyes are fixed, ensuring precision before the kill: a stare so steady as to haunt their victims who are often unaware of an imminent demise. Like those of a judge on his high bench, or of a teacher surveying and gauging accurately the shifting, shiftless students, those eyes condemn their prey with judgement. Imagine that penetrating, yellow gaze upon you.

Passage 2

Owls, often associated with Athena, goddess of wisdom and war, can be regarded as totems of protection. It is said that the feather of an owl can repel illness and negative influences. In some countries, a dead owl nailed to a stable door is believed to ward off predatory attacks by eagles on young animals. The silent passage of the owl through the forest night can be seen as a metaphor for the observation of ourselves by the gods, who make no comment but note all that we do (or do not do) in our passage through life. An unnerving metaphor perhaps, but also possibly a comforting one.

I am not the only one to believe this. The Zuni, a Native American tribe of the Pueblo peoples, believe that placing an owl feather in a baby's crib guards the baby from evil spirits. Essentially, the hooting of an owl signified the coming of death upon an individual. But leaving an owl feather in the crib was an attempt to confuse the owl so that death would not be invoked upon the infant. For me, it is unclear if this means that the owl was actually a true, positive, benevolent force. Regardless, this simply meant at the very least, that it was benign.

I remember coming home after school to my *Nonna's** house and seeing a large owl tailored from twine hanging on the frame of the front door. I am not really the superstitious type. I do not believe that a rabbit's foot is lucky or that adorning my car with a trinket of Saint Christopher will preclude me from an accident. Yet, when I used to walk under her door, I felt all of my troubles melt away like snow. I felt invincible, protected, safe. Perhaps this was just really from the comforts that Nonna had to offer me: a warm afternoon snack, afternoon cartoons, and her little quips and anecdotes about her life in bucolic Tuscany. "Owls are good luck *nipote**. They keep the wolves away from the sheep. Just look at the eyes. Like daggers into a dark spirit's soul. No malicious force would dare cross an owl." Nonna would "hoot" at the owl any time she felt as though she was being watched. That strange, yet familiar feeling of discomfort like there was a presence in the room faded with each "hoot."

She passed away thirty years ago and since then, I have kept my own version of her owl hanging wherever I lived, from my childhood bedroom, my dorm room, and then eventually to its current resting place, my own home. Sometimes I "hoot" at the owl, remembering her. You may smile in a derisory, patronising fashion at this, but it has worked so far.

**Nonna - Grandma* **Nipote - Grandchild*

1. According to both passages, owls are depicted as

(A) native crafts
(B) traditional artifacts
(C) serendipitous charms
(D) despised totems
(E) cultural symbols

2. In the first paragraph of Passage 1, the owl is depicted as

(A) a foreboding symbol that signals famine
(B) a supernatural being that judges all
(C) an animal that foreshadows future events
(D) a creative creature that is also pragmatic
(E) a magical entity that heralds good fortune

3. In lines 15-28 ("Because of…children"), the author of Passage 1 supplies which of the following?

(A) Various societal perspectives on the existence of sorcery and dark ideas
(B) Several cultural viewpoints indicative of the symbolic nature of an animal
(C) Different historical accounts of a particular phenomenon
(D) A variety of sociocultural beliefs on a very controversial topic
(E) Mystical thinking as support of a single definition of the owl's powers

4. In Passage 1, the author uses "myths" (line 29) and "myths" (line 30) in what ways?

(A) The first is given a new definition and the second is used in a clichéd manner.
(B) The first is associated with cultural views and the second with fear.
(C) The first is related to certain societal beliefs and the second to untrue stories.
(D) The first implies duplicity while the second suggests truth.
(E) The first suggests scientific facts while the second suggests unsubstantiated claims.

5. In lines 38-41 ("But, it…creature"), the author of Passage 1 implies that

(A) a common fear underlies the truth in cultural perceptions
(B) cultural superstitions are essentially meaningless
(C) folk legends only apply to the indigenous
(D) tradition reveals fallacies in mystical thinking
(E) acceptance of a time honored tradition brings people together

6. In lines 50-53 ("Like those…judgement"), the author of Passage 1 makes use of

(A) historical facts
(B) scholarly analyses
(C) citations
(D) analogies
(E) personal anecdotes

7. Unlike the author of Passage 1, the author of Passage 2 focuses on which of the following?

(A) Scientific theorems
(B) Anthropological evidence
(C) Literature reference
(D) Greek mythology
(E) Personal experience

8. The primary function of line 67 ("I am...this") of Passage 2 is to

(A) shift the focus from cultural mythology to scientific fact
(B) submit further evidence that owls are symbolic sentries
(C) contest a widely accepted Western view by discussing superstitious practices
(D) introduce the author's personal experience with owls
(E) support claims about the gullibility of past cultural traditions

9. According to the author of Passage 2, a "rabbit's foot" (line 82) and "trinket of Saint Christopher" (line 83) are examples of

(A) divine rituals
(B) native adornments
(C) sorcerous trinkets
(D) superstitious items
(E) sacrificial offerings

10. In lines 86-89 ("Perhaps this…Tuscany"), the author of Passage 2 suggests that his grandmother

(A) only offered an after school snack as a reward
(B) yearned for her former rustic lifestyle
(C) was the real source of protection
(D) often exhibited exquisite wit
(E) wanted to teach the author time-honored traditions

11. According to the statement in lines 89-93 ("Owls are...owl") of Passage 2, Nonna would likely regard line 26 ("the bird...afraid") of Passage 1 as

(A) a popular misinterpretation, since owls are otherworldly creatures that save those in need
(B) a gross misunderstanding, as only evil beings should be afraid of an owl
(C) a common occurence, because an owl's physical features reveal a truly malevolent creature
(D) an incorrect observation, for only those with children should fear an owl
(E) a cold reminder, because many mistake cultural practices as mere superstition

12. The last paragraph of Passage 2 suggests which of the following?

(A) The grandmother believes in the superstition surrounding owls.
(B) The narrator may believe that an owl can ward away evil.
(C) The narrator never fully understood his grandmother's beliefs.
(D) The narrator only remembers his grandmother when moving homes.
(E) The grandmother gave her twine owl to the grandson.

13. The difference between the attitudes of the Kenyans and Native Americans in Passage 1 and those of Nonna and the author in Passage 2 toward owls can be characterized as

(A) superstition versus practicality
(B) protection versus wrongdoing
(C) adulation versus acceptance
(D) fear versus comfort
(E) tradition versus unorthodoxy

Self Evaluation

Self Evaluation is important if you want to see an improvement on your next comprehension passage. Each passage has a set of possible reasons for errors. Place a check mark next to the ones that pertain to you, and write your own on the blank line provided. Use this form to better analyze your performance by filling it out regularly and accurately so you can recognize the pattern of your most common mistakes.

If you don't understand why you have made mistakes, there is no way you can correct them!

1st Long Reading Comprehension: # Correct:____ # Wrong:____ # Unanswered:____

- ○ Did not understand the question, line reference, or answers
- ○ Did not underline the line reference
- ○ Read too much or too little around the line reference
- ○ Summarized the line reference instead of answering the question
- ○ Couldn't find the false words
- ○ Couldn't choose between two possible answers
- ○ Did not use tone to help eliminate answers
- ○ When stuck between two answers, guessed instead of looking for additional facts
- ○ Couldn't finish in time
- ○ Other:____

2nd Long Reading Comprehension: # Correct:____ # Wrong:____ # Unanswered:____

- ○ Did not understand the question, line reference, or answers
- ○ Did not underline the line reference
- ○ Read too much or too little around the line reference
- ○ Summarized the line reference instead of answering the question
- ○ Couldn't find the false words
- ○ Couldn't choose between two possible answers
- ○ Did not use tone to help eliminate answers
- ○ When stuck between two answers, guessed instead of looking for additional facts
- ○ Couldn't finish in time
- ○ Other:____

3rd Long Reading Comprehension: # Correct:____ # Wrong:____ # Unanswered:____

- ○ Did not understand the question, line reference, or answers
- ○ Did not underline the line reference
- ○ Read too much or too little around the line reference
- ○ Summarized the line reference instead of answering the question
- ○ Couldn't find the false words
- ○ Couldn't choose between two possible answers
- ○ Did not use tone to help eliminate answers
- ○ When stuck between two answers, guessed instead of looking for additional facts
- ○ Couldn't finish in time
- ○ Other:____

4th Long Reading Comprehension: # Correct:____ # Wrong:____ # Unanswered:____

- ○ Did not understand the question, line reference, or answers
- ○ Did not underline the line reference
- ○ Read too much or too little around the line reference
- ○ Summarized the line reference instead of answering the question
- ○ Couldn't find the false words
- ○ Couldn't choose between two possible answers
- ○ Did not use tone to help eliminate answers
- ○ When stuck between two answers, guessed instead of looking for additional facts
- ○ Couldn't finish in time
- ○ Other:____

Single Long Comprehension
7 Questions Total, Pages 128-129

1. Correct answer: (B)
The author discusses watching both French and British TV because of his location. He then dissects the broadcasting of the two countries before conceding that sometimes he'll watch American TV. We don't know if he's stereotypical, eliminating (A), and the passage is mainly about the author himself, eliminating (C), (D), and (E).

2. Correct answer: (B)
The author describes the misogyny in French television by writing, "women do appear, but rarely as central performers in a program…they are always supporters to the central male 'star of the show.'"

3. Correct answer: (A)
The author goes on describing the host by writing he "thinks that he is irresistible," or that he is "conceited."

4. Correct answer: (E)
French television is morally upright, not "depraved." "French television is placid, urbane, patronizing and boring," eliminates (A), (C), and (D). Then, "There is no variation throughout the week," eliminates (B).

5. Correct answer: (C)
The author writes that British television "reflects the full spectrum of UK society." He then claims that "As a result, television is a much more important element in the society of the UK: in France, it is, by and large, ignored," implying that this is not common for French TV.

6. Correct answer: (E)
"However" indicates a contrast. Here, the author writes, "The show is total nonsense...However, from the moment the opening bars of the show's opening theme are sounded, I am hooked." This means the author contrasted, or "juxtaposed," the show being total nonsense to him still being hooked.

7. Correct answer: (D)
The author does not like French TV, and only watches "Murder, She Wrote" when the news is not on. So, if the author had to choose, he would choose British news because it "reflects the full spectrum of UK society."

Single Long Comprehension
8 Questions Total, Pages 130-131

1. Correct answer: (D)
The author writes in lines 14-15 "today, the latest fad makes its way into the time-old theaters: 3D." Then, in lines 84-87, "If the production of 3D cinema can continue to improve...it may no longer be a fad," explaining "the future prospects" of 3D film.

2. Correct answer: (B)
In the first paragraph, the author writes, "a movie is relaxed, informal, and cheap, with just as much excitement." "Cheap" points to "affordable" and "excitement" points to "thrilling."

3. Correct answer: (C)
The author tells the reader the common misconception is: "3D films really aren't something new created with the most up-to-date technology," and then corrects this misconception by saying, "3D film has existed for nearly a century now." These statements discuss how long 3D films have been around, or their "longevity."

4. Correct answer: (D)
The author tells us that "red carpet actors" are "the 'it' crowd," meaning the celebrities or "famous" people.

5. Correct answer: (A)
The author describes "the capital allure" by writing, "Because you are provided with a pair of flimsy 3D glasses…the movie dealers reason that you should be willing to pull out a few more bills…viewers are given the latest technological feat and the added spice to special effects, so it's only to be expected that they pay a little more." This explanation provides the "justification" of the "movie industry to charge higher prices."

6. Correct answer: (E)
The author writes, "3D showings have boosted cinema revenues significantly…the 3D version out-markets the 2D by hundreds of thousands of dollars," eliminating (C). Then, "the number of 3D screen installations in theaters around the country more than doubled in 2011," eliminating (B). Next, "the people seem to flock to the concept of 3D film," eliminating (D). And finally, "directors…can also re-release timeless (and finished!) films in the latest fashion," eliminating (A).

7. Correct answer: (B)
The author writes, "In this day and age, no technological innovation can stay fresh forever," meaning that 3D movies must continue to be at the forefront of technologal progress if they are to "continue to prosper."

8. Correct answer: (C)
The author introduces 3D films, then discusses their positive aspects, like their beauty and interest, and their negative aspects, such as increased prices of tickets. To eliminate the others, consider that the passage does not provide "a general description of an industry," but rather a specific analysis of a subcategory within an industry (A), the passage is not concerned with anecdote (B), there is no "scholarly inquiry" (D), and the author does not take an "unorthodox viewpoint" (E).

Single Long Comprehension
12 Questions Total, Pages 132-133

1. Correct answer: (C)
The author uses this LR to moderate the quote in the first sentence, qualifying the statement.

2. Correct answer: (B)
In the LR, the author refers to these highwaymen as "common" and "vicious," two words which are synonymous with the answer choice (base and cruel). To eliminate the other answers, consider that the highwaymen were thieves (A), were not complex (C), were not travelers (D), and were very dangerous (E).

3. Correct answer: (E)
You must read around the LR for context. In lines 10-11, the author states "the journey was excruciatingly long, exhausting and uncomfortable." He then goes on to say in lines 12-13, "It was prone to accidents and robbery."

4. Correct answer: (B)
According to the author, before the Industrial Revolution traveling was "prone to accidents and robbery" (lines 12-13) insinuating that the traveler was vulnerable to many hazards. But due to the Industrial Revolution, it became "imperative to be able to move smoothly and safely from factory to city to port" (lines 32-33), implying that the traveler could now feel safer about traveling.

5. Correct answer: (A)
Macadam improved the roads and Stephenson made travel more efficient, both during the Industrial Revolution. This means they were "innovators during" that time. In (B), "environmental" is out of the passage's scope and in (C), "Roman empire" is false. The author makes no suggestion that the men are involved in farming, eliminating (D) and (E).

6. Correct answer: (D)
In order to understand what "market forces" means, one must read the context in which the phrase is mentioned. In the previous sentence, the author states that travel had to be smooth and safe "from factory to city to port" suggesting the concept of commerce. In the following sentence, the author mentions "traffic of goods" and "worldwide trade" further building on this concept.

7. Correct answer: (C)
The answer comes after the LR. The author states that "the idea of empire-building followed" after international trade began.

8. Correct answer: (D)
Because the LR starts with "Certainly," you must read the surrounding lines. The author states "if the nineteenth century can be regarded as a century of industry and progression, the twentieth century can be regarded as a century of destruction and war." War follows progress.

9. Correct answer: (C)
Line 51 begins with "Yet" and line 59 begins with "Or possibly not" signifying a shift from what had been written earlier.

10. Correct answer: (E)
Since the whole passage follows a chronological progression from the pre-1800s to now, the answer choice must also take this progression into account. Travel used to be "excruciatingly long" but is now "achieved in the shortest time possible," so it is commentary on how travel has advanced.

11. Correct answer: (D)
The tone of this paragraph is (-), which eliminates (A) and (C) because of their (+) tone. The author is not scared (B), nor confused (E), but if you consider the language of the passage (shuffle, disheveled, contemptuously, exhausted, etc.) you can see the author is exasperated, or extremely annoyed.

12. Correct answer: (A)
When the author uses the phrase "the highwayman," two things should be noted: First, "the" suggests that the reader has encountered this word, and what it means, earlier in the passage, and second: this word was used in a previous LR (question 2).

Double Long Comprehension
13 Questions Total, Pages 134-136

1. Correct Answer: (E)
Both passages offer cultural evidence that owls are regarded symbolically as representing "wisdom" (line 5, P1), "warning" (line 23, P1), and an ability to "repel illness and negative influence" (line 58, P2). Considering the mix of tone, eliminate (D) which is only (-) and (C) which is only (+). In (A) crafts only refer to P2 while (B) artifacts refer to an inanimate, physical item.

P1 - Passage 1 P2 - Passage 2
LR - Line Reference
(+) - Positive
(-) - Negative
All quotes in answer choices can be found in or around the line reference.

2. Correct Answer: (C)
In the LR, owls are associated with the future: "harbingers" (line 6) and "prognosticating" (line 12) while symbolizing both "wisdom" (line 5) and "ill fortune" (line 6), eliminating (B) and (D). (A) and (E) are wrong because they depict owls as either only (+) or only (-) when they are seen as both.

3. Correct Answer: (B)
The author of P1 uses various cultural understandings (Kenyan, Native American, Cameroon, Malaysian) of the owl's symbolism. Eliminate (E) because there were several symbolic interpretations of the owl, not just a singular one. Owls were not limited to (A) sorcery. The author did not write a (C) historical account nor did he suggest any (D) controversy.

4. Correct Answer: (C)
In the LR, the author uses "myths" (29) to represent several cultural interpretations while "myths" (30) refers to its conventional definition. Eliminate (D) because "myths" (29) were not deceitful and "myths" (30) are not truth. "Myths" (29) are not (E) scientific nor were they (A) given a new definition. Eliminate (B) because "myths" (30) does not refer to something mysterious.

5. Correct Answer: (A)
The author writes that the phenomenon suggests an "interesting, universal" (+) "fear of the unknown" (line 42). Eliminate (B) since they are meaningful. Eliminate (C) because this concerns "indigenous or otherwise." Eliminate (D) because fallacies are (-). The author does not suggest that (E) people are united, just that they "share similar sentiments" (line 40).

6. Correct Answer: (C)
The author writes using comparisons: "like" a "judge on his high bench", or like "a teacher surveying," which are analogies.

7. Correct Answer: (E)
The author of P2 writes in first person about his experience at his grandmother's house in the third paragraph. The author does not include (A) science, or (C) literature. Eliminate (B) and (D) because both authors use these devices.

8. Correct Answer: (B)
After the LR, the author of P2 writes about the Zuni who share similar cultural symbolic interpretations of the owl as those "countries" (line 59) in the first paragraph. Eliminate (A) because the author is not including science and (E) since the author does not state that these traditions are foolish. Eliminate (D) because the author does not refer to his own experience with an actual owl and (C) because the LR suggests further agreement, not a contrasting statement.

9. Correct Answer: (D)
The author of P2 writes that he is not "superstitious" (line 81) and uses the "rabbit's foot" and the "trinket" as examples. Eliminate (A) and (E) since the examples refer to physical items. The author never states that these examples are (B) native or (C) magical.

10. Correct Answer: (C)
The author of P2 writes that with his grandmother, he felt "invincible, protected, safe" (line 88). Eliminate (B) because the author does not write that she wanted to go back to Tuscany or that she was (D) witty. The author does not write that his grandmother wanted to (E) teach him the owl's symbolism nor did she (A) reward him with snacks.

11. Correct Answer: (B)
Nonna believes that owls' eyes are "Like daggers into a dark spirit's soul," and so only the dark spirits should fear them. She would disagree with the LR of P1. Eliminate (C) because Nonna does not mention that owls are evil and (D) because she does not mention children. Nonna does not indicate that owls are (A) "otherworldly." Nonna does not believe that an owl's powers are (E) superstitious, but rather real.

12. Correct Answer: (B)
The author of P2 writes that "it has worked so far," suggesting he believes the owl has protected him, eliminating (C). Eliminate (A) because the LR is about the author's use of the owl. The author remembers his grandmother every time he hoots at the owl, not just when he is (D) moving. (E) is wrong because the author has kept his "own version of her owl," not her owl.

13. Correct Answer: (D)
The Kenyans and Native Americans view owls as generally evil (2nd paragraph, P1), eliminating (B) and (C). Nonna and the author of P2 view owls as sources of protection (+) (3rd and 4th paragraph, P2), eliminating (E). (A) is wrong because Nonna and the author of P2 believe in the mysticism of the owl, too.

Chapter Ten

Questions 1-6 are based on the following passage.

This passage examines the role that Shakespeare's plays have in today's society.

Of the thirty-five plays included in the First Folio collection by Hemminge and Condell of the Works of Shakespeare, fourteen are Comedies. What is more surprising is that so many of the plays in this genre are still regarded as amongst the best of all the works he produced. Tragedy spans the ages, but Comedy is much more ephemeral, trapped in the conventions and mores of the time in which it is written. Although there are productions of a certain few today, the Comedies have been regarded, by and large, as plays that are more difficult to attract a modern audience, either because of their setting or because the puns and ironic language of the plays belong to a society far removed from those of today.

Yet, the other comedies are not only as relevant today as they were when they were first penned, but also just as popular. Is there anyone who, at school, has not been introduced to and been surprised by the enjoyment found in Shakespeare's comedies? Broadway and Hollywood have gleefully turned them into musicals such as "The Boys from Syracuse" (based on "The Comedy of Errors") and "Kiss Me Kate"(The "Taming of the Shrew"). On the screen, stars such as Denzel Washington (Don John in "Much Ado"), Al Pacino (Shylock) and Elizabeth Taylor (Kate) have been eager to show their quality in Shakespeare's comedies (although perhaps earplugs should be used as protection against Miss Taylor's rather breathless, one-note screech of delivery). Today's audience experiences the same feeling of satisfaction as the curtain falls as did the audience of the seventeenth century; perhaps more so, for the fact that a play seems as relevant today as it did five hundred years ago gives weight and depth to what it unfolds about life in general and relationships in particular.

One comedy in particular - "A Midsummer Night's Dream" - exemplifies clearly the truth that exists in Shakespeare's writing. While the play appears to be about the significance of a wedding, what lies at his heart is an examination of love. Shakespeare defines for the audience the difference between real love and physical love. It is only when the four lovers have each felt that they are being cheated by love that they can see love as it really is. It is only when Oberon witnesses the selfishness of the revenge he takes on Titania that he can understand that love includes forgiveness and the negation of self in order to flourish. It is only when Bottom wakes from his "dream" that he was once loved by the essence of beauty that he can realize himself as a human being. It is only when the audience recognizes their own dance in pursuit of love enacted on the stage that they can understand why the pursuit of love is so important to their feeling of completeness.

This is why the play resonates with people today. In all his comedies, there is the discussion about that element of our life that is most important to us: love, the need to discover it and cherish it, the need to give it and accept it and return it. Only love can help us break out of this solid body that encases our soul.

1. The primary purpose of the passage is to

(A) discuss the longevity of a certain author's work
(B) question the important of love in modern society
(C) place the work of Shakespeare in a global context
(D) highlight two disparate definitions of a word
(E) give cultural context to "A Midsummer Night's Dream"

2. The author uses the word "ephemeral" (line 7) to describe Shakespeare's comedies because they

(A) will never be as popular as the Tragedies
(B) are as popular now as they were originally
(C) can still be understood by laymen
(D) were crafted for a specific context
(E) are considered his weaker works

3. The parenthetical statement in lines 27-29 ("although perhaps…delivery") primarily functions as

(A) a director's note
(B) necessary information
(C) a grave admonition
(D) an objective fact
(E) a humorous aside

4. In context of the third and fourth paragraphs, the author believes that "A Midsummer Night's Dream" (lines 36-37) illustrates

(A) the tedium of Shakespeare's contemporary society
(B) an anomaly among Shakespeare's themes
(C) the reason Shakespeare's plays still endure
(D) that Shakespeare's Tragedies remain popular
(E) a Comedy that does not have lasting power

5. Word repetition is used in lines 42-50 ("It is...being") primarily to

(A) add a lyrical quality similar to Shakespeare's
(B) provide emphasis to the author's argument
(C) contradict what certain critics contend
(D) support the author's revolutionary theory
(E) suggest a fault in previous interpretations

6. In the third paragraph, the author's argument is developed primarily by discussing

(A) a series of unrelated events
(B) a popular misconception
(C) the jargon of a community
(D) the historical context of an idea
(E) the duality of a concept

Questions 1-9 are based on the following passage.

This passage is from a series of autobiographical essays about an adventurous young man living in Sudan, south of Egypt.

I lived and worked in Khartoum for four years. One afternoon, about a month after my arrival, a friend took me to Shambart Bridge. We stood at the very centre of the bridge and gazed around us. On the Eastern bank laid the administrative and business capital of Khartoum, the solid buildings of which include the Presidential Palace where General Gordon had his final, fatal confrontation with the forces of the Mahdi, the great Mosque, the labyrinthine *souk* and the Hilton Hotel. On the Western bank sprawled the traditional Arab city of Omdurman with its palm shaded gardens, its square, white-walled traditional buildings and dust roads along which donkeys pulled overcharged carts. Between these two cities and below our feet flowed the River Nile. In truth, the Shambart Bridge spans two River Niles. It marks the point where the White Nile that has its source far South in the area of the Great Lakes of Africa, is joined by the Blue Nile that has tumbled down through the Highlands of Ethiopia. On the western side of this juncture, the water is stately, smooth, and clear; but on the eastern side, it is troubled and darkly brown from the silt it carries from its mountain source.

The two rivers may meet here but they do little more than shrug shoulders together. They do not mingle until they have flowed, side by side, for many miles northwards. It is bizarre to realize that although there is some cultivated land on each bank of the river, it is no more than a verdant strip of less than five hundred meters in width. The fertility halts with no warning. Thereon it is replaced abruptly by unremittingly hard, flat, grey-brown, baked earth that stretches endlessly away into the anonymous blaze of the heat-hazed horizon. It would seem that nothing lives out there; nor could that bleakness ever have held life.

There is a road that goes directly from North Khartoum to Port Said in the North Eastern corner of Sudan. It is narrow, just wide enough to squeeze two thundering lines of lorries and military jeeps and a few private cars, all of which are halted for police checks at regular intervals. There are no traffic signs but, now and again, one comes across a small courtyard of dusty buildings, an antique petrol pump and large urns containing water for the passing desultory group of camels and their herder, that follow the road along its verge. No other sign of habitation is visible. Somewhere to the west of this road but not visible is the Nile. To the East, the land appears to be rising and one becomes aware of barren rock and drifting sand. The road achieves the hill and begins the descent. Sand has drifted across the road in places and what seem to be dunes appear in the distance. In the far distance there appear to be shapes that might be man-made: it is hard to tell at this distance. As they become closer, they resolve themselves in to a wall against which the sand has drifted. Behind this wall there appears to be what seem like stunted pyramids, a myriad of them.

This is Meroe, although there is no sign to tell the visitor that this is all that is left of this ancient city of the Kush, a civilization that came before the Pharaohs of Egypt. There is nothing else here: just about two hundred small pyramids, each windowless but with an entrance porch facing to the East, away from the Nile. This is the burial ground of the Kushite kings, deserted and decaying. There is no sign of information – at least Shelley met his "visitor from an antique land" - to offer an explanation for their isolation, just the soft fall of the visitor's footsteps in the piling sand and a distant sound of lorry wheels on the far road. The visitor shudders a little at the eeriness of the place. For how many aeons have they stood here, alone with their secrets?

The day that I saw Meroe will always be in my memory: of that I am sure. I was with friends, and we returned to the road silently, feeling dwarfed, and drove onwards through the desolate landscape. A little further along the road there was a junction and we turned left. A half hour later we arrived in Shendi, a small town on the bank of the Nile. We were surrounded suddenly by palms and donkey carts, and market stalls. There was a little white walled cafe beside the river where we sipped thick black coffee, and glasses of cool water. We watched a young girl milking a patient goat whilst her brothers threw stones and tried to hit a heavy branch that was being dragged along by the currents of the Nile.

Then we climbed back into the car and went home to Khartoum.

1. In line 22, the word "troubled" most nearly means

(A) anxious
(B) turbulent
(C) somber
(D) mysterious
(E) dangerous

2. The author's statement "They do…northwards" (lines 25-27) suggests that

(A) the rivers flow parallel for some time prior to combining into one
(B) the two rivers will meet at least once before separating again
(C) there is arable land surrounding both of the rivers' banks
(D) the rivers flow in separate channels which will never meet
(E) the rivers provide fertilization to the surrounding soil

3. The description of the land surrounding the rivers in the second paragraph suggests that

(A) the fertility of the land bordering the river is such that it produces a high yield of crops
(B) horticulturists rely on a complex system of irrigation canals and reservoirs
(C) the region described is utterly devoid of any rainfall throughout the year
(D) the River Nile is a catch basin for all rain that falls in the surrounding desert
(E) though there is evidence of some vegetation along the river, the greater area does not support life

4. In context, the word "anonymous" in line 33 most nearly means

(A) unidentified
(B) incognito
(C) secretive
(D) nondescript
(E) unique

5. In line 51, "achieves" most nearly means

(A) attains
(B) climbs
(C) conquers
(D) completes
(E) reaches

6. According to the information in the fourth paragraph (lines 60-74), the author suggests all of the following about the pyramids of Meroe EXCEPT:

(A) They exist in quiet seclusion.
(B) They are lightly toured.
(C) They house the pharaohs of Egypt.
(D) They are shrouded in mystery.
(E) They are indeterminably old.

7. The tone of the sentence in lines 75-76 ("The day… sure") is one of

(A) conciliation
(B) hesitance
(C) nostalgia
(D) diffidence
(E) conviction

8. The narrator's reaction in lines 77-78 ("we returned... landscape") conveys a sense of

(A) disconnection and confusion
(B) depression and isolation
(C) self-loathing and anxiety
(D) remoteness and insignificance
(E) enlightenment and satisfaction

9. As depicted in lines 75-88 ("The day...Nile"), the contrast between Meroe and Shendi is one of

(A) poverty to wealth
(B) irrelevance to relevance
(C) stillness to activity
(D) community to isolation
(E) vibrancy to monotony

Questions 1-12 are based on the following passages.

The following two passages discuss the phenomenon of computer-generated literature. The first passage is taken from a 2003 news column on new media and innovation, the second is from a 2006 article on successful story-creating computer systems.

Passage 1

A seven eve will typify the gaudy scoop. A typed euros will gaily gauche the scaly scampi. The twiggy jived hence erupts the viable vision.

Believe it or not, the last three sentences were taken from a book. It's a virtual book, a digital product of The Literature Factory, which is a computer program that acts as a kind of automated "writer" that compiles letters into words, words into sentences, and sentences into a book-length work. Whether or not most readers consider this output literature, computer systems that generate language raise interesting questions about language and the nature of meaning.

Andy Fundinger made The Literature Factory for use in Second Life, a three-dimensional online environment where multiple users can build digital objects and interact with each other. An engineer by training, Fundinger's interest in the project was technical rather than literary. Nonetheless, his inspiration came from a well-loved book, <u>One Two Three Infinity</u> by physicist George Gamow. In the classic text, which explores the possibilities of math and science, Gamow describes a long automatic printing press that prints books on its own, circumventing the need for authors altogether.

Fundinger thought scripting an approximation of this idea in Second Life would be an interesting challenge, so he went to work on it, using a couple of his own desktop computers as external servers. Two other programmers designed visuals for the "factory." This means that visitors can look down from grated walkways and watch as large cylinders called Word-o-Mats spin through different letter combinations, discarding nonsensical ones until they make a word of English. The words are then picked up by smiling robots that drop them one by one into different bins.

The behind-the-scenes functionality is relatively simple. The Word-o-Mats make a request to the server, which checks the letter combinations against a dictionary to make sure the word is real. That word is then sent back to Second Life and into a bin, which checks periodically with the server to find out when new words have been created. Meanwhile, the sentence-maker connects to the server every 90 seconds and tells it to make a sentence from the words in the bin using one of a few basic sentence forms, such as noun-verb-the-adjective-noun. As the sentences are created they are copied into a digital book, thus creating a work of literature - or something like it.

Many readers would argue that the resulting collection of sentences is not really a work of literature, either because it lacks a plot or because there is no inherent meaning in its word salad. But is understandability — or even intention — the only measure of art? In the early twentieth century surrealist artists created exquisite corpse poems as a group, with each participant contributing only some of the words or lines. In a sense these works were written blindly, with no one "mind" creating them. So it may not be too far-fetched to suggest that the programmed creativity of Fundinger's robots rivals theirs.

Passage 2

With his artificial intelligence-based computer system, MEXICA, Rafael Pérez y Pérez is exploring the place where creativity and automation meet. Fed only basic details, MEXICA is able to generate very short stories, mini-epics about love and violence between knights, kings, and other ancient inhabitants of México City, the people known as the Mexicas.

Though the stories are short and simple in construction, readers gave them high marks for coherence, structure, content, and feeling of suspense. In an online survey that asked readers to compare stories produced by MEXICA, other computer systems, and one written by a person, a story created by MEXICA was ranked the highest.

Computerized storytellers similar to this have been in existence since the 1970s. So what is it that makes MEXICA uniquely successful? In a paper introducing his system, Pérez y Pérez, a researcher at at Autonomous Metropolitan University in México City, writes that although emotions are an integral part of the creative process, many computer models of creativity do not account for them. MEXICA, on the other hand, attempts to do this by tagging characters with their emotional connection to each other, then using those connections to drive plot development. Furthermore, the stories created by MEXICA are not the result of an explicit goal-oriented activity, but are created by a process that leads from one scenario into the next. In other words, it functions somewhat like the creative writer who says she "knows" her characters but not exactly what the characters will do or how the story will end until she begins writing.

The notion of a machine that can make art, which is thought to be an essentially human ability, is frightening to some. But the value in a system like MEXICA is not in replacing human creators but in teaching us how the creative process works. For example, in designing a building an architect relies on blueprints and scale models, which are tools that help him to externalize and better understand his own ideas. Likewise, computers are tools that can help people visualize complex systems. We are far from being able to create a system capable of making literature like human beings do, but if we can build a system that generates adequate short stories, we have gained a better understanding of how literature is created.

1. Which statement best characterizes the ways in which the authors of Passage 1 and Passage 2 consider computer-generated literature?

(A) The first deifies the ability and complexity of literature-generating software while the second fears the consequences of digital writing.
(B) The first speculates the external applications of this program towards other media while the second discusses the high performance of literature creating software.
(C) The first takes an absolute stance on an issue while the second wavers between praise and scorn.
(D) The first is more concerned with what literature entails while the second delves into why literature is important to culture.
(E) The first examines the process of creating nonhuman writing while the second exalts a specific program while examining its effects.

2. George Gamow (lines 21-22, Passage 1) would most likely regard MEXICA (Passage 2) with

(A) disdain
(B) appreciation
(C) caution
(D) indignation
(E) righteousness

3. Which of the following would be an example of the "interesting questions" mentioned in line 12?

(A) Will computers that create literature ever be available on the open market to consumers?
(B) Are official documents becoming a resource that can be generated with no human interaction?
(C) Can a randomly generated and fundamentally nonsensical string of words be considered a novel?
(D) Is language inherent to just humans, or do other animals share the ability to communicate complex ideas?
(E) When will computers be able to convincingly reproduce music?

4. In the third paragraph of Passage 1, the author refers to George Gamow primarily to

(A) explain the prime inspiration behind a creation
(B) provide support for an argument
(C) add depth to a superfluous endeavor
(D) dispute the necessity for original works
(E) contrast his original idea to a similar work

5. Both authors mention "art" in the final paragraphs primarily to

(A) make a claim about the advancing field of literacy
(B) dispute the value of computers
(C) link writing to a visual form
(D) question what defines a concept
(E) deride an approach to the writing

6. In line 63, the word "rivals" most nearly means

(A) competes
(B) opposes
(C) testifies to
(D) equals
(E) disputes

7. According to the third paragraph of Passage 2, Pérez Y Pérez feels MEXICA outperforms other computer-generated storytellers for all of these reasons EXCEPT

(A) linking scenes to one another
(B) establishing an emotional connection for each character
(C) creating goal-oriented activities
(D) developing characters before developing plot
(E) using characters to drive the storyline

8. Computer-generated stories would most likely be "frightening" (line 100) to

(A) "Andy Fundinger" (line 14)
(B) "Two other programmers" (line 30)
(C) "Rafael Pérez y Pérez" (line 66)
(D) "a person" (line 77)
(E) "the creative writer" (line 94)

9. The "blueprints and scale models" (line 104) are most similar to

(A) an advertisement printed with a coupon
(B) a bullet-point outline of an essay
(C) a studio recording of a new song
(D) a weekly circular detailing the sales at a supermarket
(E) a recipe published on a cooking website

10. In the last paragraph of Passage 2, the author contends that the principal benefit behind computerized storytelling is

(A) the promise of more affordable books
(B) a deeper understanding of the creative process
(C) more logical plot lines than are used today
(D) the fear it will generate in users
(E) a resurgence of lost literary forms

11. Both the "readers" (line 52) and the author of Passage 2 would agree that

(A) automated writing will replace human writing in as soon as the next decade
(B) automated writing programs are becoming too easy to create
(C) computers are already creating novels that are available for sale today
(D) computer generated literature will never fit the clear definition of writing
(E) computers today cannot yet produce stories of the same stylistic level and fluency as humans can

12. Both authors would most likely agree that computerized literature

(A) is an interesting field of study
(B) will one day cause society to lose its creativity
(C) is a useful tool for teaching the basics of writing
(D) is written as well as a story by a human
(E) is a threat to the art of human literature

Questions 1-13 are based on the following passage.

This passage is centered on tourism in Paris, and how the experience could be radically different were a tourist to visit rural France, which the author considers the "real" France.

Oscar Wilde once wrote that when good Americans die they go to Paris. One cannot vouch for the truth of that observation but it would be fairly accurate to point out that ever since Benjamin Franklin became the first American Ambassador to France, Americans have followed his trail with increasing ardor. Andrew Jefferson followed closely on Franklin's heels and spent a year in the city before returning to America and higher office. Later, Harriet Beecher Stowe stayed for a while, James Fennimore Cooper worked there, Henry James passed some languid time there. American writers and artists, such as Edwin Hopper and F. Scott Fitzgerald, arrived in droves. Ernest Hemmingway et al, dubbed "The Lost Generation" by Gertrude Stein, roamed the Left Bank, throwing back the absinthe and generally living up to the title. Two World Wars within the first fifty years of that century brought in an enormous number of Americans - plain, straightforward G.I. Joes, who passed through a misty and secretive Paris with little more knowledge of this foreign (in more than one meaning of the word) capital city other than the phrase, "Je suis Américain."

The Parisians adored them then and have continued to welcome all Americans - and their dollars – ever since. In return, vacationing Americans have made Paris the first stop on their European tour. A morning up the Eiffel Tower, an afternoon in the Louvre, a romantic (if chilly) evening dinner floating along the Seine are all on the list of "must-do." Perhaps, a visit to Versailles (far too crowded with polite and eager groups taking photos) and a visit to the flea market (far too expensive but the vendors are charming) are determinedly succeeded by a reverent tour of Notre Dame (an anxious eye cocked for the Hunchback who never appears) and an exhausting climb up all those steps from Montmartre to Sacre Coeur (sadly no longer full of French children dancing with Gene Kelly). Oh, how sophisticated are the shops and boutiques! How elegant and stylish are the French women! How charming are the pavement bistros! How so very, very Paris! And then the tourist mounts one of those incredibly sleek and comfortable French trains that hurtles them, at high speed, on to the next European capital. "Well!" the tourist exclaims, "Paris is simply wonderful, and that is France, done!"

Well, yes – except that Paris is not France; nor is France in any way a mirror of Paris. There is a wide divide between those who live in Paris and those who live in any one of the departments in the rest of the country. Those who live away from the capital accuse the Parisians of being completely oblivious to life outside those historic gates of the capital city and regard inhabitants of Paris as *snobs*. Parisians believe that to live in the country of France is to label oneself as *provincial*. Should anyone from beyond the pale, out there in the wilderness of rural France, actually manage to arrive in Paris and gain a successful foothold in Parisian society, then they are labeled as a *parvenu*. The seat of power and influence is in Paris, and, as a result everything that affects the whole country is decided only in terms of how Paris will be affected.

Thus, whilst public transport from Paris to the other major cities of France (Lyon, Marseilles, Toulouse and Bordeaux) is provided by the famous TGV (Transport Grande Vitesse) trains, rail lines to smaller cities and towns are scarce and poorly timetabled. The French motorways provide communication to those cities, but in rural areas, the roads are narrow. If one has no car, then one is stranded. There are few buses in the countryside and no long distance coaches. As a result, all over France, small towns and villages are decaying and empty.

How very ironic! For if tourists were able to tear themselves away from "Gay Paree" and explore the real France, they would find a countryside of tranquillity, history, care and beauty. Villages and towns that have been there since mediaeval times, with half timbered houses and little churches beside slowly moving, winding rivers and streams, the beauty of the French countryside is breathtaking and the regard for the ceremonies of daily life by those who live there is unchanged. Here you can still find the local bakery that opens every morning (except Monday) at 7:30, with a dozen different kinds of breads and, baguettes, and croissants. There is the local butcher with pork and beef and chickens (still with their heads) and pots of home-made patés, the van with the fish fresh from the coast. There is the café–tabac with its newspapers and magazines, its cigarettes and lottery tickets. Old men sit, hunched over the table filling in the lotto form, sipping the small cups of bitter black coffee. Walk down the cobbled Grand Rue from the old town with its ruined castle and it will take you a while, for all whom you meet will pause to say "bonjour," to say a word of greeting to your dog, and to warn you that the cold weather will be here next week and ask if you have bought in your logs for the wood stove yet. It is what the tourist yearns for.

The Parisians have forgotten about all that. The tourist will never forget it. And good Americans when they die will have no choice but to go to Paris.

1. In the first paragraph, the author backs up Oscar Wilde's statement "when good…Paris" (lines 1-2) by

(A) listing some famous personalities who moved to the city over many centuries
(B) stating that France was initially occupied only by Americans
(C) highlighting that American soldiers settled in Paris and the surrounding countryside
(D) comparing the people who left America in the 17th century with those who left in the 20th century
(E) suggesting that most American political figures prefer to vacation in France

2. In line 21, what are the two meanings of the word "foreign"?

(A) Exotic and expensive
(B) Different and unknown
(C) City and country
(D) Unfamiliar and aggressive
(E) Indigenous and native

3. In lines 31-39 ("Perhaps, a...Kelly"), the author uses parentheses in order to

(A) add extra, valuable information
(B) bring humor to a grim subject
(C) deride a less progressive culture
(D) assume what the reader thinks
(E) debunk tourist expectations

4. Lines 39-42 ("Oh, how…Paris!) are distinctive for their use of

(A) redundant opinion
(B) trendsetting terms
(C) colloquial criticisms
(D) repetitive emphasis
(E) thorough observation

5. In context of the passage, lines 39-46 ("Oh, how …done!") serve to highlight

(A) aspects of Paris that the author enjoys
(B) the author's never-ending love of France
(C) a tourist's proclivities for everything French
(D) the extent to which a tourist is duped by the French
(E) the author's contempt for a superficial tourist experience

6. The authors reaction to "the tourist" in line 45 would be best described as

(A) content now that they understand French culture
(B) frustrated at the tourist's limited expectations of France
(C) joyous at the fervor of their love for France
(D) angered because they did not truly experience Paris
(E) happy to see all Americans in love with Paris

7. The author uses italics in lines 51-59 ("Those who…*parvenu*") primarily in order to

(A) deride certain kinds of people who reside in Paris
(B) refer ironically to common stereotypes from foreigners
(C) quote popular words used in rural France
(D) imply skepticism towards the choice to move to the country
(E) highlight the way the French typically perceive one another

8. In the third paragraph (lines 47-62), the author suggests that the rural French and the Parisians

(A) are united in their love for France and therefore have little quarrel
(B) would like to separate France into an agrarian country and an industrial country
(C) are at odds over the centralizing control exerted by Paris over all of France
(D) share a mutual acrimony for each other that is largely undeserved
(E) have learned to effectively collaborate on all political issues

9. The condition of the French transportation system is mentioned by the author in the fourth paragraph (lines 63-73) in order to provide

(A) a cogent argument for the need to travel to the French countryside
(B) a warning to all foreign tourists not to rely on public transportation
(C) an illustration of advancement in France's industrial prowess
(D) an example of a possible source of contention between Paris and rural France
(E) a country-wide call for political reformation

10. The author's statement "How very ironic!" in line 74 suggests that

(A) the booming success of Paris is actually damaging the prosperity of the French countryside
(B) the French government should not be as proud of Paris as it is
(C) tourists tend to favor the decaying countryside to the city
(D) Parisians do not value a life of routine in the way that the rural French do
(E) most Americans in France are still artists, politicians, or soldiers

11. In context of the last paragraph, the author states that the bakery "opens every morning (except Monday) at 7:30" (line 84) primarily in order to

(A) express frustration at the hours of operation for the small business
(B) highlight the relaxed pace of towns in the countryside
(C) alert the reader to cultural differences present when visiting France
(D) establish a level of intimacy between the reader and the author
(E) give an account of what everyday life is like in any city of France

12. The word "It" in line 98 refers to

(A) the efficient Parisian transportation system
(B) the shops available to modern tourists
(C) the colder weather that France is known for
(D) the hospitality offered by the rural French
(E) the absence of tourism throughout Europe

13. Which of the following best characterizes the development of the passage?

(A) Liberal viewpoint to conservative viewpoint
(B) The author's opinion to a general fact
(C) What something seems to the unfortunate truth
(D) Sarcastic commentary to scholarly debate
(E) Touristic musings to governmental concerns

Self Evaluation

Self Evaluation is important if you want to see an improvement on your next comprehension passage. Each passage has a set of possible reasons for errors. Place a check mark next to the ones that pertain to you, and write your own on the blank line provided. Use this form to better analyze your performance by filling it out regularly and accurately so you can recognize the pattern of your most common mistakes.

If you don't understand why you have made mistakes, there is no way you can correct them!

1st Long Reading Comprehension: # Correct:____ # Wrong:____ # Unanswered:____

- ○ Did not understand the question, line reference, or answers
- ○ Did not underline the line reference
- ○ Read too much or too little around the line reference
- ○ Summarized the line reference instead of answering the question
- ○ Couldn't find the false words
- ○ Couldn't choose between two possible answers
- ○ Did not use tone to help eliminate answers
- ○ When stuck between two answers, guessed instead of looking for additional facts
- ○ Couldn't finish in time
- ○ Other:____

2nd Long Reading Comprehension: # Correct:____ # Wrong:____ # Unanswered:____

- ○ Did not understand the question, line reference, or answers
- ○ Did not underline the line reference
- ○ Read too much or too little around the line reference
- ○ Summarized the line reference instead of answering the question
- ○ Couldn't find the false words
- ○ Couldn't choose between two possible answers
- ○ Did not use tone to help eliminate answers
- ○ When stuck between two answers, guessed instead of looking for additional facts
- ○ Couldn't finish in time
- ○ Other:____

3rd Long Reading Comprehension: # Correct:____ # Wrong:____ # Unanswered:____

- ○ Did not understand the question, line reference, or answers
- ○ Did not underline the line reference
- ○ Read too much or too little around the line reference
- ○ Summarized the line reference instead of answering the question
- ○ Couldn't find the false words
- ○ Couldn't choose between two possible answers
- ○ Did not use tone to help eliminate answers
- ○ When stuck between two answers, guessed instead of looking for additional facts
- ○ Couldn't finish in time
- ○ Other:____

4th Long Reading Comprehension: # Correct:____ # Wrong:____ # Unanswered:____

- ○ Did not understand the question, line reference, or answers
- ○ Did not underline the line reference
- ○ Read too much or too little around the line reference
- ○ Summarized the line reference instead of answering the question
- ○ Couldn't find the false words
- ○ Couldn't choose between two possible answers
- ○ Did not use tone to help eliminate answers
- ○ When stuck between two answers, guessed instead of looking for additional facts
- ○ Couldn't finish in time
- ○ Other:____

Single Long Comprehension
6 Questions Total, Pages 142-143

1. Correct answer: (A)
In the transition between the first and second paragraphs, the author writes that Shakespeare's plays "belong to a society far removed from that of today," but that some comedies are "as relevant today as they were when they were first penned." He then goes on to discuss "A Midsummer Night's Dream" in particular and why it has lasted.

2. Correct answer: (D)
Shakespeare's comedy is "ephemeral" because it is "trapped in the conventions and more of the time in which it was written," or, written for a specific time by someone of that time.

3. Correct answer: (E)
Here the author is making a joke. The comment is not from the director (A), it is not in any way important (B), it is not a (-) tone (C), and it is not a fact (D).

4. Correct answer: (C)
In the LR, the author writes that the play "exemplifies clearly the truth that exists in Shakespeare's writing." Then, in the last paragraph, he claims the play "resonates with people today" because of its theme of love, making it an example of why some of Shakespeare's work can last.

5. Correct answer: (B)
Each statement further exemplifies the point the author is making about love as the enduring factor of Shakespeare's plays. To eliminate the other answers, consider that the statements are made primarily to be lyrical (A), there are no critics (C), the author's theory isn't revolutionary (D), and he is presenting his own interpretation, not discussing another's (E).

6. Correct answer: (E)
The author discusses in lines 40-42 the difference "between real love and physical love." He then goes on to illustrate this duality by using examples from the play.

Single Long Comprehension
9 Questions Total, Pages 144-145

1. Correct answer: (B)
The author writes, "On the western side...the water is stately, smooth, and clear; but on the eastern side, it is troubled and darkly brown from the silt." "Troubled" is the opposite of "smooth and clear" or turbulent.

2. Correct answer: (A)
If the rivers "do not mingle until they have flowed, side by side, for many miles," it suggests that before they meet, they first have flowed "parallel for some time."

3. Correct answer: (E)
The author writes, "although there is some cultivated land on each bank of the river, it is no more than a verdant strip of less than five hundred meters in width. The fertility halts with no warning," suggesting that there is "some vegetation along the river" but it is not much. So, "the greater area does not support life."

4. Correct answer: (D)
In context, the author uses the word "anonymous" to describe the infertile area surrounding the river. He then refers to this area in the following sentence using the word "bleakness" which is most similar to "nondescript" or unremarkable in any way.

5. Correct answer: (B)
In the context of the sentence, "achieves" most nearly means the opposite of "descent," so to ascend or climb.

6. Correct answer: (C)
In this paragraph we learn that Meroe used to be the "ancient city of the Kush, a civilization that came before the Pharaohs of Egypt." The author also writes, "This is the burial ground of the Kushite kings." Therefore, the pyramids of Meroe would not "house the pharaohs of Egypt."

7. Correct answer: (E)
The tone of this sentence is (+), eliminating (B) and (D). The author is not reconciling anything, eliminating (A). While "nostalgia" looks appealing, since the author says "the day…will always be in my memory," it is not the same as saying he has a desire to return to that place, leaving (E).

8. Correct answer: (D)
The clues in this LR are the phrases "feeling dwarfed" (insignificance) and "desolate landscape" (remoteness).

P1 - Passage 1 P2 - Passage 2
LR - Line Reference
(+) - Positive
(-) - Negative
All quotes in answer choices can be found in or around the line reference.

9. Correct answer: (C)
The author describes Meroe as a "desolate landscape" in that "there is nothing else" there, pointing only to "stillness." Then, the author describes Shendi as bustling in comparison to Meroe, pointing to "activity."

Double Long Comprehension
12 Questions Total, Pages 146-148

1. Correct answer: (E)
The author of P1 discusses how computer literature is created. The author of P2 describes one form of computer literature and its creator before discussing what impact machine-crafted writing will have on humans. To eliminate the others, consider that the author of P1 isn't glorifying the complexity of the literature (A) nor its external applications (B), and the author of P2 has no scorn towards the machines (C) nor is general culture and society the main idea (D).

2. Correct answer: (B)
In the third paragraph, George Gamow describes an "automatic printing press that prints books on its own," and so he would be pleased (+) to see his idea come to life. The (+) eliminates (A), (C), and (D).

3. Correct answer: (C)
The "interesting questions" concern "computer systems that generate language," such as the "randomly generated and fundamentally nonsensical string of words" exemplified in lines 1-3, and whether this "language" can be considered to have meaning.

4. Correct answer: (A)
In the third paragraph, the author writes that Andy Fundinger's "inspiration" behind the computer literature system, "came from a well-loved book, One Two Three Infinity by physicist George Gamow."

5. Correct answer: (D)
The author of P1 brings up the "concept" of art to question what is a "measure of art." Similarly, the author of P2 brings up the idea "of a machine that can make art," thereby questioning "a concept" that is generally understood to be "an essentially human ability."

6. Correct answer: (D)
Try replacing the word in the sentence with the answer choices, and you'll see that "equals" fits because the author believes the "programmed creativity" of the computer parallels the work made by "the early twentieth century surrealist artists."

7. Correct answer: (C)
In the third paragraph, the author of P2 writes that "the stories created by MEXICA are not the result of an explicit goal-oriented activity," meaning that these "activities" cannot be the reason "MEXICA outperforms other computer generated storytellers."

8. Correct answer: (D)
Computer literature would not be "frightening" to (A), (B), or (C) because these people helped develop the systems. (E) would use computer literature to gain new understanding about writing, leaving (D), who was found to be a worse writer than the computers.

9. Correct answer: (B)
"Blueprints and scale models" are "tools that help [an architect] to externalize and better understand his own ideas" before building. Similarly, an "outline" is used to "design" an essay before it is written.

10. Correct answer: (B)
In the last sentence, the author writes "if we can build a system that generates adequate short stories, we have gained a better understanding of how literature is created." So, computer literature can supply us with "a deeper understanding" of literature in general.

11. Correct answer: (E)
Both the "readers" and the author of P2 are unsure how legitimate computer literature is. To eliminate the other answers, consider that neither thinks computer literature will "replace" human writing (A), the programs are not easy to create (B), no coherent novels have been created (C), and the author of P2 and the "readers" are in disagreement about the future (D).

12. Correct answer: (A)
Both authors feel generally (+) about computer literature, immediately eliminating (B) and (E). However, neither feels the literature is yet on par with that of humans (D), nor that it's strong enough yet to teach us about writing (C).

Single Long Comprehension
13 Questions Total, Pages 149-151

1. Correct answer: (A)
To find how the author "backs up" the statement, read on. In the following sentence the author writes that "...it would be fairly accurate to point out that ever since Benjamin Franklin became the first American Ambassador to France, Americans have followed his trail with increasing ardor," which he follows with a list of "famous personalities who moved to the city."

2. Correct answer: (B)
We can eliminate (C), since the author is only talking about the Paris, not the country of France. In (A) and (D), "expensive" and "aggressive" are unsupported. The answer also cannot be "indigenous" because the author is talking about the city of Paris, not something occurring naturally, but manmade.

3. Correct answer: (E)
In the parentheticals, the author tells the reader what the tourist will actually encounter. For example, "Perhaps, a visit to Versailles (far too crowded with polite and eager groups taking photos)" shows us that "Versailles" is a place tourists flock to, but the parentheticals tell the reader what the tourists will actually experience, thereby debunking "tourist expectations."

4. Correct answer: (D)
What should stand out to the reader as "distinctive" in these lines is how the author uses the word "how" repeatedly and follows this repetition with exclamation marks, thus creating "repetitive emphasis."

5. Correct answer: (E)
In context of the passage, the author's tone in this LR is (-), eliminating (A), (B), and (C). We know the tone is (-) because the author writes in the next sentence, "Paris is not France; nor is France in any way a mirror of Paris," suggesting that the author thinks the tourist's experience was "superficial" and disagrees with the tourist's proclamation that he or she has seen France.

6. Correct answer: (B)
From the last answer, we gathered that the tone of the author's reaction is (-), eliminating (A), (C), and (E). "Angered" is too (-), leaving (B).

7. Correct answer: (E)
In the sentences in which these italicized words appear, the author tells you that this is how the French "label" themselves or how they are "labeled" by one another, which is synonymous with how they "perceive one another"

8. Correct answer: (C)
The author writes, "There is a wide divide between" the rural French and the Parisians because "the seat of power and influence is in Paris, and, as a result everything that affects the whole country is decided only in terms of how Paris will be affected." The rural French have no say over how they "will be affected" by what is "decided" in Paris, implying that they "are at odds" with the Parisians "over the centralizing control exerted by Paris over all of France."

9. Correct answer: (D)
This is an "in order to" question, which means the answer will be in the lines around the LR. Based on the last question, we know that the third paragraph sets up the idea that the rural French and Parisians are "at odds" over the "power and influence" Paris has over the rest of the country. Therefore, the example (about the public transportation system catering more to Paris than the rest of France) is given "in order to" show "a possible source of contention between" the two.

10. Correct answer: (A)
The author writes in the fourth paragraph that the public transportation system mainly serves Paris because that's where the tourists are. This tourism industry has led to "the booming success of Paris." But unfortunately, "as a result," only catering to Paris has meant that "all over France, small towns and villages are decaying and empty." Therein lies the irony; as Paris get better, the French countryside gets worse.

11. Correct answer: (B)
In this paragraph, the author feels (+) towards French country life, eliminating (A). Furthermore, this paragraph is about the French countryside, not all of France (C), nor is it about "any city of France" (E). The author provides no support for (D).

12. Correct answer: (D)
Here, the author is referring to the "hospitality" of those who live in rural France, as is reflected in the previous sentence.

13. Correct answer: (C)
The author starts out the passage by writing what the tourist's experience of France is, or rather the limited experience since it's solely based on Paris. But then the author goes on to write what a "real" French experience would be (consisting of rural France in addition to Paris). This progression of "what [a complete experience of France] seems" and what it actually would mean, points to (C).

P1 - Passage 1 P2 - Passage 2
LR - Line Reference
(+) - Positive
(-) - Negative
All quotes in answer choices can be found in or around the line reference.

Made in the USA
Lexington, KY
28 March 2015